AFTER THE TRAIN

After the Train

Irishwomen United and a Network of Change

edited by

EVELYN CONLON AND REBECCA PELAN

Foreword by Mary McAleese

UNIVERSITY COLLEGE DUBLIN PRESS
PREAS CHOLÁISTE OLLSCOILE BHAILE ÁTHA CLIATH
2025

First published 2025
by University College Dublin Press
UCD Humanities Institute, Room H103,
Belfield,
Dublin 4

www.ucdpress.ie

Text and notes © the editors and contributors, 2025

ISBN 978-1-0685023-0-9

All rights reserved. No part of this publication may be reproduced, stored in a retrieval system, or transmitted in any form or by any means, electronic, photocopying, recording or otherwise without the prior permission of the publisher.

CIP data available from the British Library

The right of the editors and contributors to be identified as the author of this work has been asserted by them

Typeset in Dublin by Gough Typesetting Limited
Text design by Lyn Davies
Printed in Scotland by Bell and Bain Ltd,
303 Burnfield Road, Thornliebank, Glasgow G46 7UQ

To the Unknown Woman

Contents

	Glossary of Terms	ix
	Acknowledgements	xi
	Foreword	xiii

Introductions

1	The Untold Spark *Evelyn Conlon*	3
2	After the Train: Irishwomen United and a Network of Change *Rebecca Pelan*	9

Essays

3	Irishwomen United: Nothing Was Off Limits *Ursula Barry*	23
4	Arlen House: A Pioneer of Irish Publishing *Mary Rose Callaghan*	30
5	Dublin Rape Crisis Centre *Collective Essay*	34
6	The Well Woman Centre *Anne Connolly*	39
7	DJ at the Women's Disco *Joni Crone*	45
8	Reflections on the Irish Women's Movement *Gaye Cunningham*	47
9	We All Know Where You Were at the Weekend *Mary Doran*	51
10	'You Bring the Gay Sisters and I'll Bring the Socialists' *Mary Dorcey*	59
11	Remembering Feminist Publishing of the 1980s *Mary Flanagan and Marianne Hendron*	62
12	Children Have Equal Rights in Society Here (Cherish) *Mary Higgins*	71
13	Attic Press: A Reflection *Mary Paul Keane*	77

14	Space for Radical Change *Ger Moane*	81
15	I Just Wanted To Do Something Practical *Anne O'Donnell*	88
16	The Feminist Way *Mary O'Donnell*	92
17	The Personal Really Was Political *Betty Purcell*	99
18	Reflections from Another Country: Irish Pregnancy Counselling Centre (IPCC) *Ruth Riddick*	106
19	And Sisters, We Were Controlled: Ireland in the 1970s *Anne Speed*	111
20	Fabulously Blasphemous: Finding Myself in Irishwomen United *Saundra Stephen*	116
	Notes	123
	Appendix 1: Charter of Irishwomen United	133
	Appendix 2: Chronology of Changes Relevant to Women in Ireland 1861–2024	134
	Bibliography	143
	Index	149

Glossary of Terms

AnCo	–	An Chomhairle Oilúna (AnCo) was responsible for assisting people seeking employment. In 1988, it was amalgamated with the National Manpower Services and the Youth Employment Agency to become FÁS (Foras Áiseanna Saothair), and in 2013 FÁS became SOLAS (An tSeirbhis Oideachais Leanúnaigh agus Scileanna), the training and education authority
An Garda Síochána	–	Irish Police Service
Annaghmakerrig	–	The Tyrone Guthrie Centre. A residential facility for creative artists
Aosdána	–	Aosdána is an affiliation of artists established by the Irish Government in 1981 to honour artists of significant achievement
CIE	–	Córas Iompair Éireann/Irish Transport Authority
Fianna Fáil	–	One of Ireland's main political parties
Fine Gael	–	One of Ireland's main political parties
Gardaí	–	A number of members of An Garda Síochána
Gay Byrne	–	Host of *The Late Late Show* from its inception in July 1962 until May 1999. The show was enormously popular and Byrne, though not a controversial figure himself, never shied away from discussing contentious and controversial issues
Dáil Éireann	–	House of Representatives
Leinster House	–	Seat of the Irish Parliament
Mná Na hÉireann	–	Women of Ireland
Oireachtas	–	Bicameral parliament of Ireland
RTÉ	–	Raidió Telefís Éireann, the Irish National Broadcaster
Seanad Éireann	–	Senate
Tánaiste	–	Deputy Head of the Irish Government
Taoiseach	–	Head of the Irish Government
TD	–	Teachta Dála (Member of Irish Parliament)
The Late Late Show	–	The world's second longest-running chat show
The 'Troubles'	–	A euphemistic term for the period of civil conflict in the North of Ireland, which lasted for over 30 years from the late 1960s.

Acknowledgements

We would like to thank all those who made this book possible, those who understand the importance of telling truths, a responsibility that grows in seriousness every day. We thank the teachers who understood that history matters, the writers who got down to the work and created their own welcome, the women who gave so much energy to making Ireland a better place, sometimes at great career or personal cost to themselves. We also thank the men who privately supported the fight, and those who took decisions to offer public support. But, most important, we thank all the women in this collection who agreed to revisit their pasts, not always the easiest thing to do.

Thanks to the staff in the National Library of Ireland, to Fintan Vallely for graphics work, and to our editors, Noelle Moran and Caitlin O'Neill, as well as all the team in UCD Press who contributed to the production of this book.

Evelyn Conlon and Rebecca Pelan
Dublin, March 2025

Foreword

The position of women in Irish society in 2025 bears little resemblance to that which existed in 1975, the year Irishwomen United came into existence, though what is clear from these essays is that the changes and improvements gained did not come about without a great deal of effort on the part of women themselves. This collection attests to what can be achieved when goals and pathways to essential egalitarian reforms are collectively prioritised, regardless of political and ideological differences. Irishwomen United drew on successes from the recent and distant past, by bringing together women from vastly different backgrounds in education, class, sexual orientation and politics. Extraordinarily, their mission thrived on allowing space for these differences to be expressed whilst, at the same time, retaining a clear focus on what needed to be done to improve the lives of Irish women. There was a lot of apathy to be overcome, resistance to be faced down, doubters to be persuaded, and time to be invested over and above the demands of busy everyday lives. That time had to be reinvested over and over again, for this was the work of decades not days.

That such a representative group from the 1970s and 1980s has contributed to this collection 50 years after the events, is testimony to their commitment to a cause that changed the country in significant ways. For some, the commitment continued as a life-long passion and a central part of who they are. For others, Irishwomen United was a moment in time – an exciting, stimulating, even dangerous one – that set them on a path of personal discovery about themselves and the world around them. The recurring description by contributors of the anticipation, excitement, joy, and satisfaction felt around 4pm on Sunday afternoons in a run-down flat on Pembroke Street, Dublin, is palpable, and shines bright in memories captured here. But make no mistake, though these meetings were stimulating and enjoyable, they were primarily about planning and strategising on how to change Ireland, in whatever ways were necessary. The equally strong, determined voices from organisations that were part of that change – from Cherish to women's publishing – are fascinating to read.

In 1976, I became legal advisor to, and co-founder with David Norris, of the Campaign for Homosexual Law Reform. The battle then was for decriminalisation, and it was fought tooth and claw with meagre resources, but fierce moral integrity, through the courts of this land and Europe. When the fledgling Dublin Rape Crisis Centre (RCC) was being set-up, they requested advice as to the legal issues involved, and I was privileged to be able to give that. A great deal of thought and research went into the establishment of the RCC, with initial meetings taking place from 1977 until the official opening in 1979 and thereafter. The RCC remains one of many enduring success-stories from that period. Along with other service agencies from the period, such as Cherish, The Well Woman Centre, and the Irish Pregnancy Counselling Centre, the development of women's publishing and women's studies, the creation of space for the development of lesbian and gay rights, as well as Irish reproductive rights, Irishwomen United and the network of women and groups who changed this country in so many ways, did so from the ground up, building on what had gone before, and changing course only when enough had been achieved to ensure that there would be no going back. There were minds to be changed, attitudes to be challenged and, in fairness to the Irish people, the evidence is in that a profound change of hearts and minds is now embedded in civic society. Seamus Heaney wrote perceptively that:

> What looks the strongest has outlived its term
> The future lies with what is affirmed from under.
> (*From the Canton of Expectation III*)

From under the centuries-old layers of sexism, misogyny, patriarchy, exclusion, dismissal, and condescension, a new future has emerged and not by accident or coincidence. The 'how' of it you will read here.

I heartily commend the contributors to this collection, all of whom have so generously shared their first-hand experience of Irishwomen United and the times of change, and I congratulate the editors on putting together such a fine example of Irish women's voices and history, and in creating a body of work that will continue to be relevant and exist as documentary evidence of just what can be achieved, what grace can fill the voids, when women gather to change their world.

Mary McAleese
February 2025

INTRODUCTIONS

CHAPTER 1

The Untold Spark

Evelyn Conlon

Some rooms have imaginative echo chambers built into them and can, even through thick walls, whistle out fragments of things said, plans made, promises shouted, years after the speakers have moved on to other places. An upper room of Number 12 Pembroke Street, Dublin, is one of those, although it's not strictly a confined space, more a crossroads, where minds met, argued, planned, revolted, and moved forward, leaving behind the sound of a country being changed. The women who closed the door on that room went forth and multiplied. They started new organisations, dedicated themselves to ones just come into existence, went back to where they'd started from, came in contact with other fledgling women's groups at home and away, got diverse jobs of their own, worked freelance, wrote reports, taught, spoke to other women in cities, towns and country, patiently and sometimes not so much so, spoke to men, won some battles, lost lots, and then won again. It was while I was writing *Reading Rites*[1] that they came back in full force into my memory. Towards the end of that book, I had written that:

> Among the things to happen next in my life will be a collection of Irishwomen United memories, so that perhaps its enormous effect will no longer be dismissed in a paragraph of misunderstood gossip. The job of resetting the desk begins.[2]

At the very last edit stage, that nervous morning when the book goes to the printers and the mistakes are now committed, I added the word 'hopefully' to 'happen next'. Here is that hope. When a book begins to emerge from the shadow, especially one like this which tells a story from many points of view, it gradually becomes clear what kind of editorial sympathies are needed. Somewhere mid-Monaghan, on one of my last visits northwards to Nell McCafferty, it occurred to me that Rebecca Pelan had all of those. I was delighted that she agreed to become part of this adventure, and I am truly grateful for the particular skills brought by her to this collection.

The intention moved to necessity when I, not for the first time, read a dismissive few paragraphs describing Irishwomen United (IWU). I'm not sure how the correspondent came to his conclusions, but wrong they were. There has been a stalwart myopia about the way women changed this country; I don't need to list the symptoms, but amongst the most glaring are how, in the week of the election of Mary Robinson as President, the airwaves attempted to ignore the role of women, or let's be honest, feminist or radical women, whatever way you want to name them. Indeed, one punter, about to tell the viewers why we'd voted the way we did, slipped awkwardly on his chutzpah. Questioned as to why no Irish women were contributing to this particular BBC programme, he replied that there weren't any with the required expertise. What he meant, of course, was that there were no women as brilliant as himself. Or with his own view as to how the election was won. He didn't know that a researcher listening to him in that faraway green room would send his words back home by pigeon, let us know how he had sold us down the drain.

As for that election result – the Monaghan teller could have explained it to him. As soon as the polls closed, he told the nation that he knew Mary Robinson would be elected when he saw how the citizens of his Aughnamullen parish voted. For the 40 years he'd been doing this job, he had observed the election-day manners. Men and women who always arrived together to the polling booth before ten, or between five and seven, had mostly not done so on that day, the women arriving instead, either on their own or with their neighbour-women, around noon. Hmm, he said, big change coming.

Irishwomen United was and is a symbol of how that change took root: indeed, it was at the centre of it. It's not that they were alone in the country, but they did manage to shout further about what was needed: they did not flinch from making clear, extraordinary demands. I do remember looking at the Irishwomen United Charter and thinking, *Yeah, Right*, as we outlined the need for free contraception. Gosh, we were not afraid. I also remember thinking that the 24-hour crèche idea might be a tad unworkable. I was one of the few who had actual practical experience of how the organisation of all that goes and wondered, mostly to myself, if I was a night-shift worker how the After Dark bit would pan out. Would you put the child to sleep before bringing it in? *No, wouldn't work*, I thought. But, I argued with myself, *what if I was a firewoman or a nurse on night-duty?* I had me there. Despite a few blips, the Charter did have a profound use beyond its specific declaration: cherry-picking was done, depending on one's area of interest, and language was given to outrageous demands. Not so outrageous now, we smile.

June Levine remarked on the handing on of the baton from the Irishwomen's Liberation Group (IWLG). She recognised these IWU women as more radical than the IWLG pioneers – as more organised, fearless, she said, and wished them well. My reading is that she also knew they were in for the long haul and that it wouldn't all be about singular media-worthy events.

On the June 1975 day when approximately a hundred women were meeting in Liberty Hall, I was treading my way slowly back to Ireland from Australia, by bus across Asia, complete with blue denim cap and its ironed-on slogan *Make Love Not Babies*, getting ready for what I intended to be a re-entry for a few years. Within a couple of months, I was pregnant, signed up for doing a degree in Maynooth, and attending a fascinating free module in University College Dublin (UCD) on Women and the Media, where I heard about IWU. The following Sunday I went, with a deal of enthusiastic curiosity, to my first meeting in Pembroke Street. And thus began what I can only describe as a monumental education – enlightening, aggravating, enthusiastic, contradictory, at times disturbing. In hindsight, by the time we had stopped meeting in that room many of us had found our way optimistically into the changing of the country, by setting up, supporting, influencing all sorts of groups. And by making them and their purposes known countrywide.

Of all the groups formed by members of IWU, the Contraception Action Programme (CAP) was one of the most crucial. And yes, of course, we briefly smiled at the pun; but moved on swiftly. The reason it was so crucial is that control over re-production is one of the most important personal freedoms, perhaps indeed *the* most important. When something has been achieved, it can be very easy to forget the *before*. Afterwards, when we've come to accept our access, we can fail to appreciate the importance of contraception, the significance of this volcanic re-arrangement of our lives. Therein lies the main misunderstanding of how this country was changed. The contraceptive pill became available in the 1960s. If a woman was a Catholic, it was against her religion to avail of it. The order came from the men. But very quickly Irish women heard rumours of a way around this command – a sympathetic priest could allow the conscience to do a Jesuitical manoeuvre, somersault, turn inside out, by partaking of the oral contraceptive for medical purposes. Women quickly developed these medical issues and spread the word. That marvellous, humorous aside has since been trivialised into a different remark. I was recently sent a recording of one our supposedly serious commentators having a fine old snigger with another male about it. This was on an international stage, and these were two men who have garnered respect in other fields. It's astonishing how hurtful it can still be to hear ourselves diminished in this way. I should say that I think it would be nigh impossible to make these two men understand how the sound of them borrowing our jocularity drops like the proverbial lead balloon. They can try to don it as their own worldliness, but it doesn't work, because the joke is ours.

Let me paint the picture. In the 1970s, Catholics still went in their droves to confession, lined up on church seats to enter the hallowed box. If the church was a big one, waiting queues for different boxes would be more or less equally distributed. That is until it was discovered, by Irish women, that some priests were dispensing the aforementioned sicknote for God. As indeed was happening with women in other predominantly Catholic countries. They quickly, efficiently, seriously, passed on this information to their co-child-bearing-age neighbours, sisters, friends, in the most spectacular whispers. And the queue outside some boxes got longer, and soon became mostly women. In other areas, mainly rural, where there was only one priest, women got lifts to chapels outside their own parish if needs be.

See those two characters with paisley scarves, knotted below their chins, whispering to each other before entering the chapel, oh yes, you think they're having a hearty gossip about daily, apparently unimportant, things. Indeed they are. And more. They are laying out the pattern for the destruction of church and male control over their reproductive bodies. And once they commit themselves to that brilliant move, they are beginning a revolution in every chapel in the country; that sound is of women sidling up to each other, a subversive infiltration, the signing up to the underground movement of knowledge. They hadn't left the church, no, not yet. They had merely moved the wheel, without anyone seeing what they were doing, except perhaps the individual priests who gave them their note. (Some of them would have had the full backing of the men in their lives, some would not). I think of them when I recall the contortions that commentators put themselves through to come up with reasons why the country changed, the tight-fitting ideological suits they tried to get themselves into, anything to avoid saying 'women'. It was women that did it. I do not snigger at them. I hear them whispering, telling each other about which priest to go to. I salute them, every single one of them.

The further we move from battles fought and won, the easier it is to forget. The decrescendo fading of the roused chorus allows for history to be distorted. While listening in the Abbey Theatre to the energised voices of 'Waking the Feminists' in 2015, I heard a worry articulated about the title; one actor pointed out that she had never been asleep. Perhaps the younger women did not know? I was reminded of a previous awakening of my own. The year was 1979 and I was choosing the subject matter of the mini thesis for my sociology degree – only achieved, I believe, thanks to the establishment of the Maynooth crèche. I had become interested in whispers from history, some of them finding their faint ways through those thick walls, and proposed an examination of them. I then had to spend an inordinate amount of energy having the idea accepted – surely this was not a serious enough subject matter for study? Eventually, after the intervention of a wise, if sceptical, head of department, it was approved, under the title 'The historical points of continuity and discontinuity in the women's movement in Ireland', complete with a stated explanation of the process. I set out to have a look at our foremothers, at places where they had organised, had communicated among themselves about issues that related directly to them, and also how they lived in the wider world. I examined not just the women I would have agreed with, but others who had lived lives unrelated to mine. The organisations examined included the Suffragettes, the United Irishwomen (later to become the Irish Countrywomen's Association), the Irish Housewives Association, the Women's Social and Progressive League, the Irish Women's Liberation Movement, and Irishwomen United, as well as individuals in the Trade Union Movement, women in the Republican Movement, and the Council for the Status of Women, all of whom either historically or organisationally bound together women of varying viewpoints.

By 2015, 36 years later, I'd forgotten about that, of course. But eerily they came to mind as I sat in the Abbey Theatre, listening to the sound of younger women taking up their baton. I didn't want to forget those figures waving from the past. I wanted to remind us of how they worked out their lives away from the light; how they organised in whatever way they could, including in the Irish Countrywomen's Association (ICA), which, incidentally, I have no doubt was an information hub for everything from sin to how to have fewer children, as well as baking cakes. How they got around the strictures of the church/state that was attempting to hold autocratic sway over their decisions: *Have you heard the latest? A mathematical way of working out the safe period. What you do is ... here, let me write it out for you.* Which note-sharing established the confidence to grab the next opportunity when it appeared.

I remembered the joy of finding some of these interviewees, none of whom had ever expected to be searched out. It had given me such great delight to see a glimpse of Irish women's history. I had been astounded, really, because I'd known nothing of it. And then I got angry to think of this deliberate erasure; to think that I might never have known. To feel with what spectacular success they had been forgotten, these women who did not toe the line, who continuously kept the notion of change on the simmer, so it was there for the big leaps when they came. The fact they were ignored in history books made it all the more difficult when we had shaped our demands, because we had done so without knowing enough about what had gone before us. That day in the Abbey, it was possible to despair as well as be delighted because, although it was marvellous to see this new energy, jumping over personal advancement, being not afraid, it was also heart-breaking to realise how much had been forgotten. Irishwomen United, and all that came after, seemed to be as invisible as the women I had interviewed all those years ago. Which is why we always need to keep our eyes on the history books, because every time we take our eye off the true telling of what happened, we create the necessity to begin inventing the wheel all over again. The publishing of *After the Train* is one step in the acknowledgement, remembrance, and celebration of those who went before.

Among the most philosophically challenging exercises we had to grapple with in the 1970s was the contradiction of our own stances, sometimes heartbreakingly painful. We wanted to recognise the women who had gone before us, but we also knew that we were tearing apart what many of them desired for us, that we were burying, with great glee, what they thought were the foundations of our safe world. From *Reading Rites*:

> We had to deal with the conundrum of contradiction on a most insistent level; sometimes silently. I still do. We wanted to recognise the worth of our mothers, but we were throwing all their lives and their admonitions into the fire. But we were in good company – Germaine Greer didn't like her mother. Colleen McCullough, author of *The Thorn Birds*,[3] went to live on Norfolk Island, a pinprick of a place, because she wouldn't live on the same landmass as hers. (Before turning to fiction, McCullough was a serious scientist. She ran neurophysiology departments and research labs. Funny we didn't know that until she died). We wanted to honour our mothers, but we were against them. Andrea Dworkin taught us a little about how to deal with that in *Right-Wing Women*.[4] But we knew that the contradiction had no solution. And it still hasn't, because although I still call myself a feminist, I'd be a right fool if I didn't admit that I've met some terrible, awful women, who have managed to do as much damage as the men they mirrored. We were fighting our mothers, make no mistake about it.[5]

Again, in hindsight, I'm surprised we managed to handle those contradictions as wisely as we did, learned how to disagree, not just with the past, but also within and among ourselves. And there was much to disagree about. Wages for Housework: on the one hand, why shouldn't women be paid for all the work they were doing? On the other, weren't we about getting women away from all-enveloping housework? We disagreed on what position we should take on prostitution, of course we did. On the one hand, why shouldn't we support women who were making a free choice about what they worked at. Free? Some argued that we had to be supportive, others railed at the notion that we should descend into that rabbit hole. Ita Gannon, referencing the jaded tripe that prostitution is the oldest profession in the world, asked if it was not more accurate to say that pimping was the oldest crime. We had direct experience of this contradiction – a few women working the streets had begun to drop in to the Women's Disco downstairs in the Pembroke Bar. Some argued that they should be welcome, others pointed out that the pimps had started hanging around outside, so made the place dangerous for us. Who was going to ask the pimps to move away from the door? The lesbians among us had a lot to put with – their reasons for the disco-going were more ethereal than these issues. They also had to listen to an awful lot that didn't apply to them in their lives. We worried about some of the influence coming in from organisations that did not have women's rights as their primary agenda. We learned how to respect women as our sisters – I had balked at the use of the word when it was first used, but began to see the sense of it when I watched its workings. We didn't disagree about occupying the Federated Union of Employers (FUE) boardroom in pursuit of Equal Pay, nor of our claim to space in the sea out at the Forty Foot. We discussed the issues affecting the women's movement all over the world – race, class, children versus no, sexual preferences, health, books about all these things. Some of us had a literary corner, where we devoured wonderful stories and poems that had all the hallmarks of having performed the great escape. Some of these works have stood the test of time, others not so much, which is to be expected in any artistic movement that breaks barriers. We also read the theory books, had our personal bibles, could respect some ideas while pledging to go further. When I finally got to have dinner with Betty Freidan I was an old hand at understanding her. Later, I would write fictionally about some of the days we faced, in, for instance, 'The Park',[6] 'The Last Confession',[7] and 'Escaping the Celtic Tiger, World Music and the Millennium'.[8]

In the mid-1970s, we crowded into that shabby room every Sunday afternoon, sat or stood where we could get space, heard reports from the previous week's activities, pickets, protests, workshops. We organised the week to come. Among us were writers, academics, women who would help set up Attic Press, teachers, office workers, several trade unionists, a journalist or two, one nurse that I know of. Attic Press went on to publish over four hundred titles. We produced a magazine called *Banshee*. We were the wailers broadcasting the death of the old regime: we had change, joyful change, on our minds.

Mary Robinson was taking the court cases. Mary McAleese, later, gave legal advice to those of us who set up the Rape Crisis Centre. Both of these women were elected as presidents of Ireland. We need to cherish that sentence again, so we can understand the complexities of Ireland: two female presidents, both of them outstanding in their own unique way. A disservice was done to history by the phalanx of commentators who, on the election of Mary Robinson, refused to admit that the echoes coming from that room on Pembroke Street, and rooms like it around the country, had managed to be heard on the byroads, and had changed minds.

The end of the Sunday meetings was a beginning. All sorts of women learned there that we had to have the long painstaking conversation, but that we could indeed change the country if we set our minds to it. Opinions may differ about the roots of the massive revolution that took place in Irish society; claims are made both by enthusiastic supporters and by people who had kept safely quiet at the time, but the one thing for certain is that Irishwomen United and the offshoots it helped to create were the architect's plan and a crucial part of the realisation of change. The echo penetrated the walls.

Evelyn Conlon is a writer, born in County Monaghan. She has published four novels, four collections of short stories, and, most recently, *Reading Rites*, an essay memoir. She has co-edited five anthologies, including *Cutting the Night in Two*, the first compilation of short stories by Irish women writers. A collection of essays examining her work, edited by Teresa Caneda-Cabrera, is titled *Telling Truths*. Evelyn has written about secret lives, borders, capital punishment, famine, the double standard, borders, sex and lies. She has been writer in residence at numerous libraries and universities in Ireland, and internationally. Her work is widely anthologised and translated, most recently into Mandarin, Greek, and Tamil. An adjunct professor with the Carlow University, Pittsburgh, MFA programme, she lives in Dublin and is a member of Aosdána. www.evelynconlon.com.

CHAPTER 2

After the Train: Irishwomen United and a Network of Change

Rebecca Pelan

> You've just read the daily papers. You've been listening to the radio. You're probably about to watch television. Would you know, from the attention devoted by the media to women, that females form fifty-one percent of the population?

So began the first Editorial of *Banshee: Journal of Irishwomen United* in March 1976. In all, eight issues of the journal were printed between 1976 and 1977, with 2,500 copies of the first issue being sold out of 3,000 printed, making a profit of £100.[1] The title of the publication is significant in an Irish context: the 'banshee' being a female spirit in Irish folklore, heralding the death of a family member, usually by screaming, wailing, shrieking, or keening.[2] Like many other European feminist publications, members of Irishwomen United (IWU) selected a feminine word that often has negative connotations ('she was screeching like a banshee'), and inverted it to give the name a positive and powerful meaning. Issue 2 of *Banshee* suggests, with a humorous, tongue-in-cheek tone familiar to the journal, that the banshees belonged to a Stone Age community, were a non-agricultural, pastoral people with magical powers, and whose religious and social organisation was matriarchal and based on a worship of nature; they lived by a rule of free union, and the concept of illegitimacy did not exist; they celebrated life and believed in the positive reincarnation of the soul and, importantly, 'the banshee cries the death of oppression, the rebirth of woman'.

From the beginning, the aims of IWU were clearly set out, and appeared on the inside front cover of every issue of *Banshee*:

> We are a group of women's liberationists who believe that the best perspective for struggle against women's oppression in Ireland lies in an ongoing fight around the charter of demands printed here. We came together originally in April 1975 as a few individual women interested in the idea of building a conference to discuss a charter; what its demands would be and how a campaign should be built. At this conference on June 8th, attended by approximately 100 women, we constituted ourselves as a separate group, Irish Women United – the only criteria for joining to be agreement on the demands of the charter. Irish Women United works on the basis of general meetings (discussions and action planning, at present every week in Dublin),

joint actions (e.g. pickets, public meetings, workshops at present on women in trade unions, contraception, social welfare and political theory) and consciousness-raising groups.

The mention here of April 1975 refers to a series of meetings, held in the International Bar on Wicklow Street, Dublin, where a small number of women first discussed the idea of a charter. This was followed by a day-long conference in Liberty Hall, Dublin, on 8 June 1975, during which the name Irishwomen United, along with the Charter,[3] sub-titled 'Irishwomen United – Sisterhood is Powerful', were agreed. The Charter appeared on the back page of every issue of *Banshee*, facilitating the consistent and regular distribution of the group's demands.

The IWU Charter was both radical and ahead of its time. And whilst the issue of contraception – arguably the most important one at the time for women in Ireland – was included, abortion was initially excluded from the IWU Charter on the grounds that it might alienate many women from joining the group, and also in deference to those women within IWU who were not clear about their own position on the issue.[4] This situation didn't last long, however, and a reference to abortion was included in the Charter in late 1975.

Banshee reflected the larger ethos of IWU itself, whereby liberal, radical, and socialist feminist perspectives co-existed without editorial intervention, just as seriously diverse political ideologies co-existed within the larger group. For example, members of IWU included individual members from a broad range of political perspectives,[5] as well as a substantial number of women who were not affiliated with any group or political ideology at all. The meetings were lively, often contentious, but always massively positive and energised, as evidenced in many of the essays included here.

IWU and *Banshee* existed for a period of just over two years as collectives with the specific aim of improving the lives of women in Ireland, and its achievements were extraordinary. Initially, meetings took place on Sundays in the International Bar on Wicklow Street, Dublin, and, from mid-1975 until Spring 1977, at 4pm every Sunday in 12 Pembroke Street, Dublin. Meetings were consistently well-attended and would run for several hours. Early in its existence, groups were formed to work on specific areas of IWU's focus: employment, contraception, social welfare, education, and sexuality, amongst others.

IWU substantially contributed to long-lasting changes for women in the political, social, and cultural landscape of Ireland, and much of the group's success was aided by *Banshee*. The publication received a mixed response from the press, but Christina Murphy of *The Irish Times*, thought, though not very professional, it was 'inspired, lively, and provocative'.[6] Many of the issues IWU campaigned on, and can be identified as themes in *Banshee*, were much the same as in other industrialised countries, but there is no mistaking the distinct 'Irishness' of *Banshee* as a result of its dealing head-on with contraception, abortion, and divorce, as well as overt and consistent criticism of the role and power of the Catholic Church in Irish society at the time.

From today's perspective, 1970s Ireland looks like another country. The Chronology included here[7] shows just how quickly things changed throughout the 1970s and, particularly, post-1975. Ireland's laws at the start of the 1970s left a lot to be desired in terms of women's equality, as they did in many other countries, especially in relation to property ownership, social welfare, financial independence, and much more. Again, like elsewhere, women were excluded from much of public duty.[8] Until the mid-1970s, many women in the Civil Service[9] were required to give up their jobs on marriage, under what became known as 'the marriage bar'. This restriction initially applied to the Civil Service only, and required single female civil servants to resign when they married. It also banned married women from permanent positions in the Civil Service. However, over time, the 'ban' was extended to both the public and private sectors, though there were always exceptions, especially for work that was conventionally done by and considered suitable for women, such as clerical work. From as far back as 1926, the Minister for Finance in Ireland had discretionary powers to hire married women for the Public Service in exceptional circumstances, on temporary, non-pensionable contracts. This was the situation for nurses, midwives, and teachers, for example, especially in rural areas, and they were not required to cease work on getting married. In 1941, five per cent of working nurses were married, and if they chose to return to work after marriage, they were employed on a continuous, temporary contract, and paid at the lowest point on the pay scale.[10] The 'marriage bar' ended on 31 July 1973 as a result of legislative changes. In writing this, Evelyn and I feel impelled to salute our mothers and aunts who always had jobs outside the home.

However, in addition to these more widespread inequalities, there were limitations imposed on women that were specific to Ireland. From 1935, for example, it was illegal in Ireland to sell or advertise any medicines or methods relating to contraception. In addition, it was illegal for anyone to print information about or to advocate for contraception, under the Censorship of Publications Act of 1929 and 1945. As with most types of censorship or prohibition, there were some surreptitious ways around the law: for example, the contraceptive pill became available in Ireland as a 'cycle regulator' from 1963, and, by 1969, women could obtain contraception from the Fertility Guidance Company, later known as the Irish Family Planning Association (IFPA), which bypassed the laws by accepting donations rather than payments for their services. By 1973, married couples were able to import contraceptives for their own use, by way of a doctor's prescription. However, it was 1979 before contraceptives became legal in Ireland.

In this, the 50th anniversary of the formation of IWU, we are fortunate to have access to the stories of so many of the women who were directly involved in, or witness to, IWU's activities, though not all were members of the group, and whilst some have gone on to continue the work begun during the period, others have followed paths far removed from political or feminist activism. Regardless, their stories are of crucial importance in extending our understanding of a rich seam of Irish women's history and experience that is often overlooked in the ostensibly bigger history of movements.

The most comprehensive study of the women's movement in Ireland remains Linda Connolly's *The Irish Women's Movement: From Revolution to Devolution*,[11] which traces the history of the movement, as well as the relationship between its component parts, and which critically prioritises the importance of the diversity and complexity of the women's movement over any essentialist reading of Irish feminist politics as being aligned with or belonging to any homogeneous or dominant ideology. Though some 23 years after the publication of Connolly's study, *After the Train* reflects her suggestion in 2002, that:

> The personal experience of discovering feminism is undoubtedly unique for each woman, and

there is room for several more narratives of the Irish women's movement. We have clearly only touched the tip of an iceberg in Irish feminist studies.[12]

After the Train: Irishwomen United and a Network of Change is just one such narrative. What it is not, however, is an attempt to project IWU as being more important than what went before or came after. In so many ways, its achievements would not have been possible without the groundwork laid by earlier groups or movements.

> A sober, sensible, structured organisation could never have given the jolt that was necessary, would never have grabbed the headlines, would never have shocked men and women into awareness of the inferior legal and social status of women. They may have disliked what was going on, but they could not ignore it. Most importantly, the movement provided a breeding ground for the many pressure groups which emerged throughout the seventies.[13]

But, as Yvonne Galligan points out, discussions of the Irish women's movement too often suggest a 'virgin birth' – a social and political phenomenon with no links to past campaigns for women's rights.[14] Yet we know that the demand for equal pay and better working conditions were of serious concern to the Women Workers' Union of the 1900s, and that the depleted position of women in the 1937 Irish Constitution was strongly opposed by a feminist collective at the time.[15] Equally, shortages of food and general poverty during the Second World War was the motivation for the formation of the Irish Housewives Association (IHA), which, in turn, became what Hilda Tweedy calls a 'link in the chain' between women's activism of the 1940s to the 1960s, and continued into the feminist movement that emerged in the 1970s:

> So many people think that the women's movement was born on some mystical date in 1970, when it had actually been a long continuous battle … each generation adding something to the achievements of the past.[16]

For the purposes of this discussion, a starting point on that long journey could be 7 November 1967, when the Declaration on the Elimination of Discrimination against Women (DEDAW) was adopted by the United Nations General Assembly. Ireland voted in favour of the Declaration, on the agreed understanding that it would introduce equal pay after entering the European Economic Community (EEC)[17] in 1972. The Commission on the Status of Women (CSW), consisted of seven women and six men, and was established in 1970, in order to report on the status of women in Irish society, and to recommend how women's greater participation could be achieved. In August, 1971, prior to finalising its full review, the CSW produced a report on equal pay, which focused primarily on the situation of women in the public sphere.

Also published in 1971, however, was a very different and considerably more radical publication, known as the manifesto of the then newly-formed Irish Women's Liberation Movement (IWLM), titled *Chains or Change? The Civil Wrongs of Irish Women*,[18] which explicitly outlined the barriers to equality faced by Irish women. The manifesto was launched on *The Late Late Show* in 1971, and its demands included equal pay, equality in education, access to contraception, and more. The first public meeting of the IWLM was held in the Mansion House in April 1971.

The IWLM was just one of several women's organisations that existed in Ireland in the early 1970s, some of which had been around for much longer, such as the Irish Countrywomen's Association, the Irish Housewives Association, and the National Association of Widows. However, IWLM was undoubtedly the most radical of the newer groups, and was founded by a group of women who had all been involved in political activism during the 1960s. There are various versions of its beginnings, but most commentators from the time seem to agree that the very first meeting of the then un-named IWLM, took place in 1970 in Bewley's Café, Westmoreland Street, Dublin, when five women – Margaret Gaj, Mary Maher, Máirín Johnston, Máire Woods, and Máirín de Burca – met, with the specific aim of examining how the position of women in Ireland could be linked to the ever-growing influence of the women's liberation campaigns that were taking place elsewhere. Subsequent meetings were held in Gaj's Restaurant, Baggot Street, Dublin.[19]

Though many readers will be familiar with the event that announced the arrival of the second wave of the women's movement in Ireland, the passing of time means that, for a younger generation, the event is either unknown altogether or represents for them a headline in feminist activism, and so is always worth revisiting. At 8am on 22 May 1971, 47 women, many of them members of IWLM, caught a train from Connolly Station Dublin, to Great Victoria Street Station Belfast, with a plan of obtaining condoms and the contraceptive pill.[20] They were accompanied on the journey by journalists and photographers from Ireland and beyond, and they aimed to buy as many of both items as they could, and bring them back across the border, where they were illegal. However, whilst contraception was legal in the North,[21] it required a doctor's prescription, something the women were either unaware of, or had overlooked, until they were inside the selected pharmacy in Belfast. Unable to get the contraceptives, they bought as many packets of aspirin as they could, assuming nobody would know the difference. In Dublin, the group was met by a substantial number of supporters, and by customs officers, and the women made it known that they had purchased contraceptives in Belfast. Clearly thrown by the bare cheek of the women, customs allowed them to pass through the station. What was, essentially, a clever media stunt, marked a hugely important moment in the history of the second wave in Ireland, achieved, largely, through extensive national and international media coverage.

In attracting such a high level of media attention, pin-pointed to an exact time, date, and place, Irish feminists exploited tried and tested methods that were successful elsewhere. From my own background at the time, for example, in Brisbane, Australia, the second wave appeared slightly earlier than in Ireland, and was also heavily influenced by feminist activism in America. At precisely 5pm on 31 March, 1965, two women, Merle Thornton[22] and Ro Bognor, chained themselves to the brass foot-rail of the public bar of Brisbane's Regatta Hotel, in protest at the exclusion of women from public bars. At that time, women could drink in the lounge bar, where drinks were more expensive, but not in the public bar. This was the case throughout Australia, but only in Queensland was it enshrined in law.[23] Once the chains were locked, a supporter took the key and threw it into the nearby Brisbane River. A substantial number of supporters and media attended the event. Police, called by the publican, realised quickly that they were out of their depth, and called for help from the Licensing Branch, who arrived and the chains were removed:

> The police then tried everything short of physically removing the women from the bar. While the TV cameras rolled, the flashbulbs popped and the reporters took notes, the two officers became increasingly embarrassed. They harried and cajoled and threatened arrest … but the protestors refused to leave, and eventually the police themselves left, saying, 'Have a good time girls. Don't drink too much'. As a public protest, it had been an extremely successful action.[24]

The success of the event led to a public meeting a week later, attended by a large number of women and men and, from there, it is possible to trace a cascade effect leading to major changes for women in Queensland.

The similarities between the 'contraceptive train' in Dublin and the events in the Regatta Hotel in Brisbane need no explanation. The two events – six years and a world apart – were extremely important, but they were not culminations of feminist activism. Rather, they were both important catalysts for change, in combination with the small, ostensibly personal steps that galvanised so many individual women to take part in a movement and a network for change in both countries.

The title of this collection, then, is both a playful and respectful response to the 1971 'contraceptive train', but with full acknowledgement of the connections – the 'links in the chain' – of women's activism historically. What is of more interest here, however, as reflected in the title, is what came after 'the train', in the form of IWU, though this is neither a history of the organisation nor is it an attempt to challenge or respond to the solid research already in existence on the origins of, and relationship between, the different sectors of the Irish women's movement. Rather, the collection fits within Maria Luddy's suggestion that, 'although Irish women's history has developed quite strongly since the late 1970s, we are still at the stage of recovery'.[25] The 'recovery' of women's voices remains as important today as it did when Luddy first made the suggestion in 1995, not alone for the purpose of seeing where we've been, but to evaluate what's left to be done. According to Ailbhe Smyth:

> There is so much recording and remembering, reflection and research which requires to be done before we can begin to fully appreciate the difference the contemporary women's movement has made to our lives.[26]

A significant part of that recording and remembering can be located in the field of women's writing and publishing, the roots of which, according to Smyth, are located firmly in the earlier years of the movement, and which played a crucial role, in the 1980s, in the development of women's creative and political expression.[27] The insertion of women into the world of publishing is dealt with in a number of the essays here, and the resultant proliferation of women's creative and political output since the 1980s is evidence of the level of success achieved. I recall making post-graduate research trips to Ireland, from Australia, in the late 1980s and early 1990s, and trawling through book-shops to locate what seemed like an endless array of women's fiction, drama, and poetry. What felt like a treasure-trove of material, fed into a PhD, and subsequent monograph, on the topic of literary feminism in the North and South of the country.[28]

The life of the IWLM was short-lived (1971–72), yet 'the train' has often – arguably too often – been used as a shorthand means of symbolising the radical changes that were taking place for women during the period, even though a number of other groups continued to work throughout the 1970s, either as lobbyists or as service providers for Irish women in relation to specific needs and issues.[29] Nevertheless, there existed a lull in anything resembling a collective feminist network from 1972 until April 1975, when IWU came into being, and took advantage of the opportunity for public protest presented by the UN's designation of 1975 as International Women's Year, designed to improve the status of women everywhere. In Ireland, the event was seriously neglected, with a Women's Representative Committee (WRC) being set up as late as December 1974. In contrast to the official lack of interest, however, IWU carried out an extensive range of activities throughout 1975 and 1976, some of which picked up where IWLM campaigns had left off, including: a picket of the British Embassy against the House of Lords ruling on rape; a picket of the Pro Cathedral against the Catholic Hierarchy's pastoral 'Human Life is Sacred', designed to expose how wrong contraception is; two 'invasions' of the Fitzwilliam Lawn Tennis Club to protest the club's policy of not allowing women members; similar 'invasions' of the Forty Foot swimming area in Sandycove, which, at the time, was 'men only'; and protests against publicans who refused to serve women in their public bars, or who would only serve them glasses of beer, rather than pints. IWU also undertook extensive advocacy work on social welfare, sexual violence, equal pay, and contraception, via the Contraception Action Programme (CAP), launched in June 1976.

Predictably, these activities attracted opposition. In 1976, two former members of the ultra-right wing Knights of Columbanus, John O'Reilly and Niall Darragh, formed the Council of Social Concern, based in Blackrock. The Irish Family League (IFL), under John O'Reilly and founded in 1973, became one of the most prominent organisations to campaign against the legalisation of contraception in Ireland, arguing that it would lead to an increase in promiscuity, especially among teenagers, and that if contraception was legalised, abortion would be also. Around the same time, Niall Darragh founded the Society to Outlaw Pornography (STOP), while O'Reilly helped form the Irish section of the British right-wing fringe group 'the Responsible Society'. In Britain, this group fought against the provision of sex education in schools. In Ireland, it opposed the establishment of rape crisis centres on the basis that they might lead rape victims to seek abortions. Later, the group became Family and Youth Concern with O'Reilly as Secretary, but their battle was against much more than abortion. It was 'against the spurious cause of feminism. This pernicious new thinking asserts that our bodies are our own and tries to justify to women this so-called right to control their own fertility … This is what we are fighting in Ireland now', according to Dr Mary Lucey, President (and public face) of SPUC.[30] In response, SPUC was viewed by Irish feminists as a serious threat to Irish women, and 'a cruel insult to the 150 women a week who cross over to England for abortions'.[31]

The Charter of IWU included a demand for free contraception for Irish women, something that existed only in the realm of the imagination in 1975. Yet, here we are in 2025, living with just such a reality, not to mention the existence of two women Presidents in the Republic of Ireland since 1990. And, in 2002, when Linda Connolly pondered the effects on women's lives of the new power-sharing and devolution in the North, could we have imagined that we would see two women as First and Deputy First Minister there? A great deal has happened in-between these very different time-lines, much of which will be forgotten in the history books, but if we only look at the achievements and not the steps to get there – often small, but nevertheless brave steps – then we do a disservice to the ordinary women and men who put in so much of the hard graft.

As mentioned already, the Commission on the Status of Women (CSW) was established in 1970, specifically to report on women's status in Irish society at the time, and to recommend ways of improving women's equality, and whilst there is no doubt that the position of women in Ireland in 2025 is qualitatively different from that in the 1970s, much about the lives of women in Ireland during that period remains in place today. To some extent, we are, yet again, relying on official / government momentum to address these imbalances, evidenced when, in July 2019, a Citizens Assembly[32] on Gender Equality was established to specifically consider issues, many of which echo those that existed at the beginning of the 1970s, including a mandate to examine:

> Gender equality and make recommendations to the Oireachtas[33] to advance the same by bringing forward proposals to:
> - challenge the remaining barriers and social norms and attitudes that facilitate gender discrimination towards girls and boys, women and men;
> - identify and dismantle economic and salary norms that result in gender inequalities, and reassess the economic value placed on work traditionally done by women;
> - seek to ensure women's full and effective participation and equal opportunities for leadership at all levels of decision-making in the workplace, politics and public life;
> - recognise the importance of early years parental care and seek to facilitate greater work-life balance;
> - examine the social responsibility of care and women and men's co-responsibility for care, especially within the family;
> - scrutinise the structural pay inequalities that result in women being disproportionately represented in low pay sectors.[34]

After considerable disruption due to Covid19, some 23 public meetings, and over 60 written submissions, the Assembly produced forty-five recommendations, 'which amount to a blueprint for the achievement of gender equality in Ireland'. It is difficult not to recall Gilligan's 'virgin birth' here, or the fact that this notion of a 'blueprint' is one that has been challenged by many feminists over the years. Mary Cullen, for example, suggests that:

> Feminism does not produce a blueprint for the ideal society. It's contribution to political thought is to insist that the political, social and economic relationships between the sexes be scrutinised.[35]

The recommendations of the Assembly were presented to the Oireachtas Committee on Gender Equality on 24 April 2021, and, in turn, the Committee published its own final report on 15 December 2022. Constitutional referenda were held on International Women's Day 2024, aimed at addressing Articles 40 and 41 of the Constitution, one on the relationship between women and the family, and one on caring. Voters rejected both Government proposals, with 67.7 per cent voting 'no' in the Family referendum, and 73.9 per cent voting 'no' in the Care referendum. It remains to be seen how effective the Assembly can be in the longer-term, but the similarities between the aims in 1970 and 2019 are disappointingly clear.

It was becoming obvious, as evidenced in so many of the essays here, that, by mid-1977, the women of IWU were exhausted. Realistically, given the extraordinary level of work done by the group in a period of just over two years, it would be difficult to imagine any organisation being able to maintain the same level of momentum for much longer. IWU fragmented from a position of collective action on a range of agreed issues and campaigns, albeit by women of diverse politics and ideologies, to a multiplicity of individual women and small groups interested in particular issues and services for women. This is not to suggest that the women of IWU felt the fight was over. Far from it. Nor is it meant to suggest that the women felt they were going their separate ways for good. Rather, individuals and smaller interest groups moved on, most of them knowing they had won much, but that there was more to do:

> IWU, in its political dimension, diffused into a number of organisations, which were to mobilise during the 1980s around lesbian rights, reproductive rights (culminating in the anti-amendment group in the abortion referendum of 1983), and the continued provision of services for women. The radicalism of this constituency, in particular, had an important effect on the transformation of the movement as a whole throughout the 1980s.[36]

It may have been difficult in 1975 for Irish feminists to envisage just how enormous these challenges, which still lay ahead of them, would be:

- the continued fight to legalise contraception (achieved in 1979);
- the repeal of the Eighth Amendment to the Irish Constitution (achieved in 2018). This fight took a long time and two referenda – the most hard fought and lost being in 1983, in which the lives of many of the women previously involved in IWU were entirely given over, day and night, to the campaign, and which, after the loss, had to be rebuilt in order to do it all over again.
- the battle for a successful Referendum on divorce (achieved in 1993);

The main aim of this collection is to capture the history and atmosphere of IWU via the personal recollections of women who were involved in or familiar with its activities, and to trace how the actions, begun 50 years ago, created a network of social and political changes that contributed to the transformation of Irish society. A secondary effect may be to provide a good example of how liberation is rarely achieved through big events but, rather, through periods of 'ebb and flow' or 'high and low energy'.[37]

According to historian Mary McAuliffe:

> Many of the women who cut their teeth in feminist activism with IWU would continue to be central to organisations and campaigns for better social conditions for women, reproductive rights, lesbian activism, as well as issues around rape, violence against women, and domestic violence, on into the following decades [....] The strategies of direct action employed by IWU continued to be used by various organisations and women's groups [....] Long after its demise many women who had developed their politics and activism with IWU were active and influential in Irish socio-political campaigns which contributed to the fundamental transformation of Irish society.[38]

In just over two years of non-stop activities, IWU became a way of life for many of the women involved, absorbing much of their time and energy, and it is clear from the essays included here that there was a strong sense amongst the members that they were part of something important. IWU had transformed into other shapes by 1978, but, by then, so much had been achieved, it was evident that there would be no going back.

As editors of this collection, Evelyn Conlon and I come from quite different directions. Evelyn was a member of IWU from Autumn 1975, was active in most of its campaigns, and was centrally involved in the setting-up of the Dublin Rape Crisis Centre (DRCC) from 1977. She also set-up the first crèche in Maynooth University. Having lived and travelled in Australia for a few years, Evelyn returned to Ireland in 1975. As she discusses in *Reading Rites*,[39] her return to Ireland was for the dual purpose of getting a degree and leaving Ireland again as quickly as possible, but, as is so often the case, life intervened and she was taken in another direction. By contrast, during IWU's existence, I was living in Brisbane, Australia, where my family had emigrated to from Belfast, and where quite different forms of oppression existed. My research field is literature with a focus on women, so what I know about Irish women's history generally, and IWU specifically, was gleaned from reading the work of Irish feminist scholars. And my understanding of women's reproductive rights in Ireland – even further out of my sphere – was informed by publications such as the 1984 *Irish Feminist Review*, which contained a detailed discussion of the issue in articles such as Mary Gordon's 'Fighting for Control', as well as substantial analyses of the topic in books such as Ailbhe Smyth's *The Abortion Papers* (1992).

In Ireland, women fought the inequalities that many women elsewhere experienced, *plus* specific oppressions imposed by the Catholic Church in hand with conservative post-independence politics. In Australia, women did the same, but for some, the *plus* was imposed via ultra-conservative politics.[40] Evelyn went from rural Monaghan to Dublin to Australia, where she lived, and then back to Dublin, by bus through Asia. I went from Belfast to Australia, where I lived for many years, and back to Ireland in 2001. We first met in 1993 when I interviewed Evelyn at her home in Dublin during a research visit about Irish women and fiction. We share many connections. I retired from academic work in 2017, but then enjoyed a second working life in the Dublin Rape Crisis Centre, which I joined as a volunteer in 2014, and became a staff member of until 2022.

In putting together this collection, Evelyn and I made a decision to allow the women directly involved in IWU and its network to tell their own stories. A fundamental principle of social science research is to anonymise interviewees, something that is most often done when the aim of the research is about a larger group or event, or to protect the identity of individuals. Although *After the Train* is, essentially, about a larger political group, its focus is precisely on the individual 'voices' and experience of the women involved in that group, and which, as a result, have been foregrounded in this collection.

In her introductory essay to this collection, Evelyn alludes to a moment when she read a few dismissive paragraphs on IWU by a prominent, male historian, and was prompted to return to the idea of this collection, something that had been in her mind for some time: for posterity, for the joy of it, but most of all for the purpose of setting the record straight on what had become, certainly for many mainstream commentators, something of a note in the margins of feminist activism and women's history in this country. And she asked me to join her in addressing that record, something that has been my privilege. Sincerely, we both hope you enjoy reading this collection as much as we have enjoyed putting it together.

Rebecca Pelan PhD, has worked in Ireland (North and South), Australia, and America in the fields of English, Irish studies, and women's studies, and has published extensively on Irish fiction and drama, with a focus on women's writing. She has been General Editor of *Irish Feminist Review* (Galway 2002–07), on the Editorial Board of *Hecate* (Australia), and the *Australasian Journal of Irish Studies* (Australia). Rebecca was the 2011 MM Fort Visiting Scholar in European Studies at Columbus State University, Georgia, where she was also guest editor of *ANQ* (formerly *American Notes and Queries)*. Her book, *Two Irelands: Literary Feminisms North and South* was published by Syracuse University Press. Between 2014 and 2022, Rebecca was a volunteer and staff member of the Dublin Rape Crisis Centre.

ESSAYS

CHAPTER 3

Irishwomen United: Nothing Was Off Limits

Ursula Barry

Sunday afternoons were a highlight of my weeks and weekends for a very special couple of years in the mid-1970s. The gathering of young, passionate women who made up Irishwomen United (IWU) was linked with the strongest belief that, not only could change happen, but that we would be central to making it happen. This was exhilarating. Without any hierarchical structures, but with active committees linked to specific campaigns, such as contraception and equal pay, or the production of the IWU magazine, *Banshee*, the energy was amazing. Impassioned debates broke out around selected feminist texts and themes, as we all stood around or sat on the floor of the room in 12 Pembroke Street. And nothing was off limits: from self-determined sexuality to pornography and the sex industry, to abortion rights, and discriminatory social welfare systems. This was unique on the Irish political landscape. One of my abiding memories of an IWU debate that went on over successive weekends was on the evidence of a matriarchal society and, more specifically, whether the Brehon Laws[1] provided examples of pre-patriarchy rule, during which Margaret Mead's[2] work was brought to life and put under scrutiny.

IWU meetings consisted of much laughter, argument, revelations, proposals for actions and issues to take up. There were members of left organisations, of which I was one, groups that gravitated together around lesbian identity, and those that were linked to legislative change and service provision. Post-meeting gatherings were places where friendships were shaped, as well as support given for those going through personal crises. Intimate relationships were formed and broken apart with equal intensity and lots of drama.

Membership of IWU was open to everyone as long as they agreed with the demands detailed in the Charter, which was the basis for the organisation, and which appeared on the back page of each issue of *Banshee*. The ground-breaking demands for free, legal contraception under state-financed birth-control clinics, and the right to free, legal, and safe abortion, were issues that were linked to wider legal rights: from equal pay, to social welfare, to lesbian and gay rights. Fundamental to IWU was women's control of our bodies based on access to contraception and abortion, lesbian and gay rights, women's diverse body images, and sexist portrayals of women in advertising and the media, and, most importantly, a growing realisation of the scale of violence against women and sexual abuse. IWU was strongly influenced by the key feminist concept of 'the personal is political', and the publication of *Our Bodies, Ourselves*[3] in Boston, overturning of the traditional left or mainstream patriarchal perspective on women and women's bodies. I had accidentally come across the launch of that amazing publication on Boston Common when I was working in America on a J1 visa in 1973, and my understanding of women, our bodies, our sexualities, and our health, including reproductive health, was radically changed as a result.

Linda Connolly's history of the Irish women's movement documents the threads that link the Irish Women's Liberation Movement (IWLM) of the early 1970s and IWU of the mid-1970s:

> The Irish Women's Liberation Movement introduced new methods of direct action, spontaneous demonstrations, stunts aimed at attracting media and public attention, such as the famous 'contraceptive train' on which a group of feminists brought condoms from Belfast to Dublin with maximum publicity.... It also brought a new insistence that 'the personal is political', that what is seen as 'private' life in reality interacts with what is seen as 'public' life, and is affected by the political, social and economic structures and policies of the day.[4]

IWU, building on the recent history and achievements of the IWLM, brought together lots of different kinds of campaigning, advocacy, and creative action that was linked with well-thought-out policy positions, and no lack of stunts to capture media attention: for example, occupying the Federated Union of Employers (FUE) offices as part of a campaign to force a backdown by government over a derogation of EU equal pay directives, or invading the 'men only' Forty Foot bathing area in Sandycove, which led ultimately to access for all. Not to mention the brilliant tactic of ordering multiple brandies in Dublin pubs, followed by an order for multiple pints of Guinness, and then refusing to pay for the former unless we were provided with the latter, exposing how most Dublin pubs refused to sell pints to women at the time, and which brought about a quick change in the rules. So much was achieved. Forcing contraception onto centre-stage and, thus, into the centre of the political process, and operating on a principle of equal access for all, meant bringing the IWU's Contraception Action Programme (CAP) from a city-centre shop into stalls in working-class communities, defying the law by making information available, and selling condoms and other contraceptive devices openly. The CAP perspective on contraception access across social classes was fundamental to the IWU perspective on gender, social and economic equality:

> Fundamentally, IWU and CAP members believed in a women's movement that allowed for the equal distribution of sexual knowledge and access to contraception. In this way, they foregrounded the connection between health and economic rights. Through their demonstrations, meetings and service provision, in unconventional spaces such as shops, markets, community centres and caravans, they challenged not only the law, but also the authority of both religious patriarchy and medical expertise in Ireland.
>
> The opening of the shop drew extensive media coverage and was featured by RTÉ in their news programme and in several other news reports. An article in the *Irish Independent* remarked that the shop had sold out of its stock of condoms, jellies, creams and caps hours after it had opened and that there had been no intervention by the police. The *Irish Press* reported that the first public customer was a soldier in uniform, with £25 in sales reported after the first two hours, almost covering the £30 per week rent of the premises. While CAP members popped champagne to celebrate the opening of the shop, not all were jubilant. Leslie Quelch, president of conservative group the League of Decency, remarked that he thought the opening of the shop was 'disgusting' and that he 'hoped that the silent majority would make

their feelings known to the authorities'. However, the shop was never raided, and no arrests were made.[5]

From the very beginning, the demands of IWU were always expressed through a consciousness of the deep-seated economic inequality that shaped Irish society, reflected in the demands for free, accessible, and legal services. The authorities took a relatively hands-off approach to the activities of IWU and the open selling of contraceptives. Reflecting on the multiple strategies, including direct action, which informed those engaged in the battle for contraception, Máiréad Enright and Emilie Cloatre describe the co-existence of different tactics, some at the edges of illegality:

> The project of anticipating the limits of state tolerance was always a 'doing'; a makeshift composition, even as the infrastructure and networks become stronger and more stable. Activists moved strategically between carefully choreographed strategies of disobedience which would not expose the movement to backlash, and public radical challenge which might directly provoke enforcement of the law, either generating public support or exposing state powerlessness. As groups gained in confidence, and in experience of living with this situation, they could incrementally adjust the boundaries which illegality set to their projects by deciding to take new risks. They would decide how visible to make their illegality.[6]

IWU brought about a new emphasis on feminist theory and practice, sexual politics, and socialist thinking to activism on women's rights. They also created a strong momentum for change and, importantly, significant legal reform and service provisions were achieved. As awareness of rape and domestic violence increased both internationally and nationally, a new urgency and intensity entered debates and campaigning activities. At the time, there was yet to be a recognition that rape within marriage was not only possible, but a very real threat in the lives of too many women, and needed to be criminalised, something that only finally happened in 1990. It took 12 years from the passing of that legislation for the first conviction of rape within marriage to take place in Ireland in 2002.[7] Following strong campaigning by women's organisations and those providing services on sexual abuse and violence, more recent legislation has strengthened the legal framework around sexual offences in Ireland, and includes a clear definition of 'consent to a sexual act' as something that is 'freely and voluntarily given'.[8] However, as noted by Seosamh Grainseir in 2018: 'The issue of rape continues to be plagued by issues such as under-reporting, not least due to complainants' lack of confidence in the legal system and their treatment in and out of the courts.'[9]

There were lots of firsts achieved before, during and after the mid-1970s when IWU was highly active, such as the setting-up of Ireland's first women's refuge by Women's Aid in 1974, the passing of the first domestic violence legislation in 1976 and (limited) contraception legislation in 1979, followed, later, by the first rape crisis centre in Dublin in 1979. Significant, new developments, involving members of IWU, were evident in the Women's Right to Choose Campaign, and Open Line Counselling in 1979, the Dublin Gay Collective in 1982 (later renamed The Dublin Lesbian and Gay Collective), and the Abortion Rights Campaign in 2013. IWU activists were also centrally involved in organising the first Reclaim the Night march when many thousands marched in Dublin.

Confronted with this new reality of legalised contraception and services in Ireland, right-wing, mainly Catholic, organisations became highly visible and strongly organised at the beginning of the 1980s. Their attention was focused on preventing any Supreme Court ruling, or political and legal campaigning, that would result in the legalisation of abortion in Ireland, under any circumstances. The Pro-Life Amendment Campaign (PLAC) was launched in 1981 and got the immediate backing of mainstream political parties for a constitutional amendment inserting the right to life of the foetus ('unborn child') into the Irish Constitution. PLAC was successful and, together with spin-off organisations like the Society for the Protection of Unborn Children (SPUC) and Youth Defence (YD), they launched a series of legislative and political attacks on the very organisations that had emerged during and after IWU, in particular the Open Door and other counselling services that provided referral to Britain to enable abortion access for women in Ireland. IWU activists continued to play a vital role in the achievement of reproductive rights through their involvement in the establishment of the Anti-Amendment Campaign, the setting-up of the radical feminist Right to Choose Organisation, and the critical role played by the Irish Women's Abortion Support Group (IWASG) in supporting women accessing abortion in Britain.

A bitter, hostile, and divisive campaign resulted in the insertion of foetal rights into the Irish Constitution in 1983, a unique development internationally, which put Ireland on the frontline of the anti-abortion movement globally. There followed many decades-long courtroom and medical battles, to the cost of women and girls in Ireland, but always challenged by political campaigns, organising, and advocacy by feminist and other organisations. Foetal rights were finally removed by way of a referendum in 2018 when two-thirds of the electorate voted YES for repeal of the anti-woman Eighth Amendment clause, and for the establishment of access to free, legal abortion services in Ireland. The struggle for reproductive justice continues to the present day, reflected in the current fight for abortion access for women in all areas of the country, and for many women with fatal foetal diagnoses. Feminists, socialists, and lesbians, who had formed the core of IWU, were everywhere across the organisations that fought battles over the following decades to establish reproductive justice for women, culminating in the Repeal Referendum in 2018. Ireland is the only country that has successfully held and passed, by popular vote, a national referendum on abortion access, confounding the final, futile attempts by the Catholic-influenced, right-wing, anti-abortion campaigns to prohibit abortion in all circumstances.

My own involvement during this period was in setting up and building the Dublin 4 Anti-Amendment group in 1981, which adopted some of the strategies of IWU in building a presence in local communities, from Ringsend to Donnybrook, developing a grassroots organisation, and taking many forms of direct action. As the campaign unfolded, I became a member of the national Anti-Amendment Steering Group, joined the Anti-Amendment Bus that toured cities and towns across the country, putting up posters and holding impromptu meetings to establish local anti-amendment groups. Later, I was part of the Women's Coalition Group that organised the 'Abortion Boat' in 1992, when 150 women, from all over Ireland, took the ferry to Holyhead to highlight the abortion issue in Ireland, and to support the estimated 100 Irish women who travelled to Britain every week to access abortion services. On their return to Dublin, balloons were released with the phone numbers of abortion services written on them. The catalyst for the event was the

1992 X Case, and the taking of an injunction against a sexually abused 14-year-old girl to prevent her and her family travelling to England to access abortion.[10] The 'Abortion Boat' highlighted the journeys being made by thousands of women from Ireland every year, to access abortion services on the private marketplace of another jurisdiction. Here, again, is evidence of the threads that link the IWLM 'contraceptive train' in 1971, defying the law and bringing contraceptives from Belfast to Dublin, with the IWU's Contraception Action Programme 1976–81, which challenged the law on the illegality of contraceptives by selling them openly, and the 'Abortion Boat' of the Women's Coalition in 1992, exposing the secret, hidden abortion journeys of women and confronting the illegality of access to abortion information in Ireland.

The roots of my political activism and academic interests were strongly planted in me during my time in IWU, and I have never strayed far over the years that followed. I have had the privilege of earning a living in spaces around reproductive and sexual justice. Working within women's studies, gender studies, and social justice in University College Dublin (UCD) I enjoyed playing a part in the early programme of women's studies in Ireland, which has played a key role in the radicalisation of tens of thousands of women over the last 35 years. It was the work of the Women's Studies Forum that brought together feminist scholars from across the UCD Campus, and became the precursor to the women's studies master's degree, first established in 1980, influencing, and influenced by, developments in the US and Britain, as well as other countries in Europe. A unique feature of UCD's Women's Studies Programme was the development of an Outreach Certificate and Diploma, which brought women's studies into working-class communities in many areas of Dublin, as well as rural areas, from Clondalkin to Ringsend, and from Longford to Letterkenny. This was a critical strategy developed by Ailbhe Smyth, the first director of Women's Studies in UCD, and implemented by Annie Dillon and, later, Aideen Quilty. Research has demonstrated time and again the transformative impact of those outreach programmes, as part of the broader movement of radical community education across the island. This new dynamic in women's and gender studies was built on the tradition established by IWU, in taking the focus on women in Irish society from the academy to the community, based on that critical coming together of academic scholarship and activism. There are now women and gender studies programmes across the third level sector in Ireland, and a number of outreach programmes that have brought together academic study and activism. There is much evidence of the high level of engagement of networks of feminist activists, academics, and working-class women's community organisations, forming the backbone of much vital national, feminist, and social justice campaigning.

IWU was a central component in shaping my life and my personal vision of bringing together activism and academia, particularly around reproductive rights/justice, and to the analysis of public policy in Ireland through a gender lens, exploring social policies and their impact on gender injustice and inequality. From the 1970s to the present day, my teaching and publishing, based in women's and gender studies at UCD, has focused on reproductive justice and gender inequalities in Ireland. As Director of Women's Studies and, subsequently, Gender Studies in UCD, I was able to immerse myself in exploring feminism as well as gender theory and practices with many thousands of students over several decades. I had the pleasure of being part of the teaching staff for the class of Gender Studies in 2017–18, which became centrally involved in the struggle to repeal the Eighth

Amendment, and to create the conditions for abortion services to be provided in Ireland. In representing Ireland from 1989 to the present day on the EU Scientific Analysis and Assessment of Gender Equality (SAAGE) Network, I have had the opportunity to engage with researchers and policymakers on gender equality across the EU and to learn how diverse countries were developing and applying gender equality. This experience heightened my recognition of the importance of the EU in creating a momentum for social change in Ireland through equality legislation in employment and social protection, in setting down minimum thresholds in rights to maternity, parental, and other leave entitlements, as well as, more recently, enhancement of early childcare provision, and the launch of a European Care Strategy in 2023.[11]

IWU brought together groups and individuals committed to changing the lives of women in Ireland, and to making breakthroughs towards women's control over our bodies, human rights, and economic justice. It was an organisation that was continuously evolving, never static, with a horizontal structure that generated imaginative ways to focus attention on gendered social injustice and inequality, demanding urgent social change. When I reflect on my time in IWU and afterwards, I often remember the world-renowned quotation attributed to Margaret Mead and her political perspective: 'Never doubt that a small group of thoughtful, committed and organised citizens can change the world; indeed, it's the only thing that ever has.'[12]

There are individual women or groups of women that I meet every now and again or with whom I have more regular contact, who were part of this IWU history. We share that legacy of excitement, anticipation, and expectation of a time in our youth that really was one of revolutionary change. At times, we brought a critical perspective to bear on our views of ourselves, our bodies, our sexualities, and our political perspectives, constrained within a rigid patriarchal society, towards a better understanding of our histories, of the diverse positions we occupy in the society, as well as the wider geopolitical and economic landscapes in which we live. At other times, there was, and still is, a frustration at how slow things have been to change, of uncovering the painful histories of so many women that were shamed, silenced, and incarcerated, of the continued widespread objectification of the bodies of women and girls, and the persistence of large-scale, widespread sexual, domestic, and gender-based violence.

IWU showed the ways in which direct action, campaigning, political advocacy and service provision went hand-in-hand, and also showed the capacity of small numbers of women to generate social movements critical to social change. Many organisations and campaigns set up around reproductive rights and reproductive justice over decades have fought bruising, but ultimately successful, campaigns to establish contraception and abortion services in Ireland. IWU has played a vital role in this history. The eyes of the world were on Ireland in 2015 when same sex marriage was legalised, and again in 2018 when foetal rights were deleted from our Constitution, giving great joy and much relief to so many in Ireland, and acting in solidarity with struggles for reproductive justice globally.

Ursula Barry lives and works in Ireland. She is Associate Professor Emeritus in Gender Studies at University College Dublin, and has been a feminist activist on reproductive justice since the 1970s. Ursula represents Ireland on the EU Research Network on Gender Equality, and has written on economic inequality, the care economy, and the feminisation of poverty. She was a member of the Expert Advisory Group to the Citizens' Assembly on Gender Equality.

CHAPTER 4

Arlen House: A Pioneer of Irish Publishing

Mary Rose Callaghan

> It is the way our sympathy flows and recoils that really determines our lives.
> D. H. Lawrence, *Lady Chatterley's Lover* (New York, 1928)

An incident from Catherine Rose's early childhood is described by Colette McAndrew in her fascinating research on Arlen House, and provides a glimpse into the ways Catherine's understanding of injustice began:

> A teacher was trying to light a fire in the two roomed rural school, but without success. To the shame of at least one child present, she then called the cleaner's daughter, also a pupil, to the front of the class and insisted that the child light the fire, a task beyond the competence of a seven-year-old. The teacher, by then angry, frustrated and cold, humiliated the child in front of the class.[1]

Catherine Rose was that child witness.

Later, as an adult, Catherine's sympathy was reignited by reading the women's pages of the daily newspapers. When working for Cork Publisher, Mercier Press, she discovered her pay was less than male colleagues for the same work, a system that was common practice then, and still exists in some jobs today. Although a minority of women in the 1970s had careers in banks, in nursing, or in teaching, most had few opportunities outside marriage and childbirth. That contraceptives were illegal, as well as divorce and abortion, is well known, but the concept of 'ladylikeness' was nearly as bad. In my youth, the Archbishop of Dublin, John Charles McQuaid, frowned on women cycling, playing hockey or using Tampax on the basis that such activities might arouse unwanted passion. It's not hard to imagine what today's young women, winning gold medals in the Paris Olympics, would think of Ireland in 1975. The past is another country, which is just as well.

The 1916 Proclamation of the Irish Republic promised equality to all citizens, but, instead, life in the new state narrowed in many ways, as a result of the relationship between the state and the Catholic Church. The Censorship of Publications Act in 1935, heavily influenced by the church, damaged the careers of many writers, both male and female. Bishops controlled education and health as well as the government, and their influence is captured in contemporary newscasts of politicians kneeling to kiss bishops' rings at state occasions.

Catherine Rose worked as an RTÉ radio producer in Cork, and, at the suggestion of Mercier Press, she had written a book about Irish women's lives, but Mercier ultimately considered the book to be unmarketable, so she put it aside. Finding herself living in Galway because of her husband's job, she decided to publish her own book: *The Female Experience: The Story of the Woman Movement in Ireland*, launched in September 1975, and Arlen House was born.[2]

The book was disparaged by Christina Murphy, then Woman's Editor of *The Irish Times*, but it sparked the interest of Terry Prone, a prominent journalist. Janet Martin, former Woman's Editor of the *Irish Independent*, was also impressed, and both women became co-founders of the press along with activist and Dominican nun, Margaret Mac Curtain, who was then a history lecturer in University College Dublin (UCD). Poet Eavan Boland also signed on as an editor and was to be an inspiring influence, teaching and facilitating writing workshops over the years. Early Arlen House meetings were held in the different founders' houses with children playing in the background. Arlen House published Eavan Boland's trailblazing poetry from 1980 to 1989: *In Her Own Image* (1980), illustrated by Constance Short; *Night Feed* (1982); *The Journey and Other Poems* (1986); *Carcanet* (1987); and *Selected Poems* (1989). Arlen went on to publish many other poets.

Arlen's second publication was Janet Martin's, *The Essential Guide for Women in Ireland*, which was launched at Listowel Writers' Week in 1977. As well as containing useful information, the book advised on contraceptives and abortion, something the publishers could have been jailed for, but weren't. It was an example of Catherine Rose's courage, which was to endure for the next ten years.

Alan Hayes, the present publisher of Arlen House,[3] lists other early publications in *Look! It's a Woman Writer*, edited by Éilís Ní Duibhne – a fascinating read for anyone interested in Irish women writers. These early Arlen books mainly covered political and social affairs – health, children's rights and childcare, family status, education, biography, history, new and classic literature, and art. A pamphlet, *Make Sure You Get Equal Pay* (1977) compiled by the Trade Union Women's Forum was widely distributed, as was Evelyn Conlon's sex education book for children, the first ever to be published in Ireland: *Where Did I Come From* (1980). Mollie Lloyd's *The Change of Life* (1979/81), sold over 20,000 copies. Others included *Who's Minding the Children?* (1981) by Ronit Lentin and Geraldine Niland; *Coping Alone* (1982) by Clara Clark; Máire Mullarney's *Anything School Can Do, You Can Do Better* (1983) which sold over 10,000 copies; Stanislaus Kennedy's *But Where Can I Go? Homeless Women in Dublin*, and *Children First* by Charles Mullan, their first male writer.

Terry Prone's books *Write and Get Paid for It* (1977), and, later, *Just a Few Words* (1985) were best sellers and published under a new general imprint called Turoe Press. Turoe also published Maeve Binchy's first play *Deeply Regretted By* (1979). Eileen Kane's *Doing Your Own Research*, published with Marion Boyars (1983), was in print until 2007. Boyars also had a co-publication and distribution agreement with Arlen in the 1980s.

From the foundation of the Irish State up to the 1950s, Irish women fiction writers had been published in both Ireland and Britain. But, during the 1950s, a new conservatism had set in. Edna O'Brien was denounced from the altar, and her books, along with many others, were banned. When I was a teenager the only Irish woman writer I had heard of was Mary Lavin. No works by women were taught in my school. All the poems and plays we read were by men. I actually thought women only wrote for children. Arlen House was determined to change this by promoting new and classic fiction by Irish women.

Terry Prone was Arlen's first fiction editor. In 1978 Arlen launched a short story competition for Irish women. Maxwell House Coffee agreed to sponsor it, persuaded by Terry Prone and Mary Finan, a prominent PR executive. David Marcus, Mary Lavin, and Eavan Boland were the judges.[4] Although living in America, I submitted a story about a nun caught shoplifting, reflecting change in Ireland. The subject shocked some people, but I was delighted to be one of the runners-up. There was one overall winner in the competition, 'The Wall Reader' by Fiona Barr set in 'the Troubles', and the rest were equally placed. Picked from over 1,000 submissions from all over Ireland, they were published as *The Wall Reader*, a thin paperback, which became an unexpected best-seller. The launch was held in the Berkely Court, one of Dublin's most exclusive hotels at the time, where Irish coffee and coffee cake were served in abundance. I still remember the thrill of attending, and even remember what I was wearing. The winner was presented with £100, and runners up £50. Subsequent Maxwell House competitions allowed poetry as well as short stories to be submitted, and these competitions became the start of a career for many Irish writers.

My success led to the publication of *Mothers*, my first novel. The story of three generations of unmarried mothers was launched in Dublin in 1982, and later in New York by Marion Boyars. The book sold well, despite some early reservations that it might negatively influence the upcoming referendum to change the constitution. I have the warmest memories of Catherine Rose and everyone at Arlen House. My first novel was also their first new fiction, since their previous novels had been classical reprints.

Between 1980 and 1987, inspired by London's Virago Press, who had begun republishing literary classics by women, Arlen House started resurrecting our own forgotten novels. Writers like Kate O'Brien, Kathleen Keane, Janet McNeil, Anne Crone, and Norah Hoult were republished with great success. *The Ante Room* by Kate O'Brien had an introduction by Eavan Boland. As a consequence, Arlen House sponsored the Kate O'Brien weekend in her native Limerick, which is still running today. It was organised by the poet Louise C Callaghan, an Arlen House staff member at the time.

Arlen House aimed to encourage women in every aspect of life. In 1981 they announced a Women's Literary Competition bursary for women writers, including women in prison, which would enable the winner to buy writing materials. The press also founded the Women's Education Bureau (WEB), which ran workshops for aspiring writers. A magazine was also founded, *The Web*, of which Eavan Boland was the general editor, while Evelyn Conlon and I were guest editors of the first edition. Sadly, the journal folded after one issue because the Arts Council ceased funding it. By this time, Arlen House was running into trouble financially and, in 1987, the press was bought by two female investors. Hope was running high for its continuation under new ownership, but, sadly, it closed down before any books were published. The buyers didn't realise that publishing is a labour of love and doesn't always make money. A revival was promised in 1988, but didn't occur.

Eavan Boland's *Selected Poems* was published by WEB/Carcanet in 1989, after Arlen House had folded. By now a prominent poet, Eavan remained a passionate encourager of women who wanted to write. WEB continued to organise day and weekend seminars at different venues. Some were held in the Irish Writers Centre, the Dominican Convent

Sion Hill, and other venues. Established writers, among them John McGahern, Jennifer Johnston, and Seamus Heaney, facilitated these workshops, where women were helped to find a voice. Catherine Rose also organised an AnCo course for apprentice writers. Another workshop, sponsored by WEB along with the Arts Council, facilitated again by Eavan Boland, was held in the Tyrone Guthrie Centre, Annaghmakerrig. Many of the participants became successful writers, and the group still meets to this day.

Mary Rose Callaghan was born in Ireland. She has lived in England and America, and now lives in Bray, County Wicklow. Her first novel, *Mothers*, was published by Arlen House in 1982, and she went on to publish nine others, a collection of short stories, a memoir and a biography of Kitty O'Shea. Mary Rose was a contributing editor for the *Journal of Irish Literature* from 1975 to 1993, and associate editor for the first two editions of the *Dictionary of Irish Literature*. She has taught writing at the University of Delaware.

CHAPTER 5

Dublin Rape Crisis Centre

Collective Essay

The agency we know today as the Dublin Rape Crisis Centre (DRCC) began life as one of the many 'key groups'[1] to emerge from Irishwomen United (IWU), a full two years before the Centre officially opened:

> During 1977 and 1978, there was a growing number of media reports about the rape and sexual assault of women in Ireland. It was decided at an IWU meeting that we needed to do something about the fact that there was no rape crisis centre or support here for women who had been sexually assaulted. An IWU group was set up on this issue, to which I volunteered. The group did a huge amount of research, contacted rape crisis centres in Britain, and spent time becoming informed on legal and other issues surrounding rape and sexual assault. *Anne O'Donnell (founder member)*[2]

The group's first meeting took place in the Students' Union Building of Trinity College Dublin, at 6.30pm on Tuesday, 26 July 1977,[3] and, by the second meeting, the provisional name of 'Campaign against Rape' (CAR) was agreed.

Susan McKay's detailed history of the DRCC,[4] written on the occasion of its 25th anniversary, as well as Minutes of early meetings held in the Centre's archive, reveal the significant amount of hard work and research that went into setting up the Centre, starting from that first meeting in July 1977, in a process that echoed the establishment of the London Rape Crisis Centre (LRCC):[5]

> In setting up the DRCC we wanted it to last, we would take our time to get it right. That now strikes me as particularly wise. When we came to the point of opening, we did an amount of pre-publicity, most of it well-received, which helped to combat the opposing abuse thrown at us. I'm astounded at the patience we manifested publicly in those first few months. (I'll say nothing about our private conversations). *Evelyn Conlon*

The extent and intensity of the research and training meant that it became clear quite quickly that meetings would, by necessity, need to be closed 'to anyone who had not previously attended, on the grounds that it was important to brief ourselves as fully as possible and late arrivals would hinder this'.[6] The Minutes indicate this was a temporary situation, but one that would allow a core group of members to carry out the essential, foundational work and, once established, the Centre could be opened up and run as a collective, along the lines of IWU.

> I keep in mind that many have forgotten whether it was Catullus or Cicero who said that memory is the treasure and guardian of all, so I tread carefully. Because each of us who sat in those rooms, learning, being shocked, galvanising ourselves, being determined, has our own unique memory of what it was like. But, if I'm to think, fast, of the word that comes to mind about the first meeting, it's 'innocence'. Now, here we were, determined to create a place where this particular violence could be brought out from the dark. But what we did not know was how addressing that would affect us personally. I've written, in other places, about the dangers of memory, how forgetting is sometimes good for us, and I certainly think that we learned how to do that as required. No doubt this is well-known best practice in jobs that deal with trauma, but we were untrained, and yet we took the blind leap. Various people came to our meetings to help us on our route – I particularly remember Mary McAleese on legal issues, John Cullen on trauma, Bean Garda Wymes, as she was known to us, on Garda procedure, and Marie Butterly from the ISPCC (Irish Society for the Prevention of Cruelty to Children), who spoke to us about incest. I remember being aghast at some of her statistics. Even we, sympathetic as we were, simply did not want to believe that some of what we were hearing was true. *Evelyn Conlon*

Amongst the others who offered support were:

- Monica Barnes from the Council for the Status of Women (CSW), who invited representatives from CAR to attend a subcommittee meeting, which was drafting a submission to the Law Reform Commission
- Dr Hazel Boland who outlined the importance of sympathetic doctors and the fact that they may have to give evidence in court
- Nuala Fennell, who established the AIM family-law group, on the importance of public image if they were to avoid alienating government bodies
- Maureen Gaffney, a psychologist with the Eastern Health Board
- Representatives from the Samaritans
- Nicola Quinn, a therapist who later provided training
- Social workers

Anne Connolly remembers:

> We were well-received when we got in touch with Garda HQ. They took us through what was involved in preparing for a prosecution. They were well-disposed to the rape victim having the support of an RCC counsellor, unlike the situation that existed in Britain, and they were very aware that the woman had no legal standing in court, she was simply a witness.

Ger Moane joined the group in 1978, along with others from IWU:

> 'Our first task was to educate ourselves about rape and sexual assault, about which there was very little discussion or understanding – it was a hidden crime, rarely reported, and rarely prosecuted. People felt mostly ashamed and were afraid to report it, and there were no obvious services or psychological support. There was little understanding of the violence and pain that rape victims experienced, it was seen as a sexual crime rather than a crime of violence.
> I have a vivid memory of a weekend training workshop with Nicola Quinn in order to develop our listening skills. She introduced us to the basic concepts of listening, mirroring, empathising, and we got into groups and worked in one-to-one sessions that unleashed quite a lot of emotions. *Ger Moane (member 1978–9)*

An early policy document reveals the level of commitment expected from members: there was a strict requirement to attend weekly meetings and training sessions, including participation in encounter groups, to attend public speaking lessons and role-playing sessions, to study and read about rape. The group also devised its own training, based on advice from more established centres, and from invited speakers to the weekly meetings, and time was spent discussing position papers, policy drafts, and discussions about theories on the subject of rape. 'It was challenging to take on a feminist analysis, which framed rape as a crime of violence. A very important consideration was the type of service we wanted to provide, and the logistics of that', *Ger Moane*. Reflecting an effort to be as inclusive and non-directive as possible, the group also acknowledged the possibility that an Irish woman who was raped might want to talk to a priest, so a list of potential names was drawn up.

After the initial two years of training and research the DRCC was officially launched on 19 February 1979, with the latest, automated answering machine (facilitated by Charles Haughey, via Evelyn Conlon), and 19 volunteers, made up of some original members of CAR, and others who were newly trained.

> We were offered the use of a room in the Women's Aid building in Harcourt Terrace ... After publicly launching our rape crisis phone service to the media, we set up a rota and took turns to staff the line. All we could offer the women who phoned was a sympathetic listening ear, an assurance that we believed them, information about where they could get professional help or advice and the offer to accompany them to court. *Anne O'Donnell*

The launch of the Centre included a press statement providing information on the 'Function of the Rape Crisis Centre',[7] which involved: counselling, advice on obtaining medical and legal assistance, emotional support, medical help (whereby someone from the Centre would accompany the woman to her family doctor, a police doctor, or another 'sympathetic' doctor), and legal advice. Anyone who wished to access the service was asked to call Dublin 601470. During the hours of 8pm to 8am every night, as well as 8am to 8pm on Saturday and Sunday, the answering service would provide the phone number of the person on duty.

> And then we got to the task. Top of the agenda was how to work this new-fangled answering machine. We could not move forward until everyone had got the amazed hang of it. That accomplished, we opened the lines. We learned, ferociously, on our feet. Everything from listening, advocating, accompanying to Garda stations, attending court. We heard historical stories from women who had never before spoken to a single person about what had been done to them. We were shocked by some things, including an early call from a man – why had we not expected that? We learned how to support each other. We learned how to still live in our own real worlds, despite what we were hearing. And when we finished our agreed terms of commitment, we learned how to forget.
>
> Of course we knew about violence against women in all its forms, but hadn't as yet experienced up close the maelstrom, the chaos, the trauma caused by rape. Many of us had been involved in the 'Reclaim the Night March', organised in conjunction with local women from Seán McDermott Street. Marches of this order had happened in other places, and we knew how important they were. The pre-publicity was occasionally side-tracked by the question of why men weren't marching with us. I went out to RTÉ to answer that, the response on the tip of my tongue being that the whole point of the event was that women should be able to walk their streets alone. I was, of course, nervous, but was, weirdly, helped enormously by the fact that the first Polish pope had just been elected. The researchers had eventually found a

compatriot priest prepared to leave the celebrations to discuss the significance of this. Thus, the intensity of the focus was happily divided. *Evelyn Conlon*

I was horrified by the first actual case that I encountered of a woman who had been subjected to years of rape, sexual assault and physical violence. Perhaps more than readings or discussion, it brought home to me the dehumanisation and brutalisation of rape, and the violence that women endured. *Ger Moane*

Speaking to the women callers was a deeply humbling experience. They were so grateful to have someone to talk to and an acknowledgement of the abuse they had experienced. *Anne O'Donnell*

And the callers were not the only ones grateful for the existence of the helpline.

I'd heard of the Dublin Rape Crisis Centre, but knew nothing about it. But when I was living in Rathmines in the 1980s, a frantic man rang my home number, thinking he was onto the Centre. I told him it was the wrong number and looked up the number of the Centre for him. The numbers were almost the same. I'll always remember the panic in his voice, and I felt so relieved there was someone to help him. *Mary Rose Callaghan*

In August 1980, the Department of Health gave the DRCC its first grant of £5,000, which was used to appoint Anne O'Donnell as full-time administrator, but it is doubtful that anyone could have predicted the many years ahead in which existing funding came under threat, and increased or different funding had to be fought for; and yet the work continued, and the numbers needing the service increased, year-on-year.

Throughout the 1980s, the agency was faced with a significant increase in the number of calls from incest victims. In 1983, for instance, the Centre dealt with 196 cases of rape and sexual assault and, in 28 cases, the rapist was a relative and the victim was under 15 years old, whilst in 1984, out of a total of 426 rapes, 152 were defined as childhood sexual abuse.[8] Seeking advice and training on the issue of incest proved extremely challenging, and there were lengthy debates within the collective as to whether they should be handling these cases at all.

During its 46-year existence the DRCC has consistently been involved in advocacy campaigns around the core issue of sexual violence, including: childhood sexual abuse (CSA); incest; sex education in schools; the reform of rape laws; treatment programmes in prisons; marital rape; male rape; support within the justice system; training programmes; and much more. One of its most important campaigns in the 1980s related to forensic healthcare, which led to the establishment of the first Sexual Assault Treatment Unit (SATU) in the Rotunda Hospital in 1985:

The Rotunda SATU commenced as a pilot in 1985, and Anne O'Donnell was involved in the working group that established it. The first training days were held on 12 and 13 Dec. 1984, in readiness for the pilot starting. Anne O'Donnell spoke on 'First Contact with the Victim' and on 'Follow Up'. *Professor Maeve Eogan, Consultant Obstetrician and Gynaecologist and National Clinical Lead SATU (HSE)*

In January 1985, the Sexual Assault Treatment Unit (SATU) was established in the Rotunda Hospital, Dublin, with 12 women doctors in place. All Garda stations and health agencies in the Eastern Health Board region were notified, and, from the beginning, a rota of DRCC volunteers was linked to the SATU, with the SATU on-duty nurse notifying the volunteer when a victim/survivor was coming in.

In 1988, Anne O'Donnell resigned, for personal reasons. She was the last of the DRCC founders to leave the collective and was missed by many. Bernie Purcell then took over as Director, followed by Olive Braiden in 1990. One of Braiden's first jobs was to appoint a board of directors, a step that rang the death knell for the collective, since securing funding, overseeing management structures, etc., all part of any Board's remit, cannot co-exist with the concept of a collective. Anne O'Donnell has always acknowledged that there was pain in letting go of the collective.[9]

Rebecca Pelan[10] – who worked in the DRCC in recent years, first as a telephone counsellor and accompaniment volunteer, then later, as a staff member on the National Helpline telephone team, and, finally, as interim manager of Volunteer Services – remembers being both surprised and incredibly impressed when she realised that the training given to DRCC volunteers today, remains remarkably unchanged from that of the very early group members who answered the first automated phone system, particularly in terms of core training, such as listening skills, non-directive counselling principles, empathy, information on the legal and medical aspects of rape, role playing, rape myths, and more, suggesting that the early 'foundational group' got it right first time.

Anne O'Donnell believes that the core group who worked together from 1977 carried out what are now standard procedures in training – such as training-needs analyses and trauma-informed practices – without being overtly aware of these at the time.[11] But there have been some changes, of course: the delivery of the training today has altered, especially since Covid19, when online sessions were introduced, by necessity, and have since become a standard component of the training programme, while the 'new-fangled' automated phone system of the early days has been replaced with a sophisticated, software-based system, accessed via an 'app' on a mobile phone, which staff and on-duty volunteers simply log in to. And, in addition to extensive clinical services, the Centre now has departments of education, communications, fundraising, human resources, and more. What has not changed, however, is that the phone line – now known as the 24-hour National Helpline – remains the core component in the work of the Centre.

> At the 2019 fortieth anniversary of the Dublin Rape Crisis Centre, held in The Royal College of Surgeons, Dublin, Anne O'Donnell and I spoke to a room crowded with DRCC staff, supporters, volunteers, councillors, all people who knew more than we did when we started. Several organisations and support groups were represented, prevalent among them the Gardaí. It was then that I remembered how much I had forgotten. *Evelyn Conlon*

And from Anne O'Donnell: 'The modest and low-key start [of the DRCC] marked the beginning of a journey that would eventually lead to the establishment of highly professional and expert rape crisis centres in many parts of Ireland'. Currently, there are 19 rape crisis centres across the Republic and North of Ireland, and six sexual assault treatment units.[12]

CHAPTER 6

The Well Woman Centre

Anne Connolly

When the Well Woman Centre opened its doors in the basement of 63 Lower Leeson Street, Dublin, in late January 1978, it was met with a deafening silence. The press launch, two days earlier, announcing Ireland' s latest new player on the emerging 'family planning' scene in Ireland, elicited zero media coverage. Worse, the two doctors scheduled to be key members of the clinical team had been advised by Professor Éamon de Valera in the Mater Hospital, to choose between a career in medicine or a career in our clinic. Understandably, they had to bow to the pressure just days before we opened. So, no public awareness, no doctors. The rest of the small team were left waiting for the first clients to somehow miraculously show up.

However, all that changed on that first afternoon when four anti-abortionist protesters picketed the entrance to our clinic, complete with gory placards and loud, colourful language. They were remonstrating against the evils that the Well Woman represented. Apparently we were part of an international conspiracy that would bring a string of horrors to Ireland – contraception, promiscuity, abortion, homosexuality, and much worse. Their pickets and sensational leaflets spelt it out in lurid detail. One phone call to the evening papers was all it took. The ensuing front page of the *Evening Herald*, with its colourful pictures, the name, address and list of services being provided by Well Woman, gave us advertising we could never have afforded, and ensured we never looked back.

Why did decent caring doctors have to choose between a career in hospital medicine or working with us? Why did the 'SPUC brigade',[1] as they became known, bother to picket us – there were other clinics in Dublin offering a wide range of what was then termed 'family planning' services, and whose leadership had bravely pioneered this 'new to Ireland' service in the preceding decade? There were now four such clinics in Dublin.

So, what made us different? Was it that our language was different: we offered a wide range of contraception (not family planning) services, and we made it clear that no marriage certificate was required to avail of them? Was it that our services were different? We clearly signalled from the start that we included non-directive pregnancy counselling services in our programme and, where chosen, we referred women to Britain for safe abortions AND provided the medical check-ups and counselling they might seek after. Was this the beginning of a concerted action by the religious far right to 'fight back' against a growing tide of liberalism, who enjoyed financial support from well-funded organisations in the United States? Was this one of the early signs of a campaign that ultimately championed the 1983 insertion of a constitutional ban on abortion, despite abortion already being a crime under the 1861 Offences against the Persons Act, and punishable by life imprisonment?

I was approached in early 1977 by Dr Tim Black, Director of the Marie Stopes Clinic in London, asking me if I would be willing to consider establishing and running a Well Woman clinic in Dublin. The late Dr David Nowlan from *The Irish Times* had recommended me. The idea of setting up a woman-centred sexual and reproductive health centre, which would enable women to make informed choices about their reproductive health and fertility, really appealed. However, I knew nothing about how to run a business, albeit a not-for-profit one. So why ask me? I was 24 years of age, had just graduated from Trinity College Dublin with a degree in History and Politics, followed by a year as Vice President of the Student Union. Not very obvious qualifications for the role.

The aim of the clinic was to provide a full range of contraception services, including vasectomy, selling condoms over the counter and by post, dispensing with any pretence that the services were for married people and only for family planning purposes. And we offered non-directive pregnancy counselling services and abortion referrals, where chosen.

It soon became clear that they asked me because, as a student union leader, I had been quite outspoken on a woman's right to control her own fertility, and included in that, her right to terminate an unwanted pregnancy. Because so few people were advocating publicly on this issue, I quickly became identified as the 'pro-abortion advocate'. Despite efforts on my part to be associated with many of the other issues of the day, it came to define me. I hadn't been the first person Marie Stopes approached, others had apparently turned down the offer.

Any history of the Well Woman Centre has to acknowledge the pioneering role played by those who went before. By the time we opened our doors, there were six different organisations, all calling themselves family planning clinics, founded from 1969 onwards: the Family Planning Association (IFPA 1969); Family Planning Service (FPS 1972); Cork (1974); Limerick (1976); Galway (1977); and Bray (1978). Shortly after the Well Woman was set up, we came together and forged a national network. We met regularly to discuss shared challenges and provide each other with moral support when needed.

The history of the family planning movement in Ireland is a worthwhile topic in its own right. It is well summarised in a 2023 article by Laura Kelly,[2] which profiles how, in 1968, a group of courageous doctors and others came together to address the lack of family planning services in Ireland. The group was led by stalwarts, such as Dr James Loughran, Dr Michael Soloman, Dr Joan Wilson, Dr Dermot Hourihane (father of journalist Anne Marie Hourihane), and Máire Mullarney (psychologist and mother of eleven children). Subsequently, this led to the opening of the first IFPA Clinic in Synge Street, followed quickly by another in Mountjoy Square, and the FPS in Pembroke Road.

Others played an even more public advocacy role. Frank Crummy and Robin Cochran, co-founders of FPS, along with Pat O'Donovan, faced a wide range of logistical as well as social/political challenges. Openly providing 'family planning' services required the sourcing of contraceptives from Britain – condoms, diaphragms, IUDs, and the contraceptive pill (available in Ireland as a cycle regulator) – as well as the need to organise laboratories for smear tests, and locate consultant gynaecologists and others willing to take referrals. This is infrastructure we take for granted now, but then it required finding sympathetic players within the system. And they did exist.

The opportunity to create such a disruptive and woman-centred service strongly appealed to the politically 'lefty', burgeoning feminist that I was at the time. So, when offered the role, I quickly agreed, despite some concerns on my part about the Marie Stopes approach and what I perceived was a 'population control' agenda; concerns that ultimately led me to break from them some years later.

Setting up the Well Woman Centre took nine months of intensive preparations, from when I agreed to take on the role in March 1977 until the day we opened our doors to the public in late January 1978. Thankfully, I had little idea of the obstacles ahead created by the prevailing socio-political climate, as well as my own lack of management expertise. I received very basic training in the Marie Stopes Clinic in London on how to run a Well Woman Centre; everything from sourcing products, designing services, and booking systems, pricing, recruitment, single incision vasectomies, insurance, to financial management and much more.

Back in Ireland, the first challenge was to secure a suitable premises, but auctioneers were not willing to help, given the nature of our enterprise. Recruiting a clinical team, on the other hand, proved surprisingly uncomplicated. The IFPA had developed family planning training courses for nurses and doctors, creating a pool of fully trained personnel. On that first day, with the support of the ever-helpful Frank Crummy, we found a saviour in Dr Norah Sheehy Skeffington, despite Professor de Valera's best efforts. And, following the headline-grabbing picketing on that day, we continued to receive extensive and, largely sympathetic, media coverage. The clients came in their droves, and so did the nurses and doctors we needed to run the clinic. Doctors like Maura Woods, John O'Keeffe, Catherine Hayes, nurses Ann O'Keefe, Lilian, and the amazing reception staff and counsellors, Mary McNeany, her sister Joan, Bonny Maher, Felice Cohen, Joan King, Noreen Byrne, and many more.

In the almost seven years I was CEO, we had the autonomy and ambition to innovate in response to what we could see were unmet needs. We differentiated ourselves from the other clinics in a number of ways: we were a woman-centred health service, seeking to 'de-medicalise', where possible. This translated into quite distinctive approaches and practices. For example, we didn't allow the use of examination stirrups; clients were 'clients' and not patients; clients and all staff were on first name terms; clients were handed a copy of their medical records when they arrived, and were free to read the nurses' and doctors' notes from previous visits. We stressed the importance of giving our clients information on the range of contraception options available to them, and for them to choose what best suited their lifestyle, within the limits of medical safety.

We listened carefully to the needs of our clients and, as a result, innovated regularly with a wider range of services than were typically then provided in family planning clinics. For example, we:

- offered the first menopause clinic;
- pioneered AIH and AID (artificial insemination by husband and by donor sperm) for women experiencing difficulty conceiving;

- used behavioural psychologists in our counselling service;
- offered pre-pregnancy health advice;
- openly ran a mail order service selling condoms, spermicides, and a range of other products;
- were the first to openly provide 'morning after' contraception. Initially, this was offered in the form of a double dose contraceptive pill, but, later, extended to provide post-coital IUD's up to ten days post-unprotected intercourse. Interestingly, we were able to do this, unlike clinics in Britain who were hamstrung by an interpretation that it would breach their abortion laws.

At the same time, the Centre was always very explicit in including pregnancy counselling in our suite of services. We offered non-directive counselling, which gave women a safe and unpressurised space to think through an unplanned pregnancy and decide for themselves whether to proceed with or terminate their pregnancies. Equally, we were very open about the fact that, should they choose to terminate, we had relationships with a number of abortion clinics in Britain, where our clients could be guaranteed safe procedures and a sympathetic staff. Most importantly, we offered those women post-abortion check-ups and the security of having somewhere to go if they experienced any problems.

When I left the Well Woman Centre in 1984, just over seven years since I first got involved, there were over 35,000 clinic clients on our books, in addition to the many thousands availing of our mail order and other services. Looking back now, over 40 years later, it all seems like another world. Back then, despite our ardent campaigning, I don't think any of us really believed that we would live to see an Ireland benefiting from relatively liberal abortion laws. The May 2018 Referendum, repealing the Eighth Amendment, was approved (64.4 per cent to 33.6 per cent), enabling the passing of the Health (Regulation of Termination of Pregnancy) Act in December 2018. This allowed for legal abortions up to twelve weeks, and in later cases where the pregnant woman's life or health is at risk. Nor could we have envisioned an Ireland where, in May 2015, 62 per cent of voters approved a constitutional change legalising same-sex marriage, the first country in the world to do so by popular vote. In the 1970s and 1980s, attitudes were changing, albeit slowly, but no-one could have known that from the prevailing orthodoxies in Dáil Eireann at the time.

In 1932 a description by British left social reformer, R. H. Tawney, describing the British Labour Party, aptly summarises the political environment prevailing in Ireland at the time: 'intellectual timidity, conservatism, conventionality, which keeps politics trailing tardily in the rear of realities'.[3] The changes in public attitudes and behaviours were enabled by a number of factors: Ireland joined the EEC in 1973, and this resulted in reforms to equality legislation, and through travel to Brussels, to the exposure of senior policy-makers to more liberal European mores. Ireland became more porous to the influences of global liberation movements, such as the civil, black, and women's rights movements of the late 1960s and early 1970s. Irish people began to travel more, and were becoming better educated through increased access to higher education. And the various scandals within the Catholic Church began to significantly erode clerical influence. However, for us in the Well Woman Centre, there were two main factors that afforded us protection against prosecution and closure: the women's movement, and changes in the media, both of which helped create a climate and appetite for change, where previously none had existed.

In the 1970s, the women's movement was comprised of two, somewhat parallel bodies. The first was a relatively cautious, and to some of us, somewhat conservative, Council for the Status of Women, founded in 1973, which functioned as an umbrella body for a large number of women's organisations. It was an important voice for women, was consulted by government, and attracted some very effective leaders, including Hilda Tweedy, Monica Barnes, and Frances Fitzgerald. Possibly unfairly, we found it too hesitant in campaigning for liberalising contraception laws. By contrast, the second, and more vocal and radical, branch of the movement consisted of the Irish Women's Liberation Movement (IWLM) and, later, Irishwomen United (IWU). Neither had any hesitations, although perhaps, understandably, the former did not include abortion in the founding six demands of their manifesto, *Chains or Change*. Nevertheless, some seven years before the Well Woman Centre opened its doors, the high-profile 'contraceptive train' in 1971, which grabbed the attention of Irish and international media alike, certainly put the issue of contraception firmly on the political agenda.

The other key enabler for us in the Centre was the media, mainly, but not exclusively *The Irish Times* and RTÉ.[4] In particular, *The Irish Times*, under the leadership of editor Douglas Gageby (from 1964 to 1986) played a major role. In the 1970s Gageby recruited some high-profile feminist writers and social commentators: Nell McCafferty, Mary Maher, Mary Cummins, and Mary Holland. Whilst abortion remained taboo, the paper was key in challenging the laws on contraception, and gave a voice to a more radical feminist perspective.

In RTÉ, broadcasters such as Gay Byrne and Marian Finucane provided important platforms for airing views that challenged prevailing orthodoxies. Gay had an extraordinary talent for getting people to phone in with personal stories they were too shamed or scared to tell even their nearest and dearest. These stories inevitably addressed the issue of unwanted pregnancies and larger-than-wanted family sizes. Gay, through both his radio programme and the Saturday night *Late Late Show*, gave the Well Woman Centre a strong platform for making our case for legalising and broadening access to contraception in this country.

In 1979, RTÉ launched *Women Today* hosted, initially, by Marian Finucane and produced by Clare Duignan, and which went out five days a week. This too proved to be a highly influential forum and an important voice for Irish women. In 1980, Marian approached us and asked whether it might be possible to interview a woman going to Britain for an abortion. One very courageous young woman agreed, and the result was a most powerful documentary *The Lonely Crisis*, involving interviews with the woman at various stages of her journey. It deservedly won Marian the Prix d'Italia Award from the Italian Press Association.

In that same year, Mary McAleese approached us to be involved in a television documentary, also following a woman over to Britain on the Liverpool ferry, and it would include interviews with some of the British service-providers. Again, a brave woman volunteered, and Mary's highly sensitive documentary,[5] along with Marian's, were important initial airings of the abortion issue. They provided important insights into the personal plights of Irish women having to travel overseas to terminate their unwanted pregnancies.

In its first eight years, the Well Woman Centre was clearly in breach of the law in providing medical and mail order contraception services, but we were never prevented from doing so.[6] We were also clearly in breach of the spirit of the 1861 Offences against the Persons Act in openly referring women to Britain for abortion and in providing post-coital/

emergency IUDs within ten days of unprotected sex. But there was never any legal attempt to challenge what we were doing. Yes, there were occasional visits by the Vice Squad on foot of complaints from members of the public and, occasionally, I was called up to attend the Harcourt Street Garda Station to answer questions. But all such encounters were not only polite, but, for the most part, warm and friendly with a sense that the Gardaí involved were simply 'going through the motions' to tick the 'done' box.

The truth is there was no legal or political appetite to stop us. The lag between the political-legal establishment and public opinion was increasing. The 'Irish solution for an Irish problem' ensured that services were available, but not quite legally. This reduced the pressure to tackle the reforms needed and bought time for the politicians in Leinster House.[7] That is until the 1990s brought a tsunami of legislative reforms, and Ireland, initially at a snail's pace and then at a run, came into line with international norms and leap-frogged into the 21st century.

At a personal level, it was an odd sort of time. Yes, I was 'read off the altar' on more than one occasion; friends told me of the outraged reactions of their family to yet another headline about the Well Woman; I was accosted on the streets; there were lurid letters and postcards, some of which I have to this day; it was very tough watching my parents try to cope. They were deeply religious, as were their network of friends, but they also strongly believed that I had to do what I thought was right. Looking back now, I am hugely admiring of how they coped and defended my right to do what I was doing. But it was also true that, like others around me, I was able to live my life in a liberal bubble, among like-minded friends and colleagues, not daunted, but energised and, sometimes, relishing the fierce opposition.

Anne Connolly founded the Well Woman Centre in January 1978. Since leaving that post in 1984, her career has been varied: MD, Magill Magazine, CEO, Youth Exchange Bureau (YEB), an MBA (UCD Smurfit Business School), Kingspan, and her own strategy management consultancy practice. Since 2006, Anne's focus has been on 'smart ageing', and setting up Ageing Well Network at the request of Atlantic Philanthropies. She is currently founder/CEO of SAVVY Health – a new specialist healthy ageing centre.

CHAPTER 7

DJ at the Women's Disco

Joni Crone

When I came home to Dublin in 1976 lesbians were invisible. I had one phone number for the Irish Gay Rights Movement (IGRM) that I'd found in *Gay News* in London. I went to an IGRM conference in Trinity College Dublin where Margaret McWilliams said, 'I am a woman first, a feminist second, and a lesbian third'. I found that inspiring. I met Joanne O'Brien who invited me to a meeting of Irishwomen United (IWU) in Pembroke Street.

Dilapidated walls, an old sofa with the stuffing hanging out, mats and newspapers on the floor, a squat. Anne Speed was talking about women's rights, workers' rights, and the urgent need to change Ireland. I'd never heard a woman with a Dublin accent speak so articulately, with such a breath of knowledge about politics and world events. Everyone else spoke very powerfully. I felt intimidated, and didn't dare speak. Then I saw two women in the corner, holding hands. That was radical back then. And I noticed other women wearing women's symbols, badges, a labrys pendant – winks and nods of recognition. I had been to the Gateways club in London, and had hoped to find a similar club in Dublin, but none existed. Terri Blanche had tried to run women's discos in Parnell Square, but that hadn't worked out. In Nesbitts pub on Baggot Street, after the IWU meeting, women were talking, pointing, ordering pints, whooping with laughter. Somebody said Tailor's Hall might be a good place to hold a disco as a fundraiser. Tailor's Hall agreed to a women-only disco on a trial basis on Monday nights, but they wouldn't let us advertise it. Ruth Smith and myself phoned everyone we knew. I called the feminists, Ruth called the bar dykes and darts players. 61 women turned up. 'I never knew there were so many lesbians in Ireland', one woman said, with a big smile on her face.

Tailor's Hall was a dingy basement, but no one cared; everyone was so excited we couldn't stop smiling. We only had a few LPs, so Gaye Cunningham played guitar and sang a few songs as a warm up, including a memorable rendition of *I'm Gonna Be An Engineer* by Peggy Seeger. Nell McCafferty landed in. 'Singin'?' she said derisively, in her broad Derry accent. 'I didn't come here for singin', I came here for a disco.' I explained that we'd have the disco after 'the singin'. I ended up playing *Midnight at the Oasis* by Maria Muldaur over and over, along with *I Am Woman* by Helen Reddy. Then the turntable went wonky and I announced an interval. The excitement and the roars of laughter had nearly drowned out the music anyway, so no one minded. We managed to get the turntable going again for a while before the barman shouted, 'Have yiz no homes to go to? Come on ladies, please finish up, yiz'll get me in trouble'. 'We're not ladies, we're lezzies', replied one merry customer.

The Pembroke Women's Disco attracted a mix of lesbian, bisexual, and straight women. Some came to dance without hassle from men, some wanted to meet friends, and lesbians wanted to meet a partner or mix with other lesbians. These were scary times. It's hard to explain to young women now that a woman walking on her own at night was very likely to get harassed. Often, women met for a drink beforehand and came to the disco in a group.

We wanted to expand, but we couldn't advertise except for a tiny notice in *In Dublin* magazine. So we printed small flyers and cards to pass the word around. It took good teamwork to keep it going. I organised and played the music, Ruth did all the promotion and getting the word out. This was before the internet and mobile phones. If an event wasn't listed in a newspaper or magazine, you wouldn't know it was happening, but no newspaper would accept our notices. Ruth sent information to newspapers all over Europe: *Le Monde*, *Der Spiegel*, *La Stampa*, even *Pravda* in Russia. We'd no way of knowing if they got printed, but we got a lot of visitors in the summer months. Ruth walked the feet off herself, traipsing all along Baggot Street, Grafton Street, Henry Street, putting flyers in shops and pubs, in chemists, anywhere she saw a noticeboard, and in Books Upstairs. The hard slog paid off. Women came from all walks of life: cleaners, waitresses, academics, artists, teachers, actresses, and older lesbian couples. Ruth and I were constantly surprised at the variety of women who found their way to the Pembroke Street disco, including a policewoman and several prostitutes. This collection of women had a diverse taste in music, which presented a challenge for me as DJ. In one night, I was asked to play jazz, blues, women's music, country music, rock music, reggae, and the latest pop singles. I got to know what the regulars liked and some songs became anthems, such as *I Will Survive* and *I Am What I Am*. The whole bar would sing along and clap. It made for a great atmosphere. Elkie Brooks, Patsy Cline, Crystal Gayle, and Anne Murray were firm favourites when I played slow sets.

After IWU broke up, the women's disco continued to provide a meeting place and a feminist network that supported a lot of events and campaigns through the 1980s. I stepped back, but Ruth Smith and Pauline O'Donnell kept the disco going through the 1990s. I, and others, continued to be involved in Lesbian Line, the Campaign for a Women's Centre, the National Gay Federation, the Anti-Amendment Campaign in 1983, and other groups. But it was the disco that kept us going through all the setbacks: the energy, the camaraderie, the sisterhood was real and palpable. Looking back, I feel proud of my sisters from the Pembroke and JJs women's discos because we kept dancing through the hard times, and we created safe spaces for women in Ireland, especially lesbian women, to jive and thrive.

Joni Crone, a Dubliner from Macken Street, joined Irishwomen United in 1976. She was involved in women's liberation, gay rights, and lesbian feminism, and she came out on the *Late Late Show* in 1980. Joni has written Community Arts Plays, and was a writer with *Fair City* in the 1990s. She also worked as a trauma therapist in Omagh for ten years. Joni currently lives in Leitrim, where she is a member of Splodar Theatre Company as stage manager and playwright.

CHAPTER 8

Reflections on the Irish Women's Movement

Gaye Cunningham

An online search for the Irish Women's Liberation Movement (IWLM) will elicit descriptions such as this:

> The Irish Women's Liberation Movement (IWLM) was an alliance of a group of Irish women who were concerned about sexism within Ireland both socially and legally. They first began after a meeting in Dublin's Bewley's Café on Grafton Street in 1970. The group was short-lived but influential.[1]

It's an accurate enough overview, but rather simplistic in suggesting that the IWLM was organised and named from that early time. In fact, the unnamed group that met in Bewley's Café in 1970 consisted of a small number of women, but steadily grew in number, leading to regular meetings in Mary Maher's house (because she couldn't get a baby-sitter, according to June Levine),[2] and then in Gaj's Restaurant in Baggot Street. The IWLM manifesto, *Chains or Change: The Civil Wrongs of Irishwomen* was published from the offices of Kevin Clear Ltd. in Waterloo Road and officially launched on the *Late Late Show* in 1971, followed by the media event known as the 'contraceptive train'.

Gaj's Restaurant was a great meeting place for those on the political left. It was owned by a formidable Scottish woman and intrepid poker player, Mrs Margaret Gaj, who died in 2011 in her 92nd year. The restaurant was a centre for radical thinkers of the day. One of my abiding memories was of winning a Women's Poker Classic around 1987. When hailed as a champion, the main astonished reaction was that I had beaten Mrs Gaj.[3] The IWLM continued to meet in Gaj's for some time, but dissipated into other groups around 1972.

At the time of that meeting in Bewley's Café, unbelievable as it may seem to young people today, some women had to leave their jobs in the Public Service, and in some private firms when they got married. The 'marriage bar', as it was known, was in force from the foundation of the State and was not lifted until 1973, as was the case in many countries at the time.[4] Contraception, divorce, and abortion were illegal. Divorce was legalised in 1996 and abortion in 2018. Children born outside of the institution of marriage were designated 'illegitimate', and women did not serve on juries until 1976 following the De Burca and Anderson versus Attorney General case. In that case, Máirín De Burca and

Mary Anderson argued that certain provisions of the Juries Act 1927 were unconstitutional, including the provision that exempted virtually all women from serving.

Shortly after attending a meeting in University College Dublin (UCD), I joined a women's group meeting every Tuesday evening, in a small cottage in the heart of Ringsend.[5] Meeting like-minded women during these meetings was a liberation that came to influence the rest of my life. Shortly afterwards, the Ringsend group joined up with Irishwomen United (IWU).

As a young woman in the early 1970s, horrified by the complete lack of rights for women in twentieth-century Ireland, I entered the fray with IWU with some conviction and a little trepidation. The direct action methods of IWU were significant and threatening to the conservative society in Ireland at the time. Starting out in what became a long career in the Electricity Supply Board (ESB), I found myself taking part in some of the activities, as well as in media appearances and pickets during my lunchtimes. I well remember taking part in a picket demanding equal pay, armed with a high-quality wooden picket made for me (on their breaks) by the friendly carpenters in the ESB yard. I also remember being collected by taxi to go out to the RTÉ studios, during a lunchtime, to take part in a debate with Adele King (aka 'Twink') on the music of Dory Previn. Twink insisted Dory was a morose, depressing songwriter, while I insisted she was a trailblazer whose portrayal of women in her songs, and the role of the Catholic Church in the oppression of women, was groundbreaking.

IWU's direct actions were many and included the occupation of the Federated Union of Employers (FUE) HQ, to demonstrate against their support for the Irish Government's application for exemption of the European Directive on Equal Pay. Imagine that: a European Directive on equal pay for women doing the same or like work as men was on the horizon, and Ireland's Government was about to plead inability to pay because we couldn't afford it. Nell McCafferty and I were first across the threshold when we entered the hallowed halls of the FUE. We went up to the first floor, occupied their boardroom, gave speeches from the balcony to the picket of women below, only to hastily retreat inside when a message came through that the balcony wasn't safe enough to carry our collective weight. That demonstration ended with the FUE promising to review their decision. The other memorable demonstrations and occupations included the invasion of the Forty Foot swimming area in Sandycove and the Fitzwilliam Tennis Club. In both these places, women were not wanted at all or were not wanted as full members.

Having sometimes been critical of the trade unions for their bureaucratic and conservative approach to women's rights, I found myself getting involved from an early stage in my union, the ESB Officers' Association. My women's rights activism and involvement in Irishwomen United influenced my engagement, and I participated in driving policies through the Irish Congress of Trade Unions (ICTU) for women's greater participation and equality in the workplace, and within the unions. I joined the Women's Committee of the ICTU which encouraged negotiations at workplace level for equality measures including crèches. We negotiated directly at government level for the repeal of regressive legislation, and for negotiations for equality and human rights. We produced practical guidelines for negotiators, such as the groundbreaking ICTU 1987 document *Gay Rights in the Workplace: Guidelines for Negotiators*, which fed into the 1990 Irish Council for Civil Liberties policy 'Equality Now for Lesbians and Gay Men'.[6] The ICTU and its constituent unions were allies of the courageous men and women of the gay rights movement. Decriminalisation of homosexuality in Ireland was not brought about until 1993, following decades of activism and lobbying, including a legal case pursued all the way to the European Court of Human Rights by David Norris. In what could be viewed as a brave move in the face of a conservative society at the time, Máire Geoghegan Quinn, as Minister for Justice, introduced the decriminalisation law. Another woman, Phil Moore was part of the delegation, which lobbied the Minister, and the story of her young son coming out to his parents, moved Geoghegan Quinn to realise that, as a mother herself, she would not like her sons to be criminalised for who they love.

The Equal Pay Act was passed in 1974 and the Employment Equality Act, outlawing discrimination against women in the workplace, was passed in 1977. This legislation would not have existed without the combined actions of women and trade unions. I like to think the direct action by IWU, in occupying the FUE offices, helped to put pressure on the Irish Government in bringing into law the principle of equal pay for women and men. Divorce legislation, defeated at first, was finally successful in 1995 after concerted action and campaigning. Around this time, I enrolled for a degree in Industrial Relations and made a lifelong friend in Mags O'Brien, who drove the campaigns for divorce. In her inimitable style, Mags is one of the great activists of our time.

I went on to have a long career in the ESB, followed by my appointment, by the Minister for Labour at the time, as a Rights Commissioner in 2008, and now Adjudication Officer in the Workplace Relations Commission (WRC). My decisions often involve examination of equality legislation, some parts of which did not even exist when I started out as a young feminist activist in 1974. I also operated as an independent consultant and investigator for ten years, between 2014 and 2024, work that often involved investigating allegations from women of ill-treatment or harassment at work, including sexual harassment.

As a country, we've come a long way since 1975. The strides made in the area of rights for women have their history in the long, difficult battles undertaken by courageous women: the fight for equal pay in the Public Sector (Murphy versus Bord Telecom) and the Private Sector (Nathan versus Bailey Gibson) being significant cases. Women's rights organisations also struggled for change: Cherish, which fought to eliminate the stigma attached to 'illegitimate' children; Women's Aid, which tirelessly confronts Irish society with the truth about violence against women; and the rape crisis centres, which continue to provide support for both women and men who have experienced sexual violence. Through my involvement in the foundation of the Dublin Rape Crisis Centre in 1979, I renewed many friendships with women who were active in IWU, such as Evelyn Conlon and Anne O'Donnell.

Those women were at the forefront of the many changes that have taken place in Irish society, and there are others who need to be remembered whenever milestones are still being reached: Róisín Conroy, co-founder with Mary Doran, of Irish Feminist Information (IFI) and co-founder with Mary Paul Keane, of Attic Press; June Levine, Canadian/Irish journalist, author of *Lyn: A Story of Prostitution*;[7] Mary Maher, American/Irish journalist and editor of *The Irish Times* women's page; Padraigín Ní Mhurchú, the last General Secretary of the Irish Women Workers' Union (IWWU); and Nicola Underwood Quinn, a psychotherapist who led groundbreaking women's bodies workshops for women, just to mention a few. At the time of writing, adding the name of Nell McCafferty to this group provides a poignant reminder of the significant legacy left by her.

There were surely many dark and dismal days in the 1970s, when Ireland was not a country for young women. But through the heady days of direct action and campaigns, we in Irishwomen United marched our way through the halls of power and to the seat of male establishments, including their public houses, where we established the right to the same customer service as the men. The breaking of the rule that women were not served pints in pubs is described in Nell McCafferty's autobiography.[8] In Nell's account, she went into one of the pubs that refused to serve women pints and, accompanied by a group of 30 or so women, ordered brandies. When the drinks were served, she ordered a pint of Guinness; when the barman refused to serve, they refused to pay – one of the lighter and more madcap moments in the history of the women's movement. We had many good times as well as bad times. House parties were a feature with great music, singing and declarations, such as *If I can't dance, I won't be part of your revolution.* I look back on those days with a nostalgic eye, with sadness at the loss of so many amazing women, but with pride that I was part of a great movement that truly changed Ireland for the better.

Gaye Cunningham was born in Dublin and now lives in County Wexford. She was an active member of Irishwomen United, and a founder member of the Dublin Rape Crisis Centre. Gaye is a former Chair of the Irish Congress of Trade Unions Women's Committee and former Chair of Women's Aid. She was a Rights Commissioner, and is currently an Adjudication Officer for the Workplace Relations Commission, adjudicating on complaints made by workers under labour and equality laws. Gaye also acts as an independent workplace relations consultant.

Chapter 9

We All Know Where You Were at the Weekend

Mary Doran

Once a week, a group of women used to meet in my house in Ringsend, around late 1974 to early 1975. Occasionally, a lone woman, or two women together, would turn up at the door having been told of the meeting, probably by someone who had attended a previous meeting. No one asked where they came from, they just joined in the conversation if they felt like it. The numbers varied every week. Some of us had come from the last of the Irish Women's Liberation group that used to meet in Baggot Street, but had joined much later than the original members, who were mainly journalists. I don't know where the women who had not been part of the Baggot Street group came from, but I assume information was probably spread by word of mouth. From that group I remember Mary Dorcey, Irene Brady, Elaine McWilliams, Gaye Cunningham, Mary McAneaney, Mary Jennings, Bernadette McLeavey, Edna Wilson, and many others.

Prior to the dispersal of the Baggott Street group, a number of women, including Nicola Quinn and Ros Pearmain, had moved to Sandymount, probably to Nicola Quinn's home, to start a consciousness-raising group, which subsequently became the Sandymount Self-Help Group. This was a closed group, in that new people could not turn up every week, and it was confined to a small group who had been together from the beginning and who had formed a bond, trusting each other. This was particularly important in relation to self-help health groups in which women shared very private issues relating to their bodies and discussed issues they may not have discussed previously, and would never dream of discussing in a larger group. The Sandymount Self-Help group went on to branch out, setting-up, or helping to set up, self-help health groups that would last for six weeks at a time, with each week focusing on a different aspect of women's health, for example, breast examination, during which there were discussions and practical demonstrations. The popular book *Our Bodies, Ourselves*[1] provided very useful guidance. Journalist Patsey Murphy and I facilitated such a group in Ballsbridge.

I went from the Baggott Street group to the Sandymount consciousness-raising group, and was part of both groups for a while, but I left the Sandymount group once the Ringsend group became established. I left because I wanted to be more politically active, and I felt that consciousness-raising was not what I needed at the time. However, with hindsight, I realise that setting-up and running these self-help groups was, in fact, very political, in that women were helping other women to gain knowledge about their own bodies and, thus, confidence in dealing with the medical profession. How else would we have learned to use a vaginal speculum? With the aid of a hand mirror, we used to look at our vaginas and even take a look at our cervixes. Some women were reluctant to do it; others, once they had managed the awkward position, overcame their embarrassment, and with the help of a more knowledgeable woman, were able to remove the mystery surrounding these parts of our bodies. It was difficult initially to position the mirror, point a torch in the right direction, and adjust the speculum to get the right view, but we learned. We also learned how to recognise thrush, and to treat it without medical intervention. The speculums we used were disposable, plastic, and transparent, unlike those used by doctors, which were stainless steel and really cold. I remember going to buy one in Fannin's at the top of Grafton Street. I tried to appear confident and knowledgeable when I asked the man behind the counter for a disposable plastic speculum. 'What kind of speculum?' he asked, and I repeated a 'plastic disposable one'. 'For nose, ear?' he enquired, mentioning orifices that were okay to say aloud. It felt as if I had been found out doing something wrong, as if I was asking for contraband. I mumbled something about having to check, and that I would be back. Obviously, I thought that maybe they could only be purchased by medics and I had failed the test. But I did return, more determined, and prepared to say 'vagina', a word not often spoken out loud at the time.

Our Ringsend group later moved to Mary Dorcey's flat in Cambridge Terrace, and more people started to come along. I remember the first night that Mary Anderson turned up and stated emphatically that she was not prepared to work with any woman who was not familiar with the Report on the Commission on the Status of Women, chaired by Dr Thekla Beere. Quite a few women looked around them, anywhere, to avoid Mary catching their eye. I went home and tried to find out what I could, which, in the days before the internet, was considerably more difficult and time-consuming than it would be today. As well as discussions and campaigns, parties were hosted at the flat in Cambridge Terrace, where women were introduced to the music of Dory Previn and others that they may not have heard before, and certainly not on regular Irish airwaves. Gaye Cunningham was usually there playing the guitar, singing along.

But from June 1975, many of us believed the only place to be at 4pm on Sunday afternoons was upstairs at the International Bar on Wicklow Street, Dublin, where the Irishwomen United (IWU) meetings took place. Initially, it was to be an umbrella group for the various women's groups around Dublin, which included the group that I was in, but it evolved into a body of individual members. There was a great feeling of camaraderie and a sense that we were doing something important. The first time I attended a meeting, I was quite surprised at the number of women present, and I felt a real sense of belonging knowing that I had found a place filled with like-minded women. I was surprised also at the number of women who had come from political groups, some of which I had never heard of, such as the Revolutionary Marxist Group, Revolutionary Struggle, and some republican groups. These women had been working away in all of these groups around the city, and it was great to join with others who wanted to achieve the same things.

Usually, a topic was selected for discussion each week, and included such things as equal pay, contraception, discrimination in education, and abortion. Other, broader issues included dual membership, feminism, and socialism. Sometimes, after the discussion, it was felt that further action was needed and a group would be established to meet during the week to work on that issue. Some of these groups published documents on the specific topics, others developed into campaigns, as was the case with equal pay and access to contraception, to name just a couple. At some point, one of the IWU groups arranged for the Sunday afternoon meetings to be held in a house at 12 Lower Pembroke Street, Dublin, and from there IWU grew substantially.

There was a large number of interest groups within the organisation, most of which had weekly meetings, and which required record-keeping, as well as the writing of letters to politicians. Other groups, with similar objectives, might join forces for a particular campaign or public meeting. These groups included campaigns on equal pay, education workshops, a contraception group, which became the Contraception Action Programme (CAP) – also known as the Contraception Action Campaign – and the welfare rights group. One of the groups, whose focus was on legal reform, prepared a submission on behalf of IWU to the Law Reform Commission on the Law of Domicile (*c.* 1975–76). Maureen Cronin, a lawyer, was central to this submission, the end of which stated that no particular issue should be considered in isolation, and reference was made to the legislation on Criminal Conversation,[2] the law on which was finally abolished under the Family Law Act of 1981.

I well remember the decision to invade the Fitzwilliam Tennis Club, which, at that time, did not allow women members. There was an important tournament coming up, and some women decided to go along and start playing tennis. A photo of them appeared on the next issue of IWU's magazine, *Banshee*. A small group of us met on the Friday night and planned to paint a large feminist symbol with the clenched fist inside on the centre court, under cover of darkness, that very night, which was the eve of an important match. We met in Ringsend with pots of paint and large brushes, and there was a discussion about whether there might be security, even a dog perhaps: *what would happen if we were caught and tried to escape or, if gates were locked, could we scale them quickly?* All sorts of potential problems were raised. Before leaving, we painted a test symbol on the back wall of my house. When my partner saw it much later, he asked if we had wanted to advertise the whereabouts of the culprits who had carried out the damage to 'private property' at the club. However, when we arrived at the grounds, the gates were wide open, and it could not have been easier. We strolled to the court, wondering if there was a trap, and someone painted the symbol while a number of us kept watch.

Never a group to miss an opportunity, the following day, on our way home from the regular protest at the Forty Foot, a 'men only' swimming spot in Sandycove, we climbed over the rear wall of the Fitzwilliam Tennis Club, where we were met by some elderly men demanding to know if we were the people who caused damage to private property the previous night. One also suggested that if a woman wanted to become a member of the club she could marry a member – *now why hadn't we thought of that?* We tried to look as though we didn't know what he was talking about, all the while carrying placards highlighting discrimination against women. The following Monday, when I arrived in work, somebody said to me 'we all know where you were at the weekend', while others grinned. I didn't know what he was talking about, but all became clear when he produced a copy of the *Sunday Press* and there, on the front cover, was a photo of me, placard held aloft, arguing with a member of the Fitzwilliam Tennis Club.

There was a great buzz in being involved in a group that was active in highlighting the way women were treated. We were involved in these actions because we believed that things needed to change, and that the only way to make sure change would happen was by direct action. These events got publicity, to some extent out of proportion with the numbers involved, but not, we believed, out of kilter with the urgency of the issues. There were always onlookers or people who were ready to tell us what we should be doing and what other thing we should be trying to change. Some also thought that we should not be on the streets, but at home, out of the public eye, not drawing attention to ourselves and these issues. There were also, of course, women who cheered us on.

The IWU subgroups were very active in preparing reports and making submissions relating to issues that were not the subject of public protest. However, these issues were not always deemed newsworthy or suitable for a photo opportunity in the way that an invasion of a male only club would be. We issued a press release in advance of most events, and it helped that many of the female journalists were sympathetic to the cause, many having been founder members of the Irish Women's Liberation Movement (IWLM). Some were still involved, particularly Nell McCafferty, who never ceased in her involvement in and support for improving women's lives.

One of the central issues of the women's movement, and IWU specifically, was skill-sharing and passing on knowledge to others. We tried to pursue this principle with regard to media interviews, for example, by ensuring that it was not always the same woman who was interviewed in a radio programme or by a newspaper. It was something of a continuous battle, however, since radio interviewers often requested a particular woman, usually someone they had heard speak previously, and they preferred not to have someone who had never been on radio before. Some years after IWU, I was explaining the idea of 'skill-sharing' to a friend who found it a difficult concept to grasp: 'you mean if someone knows how to do something, you don't allow them to do it and you ask someone else to do the job, someone who doesn't know how to do it?' I admit that it was not universally accepted, but it worked as a way of passing on knowledge and skills, and not limiting control to a small number of people.

At some point, a subgroup formed with the intention of setting up an editorial board to publish a magazine that would spread the word about why women's lives in Ireland needed to change, as well as the activities that were being organised by IWU, including highlighting discrimination against women in the areas of equal pay, education, control over our own bodies, and other issues deemed to be important and of significance to women. The magazine was *Banshee*, and an editorial board was set up to collect articles and to carry out the required activities. I am not sure that most of the board really knew what they were taking on, but we carried on nonetheless. In pursuit of the principle of skill-sharing, the editorial group that produced the first two issues of *Banshee* proposed in a report that, after three issues of the magazine, the members of the editorial collective should change. Mind you, this sometimes left gaps and, with hindsight, might seem somewhat short-sighted in that women who had acquired skills would step aside and leave the job to others who often lacked the necessary experience.

Articles for each issue of *Banshee* had to be written by members of IWU, but the authors were not named. There were records of actions like the Forty Foot incursions, the invasion of Fitzwilliam Tennis Club, the forced entry into the Federated Union of

Employers (FUE) HQ, coverage of strikes, such as Kilmartin's and Thom's. There was a list of upcoming events, actions, meetings, etc., and international news relating to women's rights. One issue of *Banshee* had an illustrated article on methods of contraception, with detailed drawings and instructions for use. There was also a list of pubs to be boycotted, either because they would not serve women, especially unaccompanied, or they would not serve pints to women on the grounds that it was unladylike for a woman to drink a pint.

When the magazine was printed, it then had to be distributed and sold. The whole operation was something that I think we underestimated. We all took a number of copies to sell to friends, work colleagues, families, and anyone else who might be interested, and we planned evenings when women would go in pairs to pubs, especially in the city centre, to try and sell *Banshee* to women. Quite often the women that we tried to engage would be with a man who might insist on telling us that their companion did not want to buy a copy, and would then proceed to tell us what we should and should not be doing, but we believed this was a good way of making contact with women. In some cases, we believed it exposed how much some men tried to control the woman who was with them. It did take a lot of time and could be exhausting, and we had discussions about whether it was worth the time spent. We distributed copies to some shops, which would take them on a sale or return basis. This was also labour intensive as it required whoever distributed the magazines to call back to the shop, numerous times, to collect the unsold copies, before being recompensed for the small numbers sold.

We also gave copies of *Banshee* to friends who lived outside Dublin, with requests they be put into shops or sold to other friends. The magazine was stocked mainly by shops in Dublin, and Porters distributed to cities outside Dublin, and it was sold in some independent bookshops and newsagents. Eason bookstore distributed it for a while, but at some point they refused to handle distribution due to the magazine's content. All of this required good record-keeping and invoicing, and we were lucky to have an accountant, Colette Cullen, whose well-kept ledgers show the importance of good bookkeeping. In the end there was a small profit, and it was hoped that, if the magazine continued, someone could be paid to do the necessary administration work. Records in the archive in University College Cork (UCC) are evidence of the level of work involved at all stages of the production and distribution of *Banshee*, even though most of the women involved were also involved in other campaign groups at the same time.

We seemed to spend a lot of time protesting. Some of the women who were involved in the trade union movement encouraged us to support working women, usually in female-only workplaces, where strikes took place for better pay and conditions, and we got involved, offering support, usually on picket lines. Kilmartin's Bookmakers was one such strike, where the working conditions were very poor. Some premises did not have proper toilet facilities for the women. Another strike was that of Thom's Directories, and was in relation to the right of the workers to join a trade union after unfair treatment and dismissal of a worker took place. After five months on strike, the women won their case in the Labour Court, but said that they were subsequently blacklisted and could not find jobs. The catch-cry became, *The union is claiming victory and the women are claiming the dole.* It was common then for companies to claim inability to pay increased wages and threaten closure. In some instances they did close, but some would reopen under a different name sometime later.

When I think of some of IWU's actions at the time, I am amazed at our confidence, and how we felt that the end justified the means: we were very clear that we were doing something important and necessary to improve women's lives. On 8 January 1976, when we burst into the Federated Union of Employers (FUE) HQ on Fitzwilliam Street, we believed that it was a completely acceptable thing to do. We decided that the employers' representatives must be confronted and questioned about why they were supporting the denial of equal pay to women, and the only way to confront them was to 'doorstep' them. We met nearby beforehand to discuss how all this would be handled, and I would say that we actually had no idea how we would achieve what we wanted to. A group of us turned up at the door of the headquarters, and when the door was opened by one of the board members, we pushed past him and headed to the boardroom. We sat around the table and demanded a meeting to discuss the issue of equal pay. I am sure that the men who were on the premises were totally shocked that women would force their way into the building and presume to sit around their boardroom table and make demands. When we refused to leave, the Gardaí were called. These were different times, and two guards stood in the room awaiting some resolution, clearly not relishing the prospect of trying to remove the women from the building. There is a photo taken, I think by Derek Speirs, of the scene in the boardroom with the Gardaí present, which was featured on the cover of *Banshee*, and appeared in a number of national newspapers. Eventually, some form of agreement was reached, and we agreed to leave peacefully, as did the Gardaí. While the FUE might not have followed up on what was discussed, it was important to demonstrate that women were going to explore every avenue in the fight for equal pay.

These activities took place following the Irish government's application to the European Commission for a derogation on the Directive on Equal Pay, which was refused by the Commission. Members of IWU were also very active in a national campaign, collecting signatures to a petition demanding that the government comply with the EC directive. I remember also collecting signatures anywhere that I went, including a grocery shop in Irishtown, where my family was known. We had no qualms about collecting signatures everywhere we went. All of this was part of a national campaign being conducted by some politicians, in courtrooms, and at all levels throughout the country.

Regular protests took place about the lack of contraception, as well as demands that women have rights over their own bodies. I noticed recently, when reading something written at the time, that the terminology used was 'family planning', 'reproductive rights' being a more recent concept. One protest was held outside the gates of the Archbishop's Palace, highlighting the interference of the Catholic Church in women's control of their bodies. The Archbishop of Dublin at the time was John Charles McQuaid, who not only ruled over the Catholic Church in Dublin, but also had a very strong influence over politicians and political issues of the day, particularly those relating to sexuality and reproductive rights.

We often held protests on Friday evening outside the GPO or the Customs House, where the Department of Health was located. I worked just off Parnell Square, and remember bringing a placard to work with me on Fridays and hiding it in the toilet, from where I collected it after work and went to O'Connell Street or Store Street to meet up with others to publicise our fight for access to contraception. The intention was to be seen by as many people as possible, many of whom would be on their way home from work, though I tried not to be seen by anyone I worked with, since they might figure out that I must have left early to get to the location.

Towards the end of 1977, when it became evident that IWU was losing some dynamism and direction, it was agreed that it would be better for the women involved in IWU to break up into smaller groups in different parts of the city and work within their own communities. It was felt that maybe smaller groupings might be more effective in reaching other women. However, it was very difficult to change the dynamic of the existing group. I think it was precisely the variety of people and the variations in political leanings and life experience that contributed to the discussion and campaigns that were organised, as well as the approach adopted. Most of the subgroups had links with each other and had members in common. Information was shared, and one meeting, which all of the subgroups attended, seemed to be the best way to operate and keep everyone informed and ensure that new members knew what was happening. Some single-action groups emerged, one of the most enduring being the group focusing on rape. Initially, a group called Women Against Rape (WAR) formed, which would engage in political action, and were very public in highlighting the legal position and working to change the law and public perception of rape. Some women felt that what was needed was to follow the example of other countries and form a group that would work with women who had been raped. Initially, this was the Rape Crisis Group and, subsequently, the Rape Crisis Centre. It was felt that, in the initial stages, women who had been raped might be wary of approaching a group for help that was making public statements and seeking publicity, for fear that somehow they or their case might be exposed to public scrutiny. The women who formed the Rape Crisis Group soon realised that a lot of research was required, along with contact with relevant experts and professionals, including the Gardaí, in order to adequately deal with the issue and the particular circumstances that prevailed in Ireland.

In an effort to examine where IWU was going, a decision was made, towards the end of 1977, to hold a conference in Trinity College Dublin (TCD), where many previous conferences, forums, etc., had been held. There were opponents against holding events in such a space on the grounds that it might intimidate or deter many ordinary women from attending, but the space was available for free, or for a very reasonable cost. Nell McCafferty suggested the title *Speak Bitterness, Speak Truth*, adopting a concept used in China, designed to encourage people to engage with each other and clear up old differences or things that might be lingering. I cannot remember clearly what the outcome was, but I know that I learned a lot, drew strength from the other women that I worked with, and am certain that we collectively brought about change and made people, including ourselves, think about issues that would not have been talked about even if they were thought about previously. I believe that it was total burn-out that eventually led to the demise of IWU. There were so many campaigns and interlinking issues that affected women's ability to survive in Ireland at the time, and there were serious challenges in continuing a long-term commitment to bring about all the changes that were desperately needed.

I would like to acknowledge and express my personal gratitude to the women who took notes, minutes of meetings, kept records of a multitude of campaigns, subsequently stored these documents, and finally donated them to the UCC archive. There is so much material archived and, therefore, available for research for others to work on and perhaps publish in the future.

Mary Doran was born in Dublin, into a family of six, and attended Sandymount High School, which encouraged equality of the sexes. Mary qualified as an architect from University College Dublin, and was involved in women's groups, including Irishwomen United. She was a founder member of the Dublin Rape Crisis Centre and subsequently the Cork Rape Crisis Service. Mary lived in New York in the 1990s.

CHAPTER 10

'You Bring the Gay Sisters and I'll Bring the Socialists'

Mary Dorcey

In 1973, I came home to Ireland after living in Paris and studying at University there. I had a French boyfriend who had been very involved in the student politics of 1968, and I shared his belief in the possibility of radical change in the way the world was run. I had been politicised by one of my brothers who brought me on anti-Vietnam War marches in the late 1960s, while I was still at school. In a sense, life in Paris was the moment I had been waiting for.

In time, I broke up with this wonderful Frenchman and chose to come back to Ireland with the idea of trying it out for a few weeks before moving to Britain or the United States. I went to a few meetings of the original Irish Women's Liberation Group, but found them too tame in their ambition, and too ready to accept the present state of Ireland as fundamentally unchangeable. This was especially obvious for me in their unwillingness to encourage any discussion of gay rights. Frustrated by this, I went in search of other feminists, and met and had one-to-one conversations with several of them over the next few weeks. The most inspiring of these conversations took place with Anne Speed one Sunday afternoon. Anne was a trade union activist, and we had met a few weeks previously at a meeting in the Baggot Inn. She had greatly impressed me with her passion and intelligence. After a detailed discussion about the aims of a new group, Irishwomen United (IWU), its methods and organisation, we agreed that it had much potential to fulfil many of the things we both wanted, and I agreed to attend the next meeting. As we were leaving to go our separate ways, Anne said: 'You bring the gay sisters and I'll bring the socialists'. And that was just what came to pass.

I remember that first public conference in June 1975 at Liberty Hall. The room was packed. We drew up a Charter of Demands and committed to weekly meetings. Those core demands were later published on the back cover of our journal, *Banshee*. Attendance at the Sunday meetings grew quickly from 19 women in August 1975 to the high 30s in October of that year, and speedily upwards. These highly influential meetings were preceded by another remarkable event in my new life in Dublin. Earlier in 1973, as part of my search for radical sisters, I stumbled across the very first meeting of the first Gay Activist group in Ireland, held in Trinity College Dublin (TCD). Soon after that, with an urgency that drove all our actions and discussions at that time, I gave a passionate and somewhat controversial speech at University College Dublin (UCD), demanding gay rights and denouncing compulsory heterosexuality as 'sadomasochism'. It was reported in *The Irish Times*, and made me somewhat notorious. It equally caused moral outrage among all who knew my family or social circle, not helped by the fact that my family name was the only one in the country.[1] After that, I began to advocate for gay rights at the first meetings of IWU, and very soon discovered there were five or so other young gay women in the room, though they had been closeted until then. Very swiftly our numbers began to grow.

SLM, the Sexual Liberation Group we had founded at TCD, organised a public Symposium in October of 1973. A packed room listened to Dr Noel Browne, TD[2] and British activist Babs Todd echo our call for the decriminalisation of homosexuality. Browne told us, to rousing cheers from the audience, that homosexuality had just been removed from the American list of psychiatric illnesses. It is difficult to overstate the furiously hostile attitude then to 'queers', and the near impossible task of finding people who would publicly advocate any position on the subject of sex, other than the 'missionary'. But for a group of 20 or so young, gay activists wreaking havoc on a dreary conformist Dublin, the world seemed changed overnight.

Much existing writing on IWU has described the lesbian faction as mostly silenced or sidelined but, in fact, we were involved in every group, on every issue, and were extremely influential with strong opinions and great energy applied to all the questions that faced the organisation. We certainly were among the most vocal and reliable attendees at the weekly meetings. All the central issues of IWU applied to lesbians, many of whom were married, were mothers, or were working for low wages and, like all women, were not allowed to own a house in their own name, or serve on a jury. From the start, when I and a few others spoke openly about gay rights, we roused passion and excitement among the wider group. Needless to say, there were many romances and love affairs, as well as friendships that have lasted a lifetime. At the very next Sunday meeting of IWU, I reported on these events and received great support. Other than me and my Italian girlfriend at the time, there were five or so lesbians in the organisation. Many women from IWU, gay and straight, regularly joined our protest meetings, our marches, and our public discussions. Many straight women joined us in solidarity, and many never went home again.

There were fun times too, with good periods of relaxation. We threw parties. We danced in the streets. We went to bed. We fell in love. We discovered ourselves to be new, extraordinary, exhilarated beings. Sexual possessiveness and enforced monogamy were the work of the patriarchy and we felt strongly about finding a better way. We denounced this national conservatism loudly and at every opportunity. We gave speeches in pubs, in dancehalls, at public conferences, at street corners, at church gates, and in cinemas, standing up in the back and shouting against the noisy opposition.

The Sunday meetings became unmissable. At every session, there would be at least one extraordinary revelation, something no one had shared before, and keeping pace with this deep intellectual and political milieu was accompanied by a strong sense of emotional intensity. We were highly organised and disciplined, despite the fun and excitement of young women finding their voices, most of them for the first time. The opposition organised against us merely strengthened our resolve.

Evelyn Conlon and I were selected, at an early Sunday general meeting, to act as spokeswomen for the group – apparently, we had become known as articulate and not shy! In the first weeks of the group, we had spoken to each other, tentatively, about the work we had begun as fledgling writers. We had both published in a few places, and knew what we wanted to say that had not yet been written about in Ireland. I think I can fairly claim that Evelyn and I helped to bring into being the passionate tide of literature by Irish women that has swept through our country since then, inspiring so many and changing lives. It is a cause of great pleasure and some pride to me when I remember those two young women, their intensity and determination, and then look up the titles of their books published over the last 40 years. Perhaps most of all, I feel this pride when I catch sight of Evelyn across the room at our annual general assembly of Aosdána members, and reflect how far we have travelled.

IWU members also published our own magazine, *Banshee*, which had a rotating editorial board. Contraception was a crucial issue for IWU from the very start. We demanded free, legal contraception, provided through state-financed birth control clinics. We campaigned for sex education programmes and the right to publish literature on sex education, all of which was condemned as sinful and outrageous by the Catholic Church and its followers, which was the great majority of Ireland's population at that time.

The atmosphere of those years was full of challenge, excitement, high-energy confrontations, debate, emotion, direct speech, tears, anger, and laughter. It was a time of women speaking honestly to each other about their lives, their hopes, dreams, and fears, as perhaps we never had before. We came to trust strangers with our deepest feelings.

We campaigned on a variety of issues one-by-one, week-by-week, year-by-year; eventually achieving them all, but later than we had hoped for. We women's liberationists and gay activists, passionate but inexperienced, transformed our country from the ground up, dragged it from the nineteenth century into the late twentieth. We were the first generation to refuse to emigrate, or to be silenced, or banished. We insisted on making noise and making our presence felt. While making ourselves furious and disgraceful hussies, we smiled, stood our ground, and said loud and clear in the streets, in the bars, in the bedrooms of Catholic Ireland: *We are different. We are unashamed. We refuse to be quiet. We dissent loudly from the nineteenth-century consensus because we have a better way, a way that will liberate women and men from guilt and shame, bullying and silence, and we are staying here until it happens. We are Irishwomen United, and our voices are impossible to silence.*

Mary Dorcey was born in Dublin and has been an activist since her schooldays. She joined the student revolution while studying in Paris and, back at home, became a founder member of The Movement for Sexual Liberation (1973), Women for Radical Change (1974), and Irishwomen United (1975). Mary is a critically acclaimed, widely anthologised writer, whose work broke new ground in the representation of women's and gay lives. She has published seven poetry collections, a collection of stories, a novel, one novella, and many essays. She has lived in New York, Tokyo, London and Paris. She is a member of Aosdána.

CHAPTER 11

Remembering Feminist Publishing of the 1980s

Mary Flanagan and Marianne Hendron

In July 2024, we – Marianne Hendron, back from Ballarat, Australia, and Mary Flanagan, over from Roscommon – repaired to a corner of our old haunt, The Palace Bar on Fleet Street, Dublin, to reminisce about the early 1980s and four extraordinary years working in feminist community publishing. In doing so, we wanted to pay our respects to the women whose energy and vision made it possible, and whose legacy endures to this day. Our heartfelt gratitude also to Liz Harper, Women's Community Press co-worker, for reading the essay and for providing us with valuable and constructive input.

What emerged from these reflections is a somewhat random stream of shared memories of a time that seems long ago, and yet, in other ways, feels very contemporary: contemporary because much of what was done then was way ahead of its time. These memories are subjective, and definitely non-linear, and only a small part of a much bigger story. The conversation meanders so there is no clear chronology. As recollections of those times are discussed, including minor disasters – paper cuts, stapled fingers, coffee spills on the galleys – as well as successes – strong community engagement, building vital, enduring relationships, being part of change movements – thoughts turn to the sad fact that three dear co-workers and friends have since died. Rest in peace dear Róisín Conroy, Sue Richardson, and Noreen O'Donohue.

Our overriding feeling is one of good fortune at having had this formative and rich experience of working in radical publishing with an extraordinary group of women. These were the days before we scattered and went our separate ways: to Australia, New York, London, or, of necessity, to live more conventional lives. Emigration pervaded the early 1980s, and was an accepted solution to the rampant unemployment and economic stagnation in Ireland at the time. Thoughts turn to the separation and loss arising from these exiles, and the profound effect on those who left and those who remained. But the band played on, good times were had, and it's only in hindsight that the reality can be fully appreciated.

Any discussion of Irish feminist publishing has to start with Róisín Conroy and Patricia Kelleher, two inspirational women, whose personal charisma was what led the two of us to spend over four years of our lives in community and feminist publishing. Our journey began in 1982, straight out of college, into a jobless market environment, with the opportunity to participate in the innovative Irish Feminist Information (IFI) training course, and then, in 1983, to set up and work in Women's Community Press (WCP) with our three co-workers, Liz Harper, Noreen O'Donohue, and Sue Richardson. Our fundamental aim was to open up expression to groups and individuals hitherto denied access, through the medium of print. Structure and process were highly important, reflected in the co-operative model and non-hierarchical organisation. We had completed Social Science degrees, and were heavily influenced by, and engaged in, the feminist and nationalist politics and social activism of the time, and we jumped at the chance to continue engagement in transformational community development work through a short-term (low) paid course.

When Róisín, along with her friend Mary Doran, founded IFI in 1978, their aim was to empower women by making information more widely available, including and especially information on women's health, and on rights and entitlements. With Patricia Kelleher, Róisín extended this project to training for women in publishing skills, and they achieved this via an ingenious move. As a response to unemployment, the government had established AnCo[1] as a training agency, and part of its brief was to provide training for women in 'non-traditional occupations'. Róisín and Patricia successfully made the case for publishing as a non-traditional area for women, as well as demonstrating their capacity to deliver such a course, and the Women in Community Publishing (WICP) training course was established. Their case was, no doubt, actively supported by Mary Liddy, who, at the time, was external training officer with AnCo. Having succeeded in taking advantage of state employment-creation initiatives, and using these funds in the cause of women, Róisín and Patricia paved the way for the setting up of Women's Community Press (WCP).

Before all that, however, IFI had pioneered *The Irish Women's Diary and Guidebook*, helping to establish its publishing credentials. Initially a calendar, the publication became an A6 sized diary and, really, this little booklet is the mother of all the publishing ideals and ideas that were to come later. Designed to be easy to carry, it was a goldmine of valuable and often difficult to access information, particularly on women's health. That it contained a menstrual calendar was radical, enabling women to chart our menstrual cycle and take steps to control our fertility at a time of few other means of doing so. The *Diary* was also a thing of beauty. The cover design was always creative: one year, it channelled the iconic modernism of Mondrian, another the optical illusion of OpArt. All graphics and cartoons were original and provocative and, of course, supplied by women.

In the early days, Róisín and Mary, along with a few committed and creative friends, worked on the design and layout on the kitchen table. Viewed through the lens of the twenty-first century, it's hard to believe that by publishing certain information these women took personal risks. IFI was open to litigation under the Censorship Act, still alive and well in those days. Providing information on 'artificial' birth control and abortion was, at the time, illegal under various pieces of legislation. *The Irish Women's Diary and Guidebook* defied this, yet despite the oppressive and conservative times, there was a huge demand for the publication. It continued to be published until 1997 with 18 wonderful editions.

IFI can be seen to be a continuation of IWU's assertion in the 1970s that information is power. Radical publishing had also taken hold internationally in the 1960s and 70s when mainstream publishing was a male-dominated industry. Glenda Cimino's Beaver Row Press in Donnybrook and Catherine Rose's Arlen House were role models, each demonstrating what was possible. In Britain, Virago Press was founded in 1973 by Carmen

Callil, followed by The Women's Press in 1977 with its clothes iron logo. In Ireland, Arlen House was set up in 1975 with its first publication, *The Female Experience: The Story of the Woman Movement*, written by its founder, Catherine Rose. It went on to publish a range of fiction and non-fiction works by women. Much is owed to Catherine Rose's vision of women's writing being promoted and celebrated. She also republished out-of-print works by Irish women writers, and introduced them to a new generation of readers. Women's literature, poetry, and women's studies were all published under the Arlen House imprint, while its sister imprint, Turoe, set up in 1978, published social studies, as well as books highlighting women's inequality.

In 1984, Róisín and Mary Paul Keane set up Attic Press as an imprint of IFI. Attic went on to publish a range of important works, feminist titles, reclamation history, new fiction, and women's studies titles. At least five titles by Nell McCafferty, who was feminist royalty even back then, were published to acclaim and controversy. These titles were published in an atmosphere of repression, sanctions, and consequences, since transgressing the boundaries of what was considered acceptable was very real: there was the refusal of some bookshops to carry certain titles, and the arbitrary and opaque nature of censorship laws, all creating challenges that are hard to imagine now. It took real courage and commitment to undertake this work.

WCP and IFI shared space in the Irish Women Workers' Union (IWWU) building, thanks to the support of the late Padrigín ní Mhurchú and the IWWU itself.[2] The premises at 48 Fleet Street was a kind of haven, if not a heaven. As WCP and Attic Press pursued their own publishing projects, and IFI continued to run the WICP training course, a whole set of relationships and cultures were blossoming in tandem. Those cultures were feminist, leftist, anarchist, and inclusive. 48 Fleet Street nurtured a strong and relaxed lesbian environment, with mutually-supportive straight colleagues, and in which being 'out' was simply a given, a natural and accepted way of being. Memory is sensory: the sights, sounds, and smells of the location, the long, long stairs leading to our offices on the top floor of the IWWU building, the bentwood chairs, the timber floors, the sounds of the CIE buses creaking down the cobbled street to the depot in Essex street, the smell from the Guinness brewery. Yet, for all the economic stagnation and bleakness of the early 1980s, our little enclave, in what was later to become trendy Temple Bar, was rich in culture and creativity. There was the Dublin Resource Centre (DRC) with printworks and café in the former CIE buildings, and the Project Arts Centre was only a shout away on Essex Street. We recall going there to see plays by the great Peter Sheridan, and innovative bands, such as The Virgin Prunes and The Atrix. Despite the straitened times, pockets of creativity and radicalism were sprouting up in central Dublin, and feminist publishing and music were part of it. Much of our social lives centred around benefit gigs for various social and political causes, with musical magic often being provided by Maria Walsh and Carole Nelson, who went on to become Zrazy.

The WICP course was way ahead of its time including, as it did, practical publishing projects, participant evaluation, and work experience. Thanks to Róisín and Patricia's extensive networks and influence, as well as their ability to use these strategically, the course included excellent inputs from luminaries in the fields of publishing and communications, and innovative supports to enable participation: Anne Hyland on yoga and mindfulness, long before workplace wellbeing was a thing; the prolific Derek Speirs on photography; and Betty Purcell on feminist journalism, to name but a very few. What they created was a culture of creativity and self-expression. IFI recruited a diverse and experienced group of participants, each bringing their skills and life experience, and it was out of this environment that WCP emerged as a worker co-operative with an ethos of inclusion, and with a non-hierarchical structure. It declared a commitment to challenging the glaring gaps in mainstream publishing, thereby giving a forum to those hitherto excluded. The subsequent publications reflected this ethos, covering working-class women's writing, reflections of feminist activists of the time, lesbian and gay men's experiences, and heroin as a human, rather than criminal, issue.

Censorship and silence persisted throughout the 1970s and into the 80s and 90s. Homosexuality was illegal when WCP, in partnership with the Dublin Lesbian and Gay Men's Collectives, published *Out for Ourselves: The Lives of Irish Lesbians and Gay Men* in 1986.[3] The law dictated and enabled a culture of exclusion, stigma, fear and silence. Many shops refused to stock this book. Printing companies were apprehensive about touching it, and one outright refused to print it. WCP faced not only resistance from the media, but also from booksellers and distributors.

The law, the churches, and social attitudes kept many in the closet. The oppression of gay and lesbian lives was endorsed by the state, the law, and, of course, the churches. For WCP, the principle of giving a voice and a platform to those otherwise excluded from the means of expression and documentation was foundational. The publication of *Out For Ourselves* was a first in many respects, giving voice to the personal experiences and political demands of lesbians and gay men who were all but invisible in the Ireland of the 1980s. 'Gay bashing', a euphemism for violence against gays and lesbians, reached something of a watershed moment in 1982 with the horrific murder of Declan Flynn[4] in Fairview Park, Dublin. We recall the atmosphere of anger and resistance at the powerful march organised by the Dublin Lesbian and Gay Men's Collectives in response. This resilience among the lesbian and gay communities paved the way for *Out For Ourselves* to come into being. It was the first book written entirely by lesbians and gay men to be published in Ireland, and we are proud of it for that reason alone, but also because of an awareness that, 40 years on, it made a positive impact on LGBTQI+ lives. It also dovetailed with the HIV AIDS era, when information and knowledge for the queer community became even more vital.

Out For Ourselves relied mainly on voluntary inputs, fundraising by the book's editorial team and the Dublin Lesbian and Gay Men's Collectives, while WCP funded the production costs. Our treasured typesetter, the late Catherine McMahon, along with Sue Richardson, did the typesetting work free as a contribution, as did WCP workers on the layout and proofing. Unfortunately, *Out For Ourselves* didn't sell well, not because it wasn't any good – it was brilliant – but due to the refusal of many shops to stock it, and resistance from the media to promote it, which meant that it was primarily friends and relatives who purchased it. It still stands as a unique testimony to the lives of lesbians and gay men of the time in Ireland.

Morale was low in early 1980s Ireland. It was a time of high unemployment, emigration, and entrenched gender inequality. The Troubles were raging in the North, with sectarian and state violence. In the South, high profile events such as the Eighth Amendment to the Constitution,[5] the Kerry Babies Case,[6] the death of Ann Lovett and her baby,[7] Mother and Baby Homes,[8] and with sexual harassment at work and on the streets in common with elsewhere, it was impossible to escape a culture of misogyny that was alive and well. It's hard to believe, but single motherhood was subject then, to stigma and discrimination and even shame. To counter this and provide support to single mothers, the organisation Cherish[9] was established. Maura O'Dea was one of its founding members, while former President of Ireland Mary Robinson was Cherish's first president. The WICP publication *Singled Out*[10] was the product of collaboration with Cherish, and it was unique in bringing together a range of information for lone parents, as well as countering the stigma associated with single-parenting.

The fact that unemployment benefits were paid at a different rate to women and men is just one example of the structural discrimination against women. Our esteemed WCP partner, Noreen O'Donohue, campaigned tirelessly on this issue and set up the campaign group Equality in the Social Welfare Code to highlight this blatant discrimination, with preliminary changes only being achieved in 1985, then further changes in 1995 following threats of legal action against the Irish government by the European Union, and finally resulting in the Equal Status Acts (2000–4).

The *Irish Feminist Review* (*IFR*), published in 1984 by WCP, edited by Caroline Butler who conceived the idea, documented key issues affecting women's rights and freedoms at the time. It provided a first-hand account of the culture of misogyny and the efforts of courageous women activists to change and improve things. The oppressive role of the Catholic Church was enabled by the state, with the constant interference by the church in secular issues and affairs of state. Hence, we had no legitimate access to contraception, to divorce, or to abortion services. In fact, there were not only legal barriers to access, there were also physical ones in the form of anti-choice objectors. For example, non-directive pregnancy counselling, such as that provided by the indomitable Ruth Riddick and Open Door Counselling, was subjected to persistent and aggressive picketing by so-called pro-life organisations. Pro-choice women, including ourselves on many occasions, had to provide a human shield against the protestors in order for the women wishing to avail of the service to gain entry to the building.

The *IFR* highlighted the sharp edge of a theocratic state, with church and state working hand in glove. *Not the Church, not the State, women must decide our Fate* was the catch-cry to be heard during marches and written on banners. The separation of church and state was a constant demand of social activists and campaigners. The *IFR* brought together the many strands of feminist activism that existed at the time. Intended to be a quarterly publication, written by women activists, its first and only issue covers such travesties as the Eighth Amendment/Constitutional Referendum on abortion. This included the case of Eileen Flynn, a teacher who lost her job because she was 'living in sin' with a partner, and the tragic death of Sheila Hodgers at Lady of Lourdes Hospital, who was denied cancer treatment because she was pregnant.

Much of the *IFR* was dedicated to the experiences of women who might otherwise never have a voice: the Women's Right to Choose Group, and the anti-amendment campaign, which shone a light on one of the most divisive culture wars of our time; Irish lesbians who discussed their experiences and aspirations; the war in the North, and women's experience of visiting loved ones in jails; the protest by the Armagh Women; and Republican women in Armagh Prison who engaged in a 'dirty protest' for political status, to mention just a few of the topics covered. But what is significant is not just the contemporaneous documentation of these momentous events and experiences, but that each article is written by the women embedded in activism on the various issues.

The lines between our own working lives as publishers and our involvement in campaigns and causes were unquestionably blurred. Such was the overlap, that many a banner and campaign leaflet was produced in the WCP office, using our precious resources for the greater good. The photocopying machine was put to many uses. Our reflections for this piece constantly reference the vital fact that we were operating in a pre-internet and even pre-technology world. We obtained our first computer in 1987 through a generous supporter and a small grant. Ideas, information, and views that are today disseminated in minutes with a few keystrokes had to be manually typed or handwritten, copied or gestetnered,[11] bound and distributed. We had access to a means of production and were committed to using these for change.

Mostly, we ignored the institution of the Catholic Church, but every now and then it drew our attention. On news of the election of a new Dublin Archbishop, some of us joined a group of other feminists outside the Archbishop's Palace in Drumcondra under the banner *Not Another Phallus in the Palace* and *Women Against Bishops Against Women* to protest about the church's treatment of women.

Disadvantaged communities inevitably bore the brunt of the economic and social problems. Sue Richardson lived her commitment to working-class rights, and this included the working-class communities that were, at the time, ravaged by the heroin scourge. WCP wanted to draw attention to the human, lived experience of this epidemic. *Pure Murder: A Book About Drug Use*[12] was the product of this ambition, and the project was led by Sue Richardson and Noreen O'Donohue. In keeping with our ethos, *Pure Murder* gave a voice to drug users and their families and highlighted the real-life devastation caused by the epidemic. It also drew attention to the state's neglect of working-class communities, and to the heroic response of the grassroots group, Concerned Parents Against Drugs.

When *Pure Murder* was published in 1984, the aim was to highlight this devastation from the perspective of those most affected, and was written largely by the people who have direct experience of the 'pure murder' that addiction brings – the users, ex-users, and their families – because they are at the heart of the matter and must be listened to. The book aimed to get their harsh reality across in the midst of all the worthless media outrage that obscured it. While Ireland continues to treat drug use and addiction as a criminal or legal issue, rather than a medical and social issue, *Pure Murder* widened the discourse and humanised those victims whose lives were devastated. The book is a credit to Noreen and Sue's ability to capture the reality of the situation. These two wonderful women couldn't have been more different in terms of political outlook and background, but they shared a deep commitment to social change and to equality, as well as sharing a wicked sense of humour. It was a deep privilege to have known and worked with them.

WCP operated on a shoestring financially. We commenced with government job creation start-up funding and kept going on piecemeal grants from agencies such as the Arts Council, the National Women's Council, and the Vocational Education Commission. Book sales accounted for a fairly small proportion of our revenue. Some funds were generated, too, from providing training to community and women's groups, but most of the time we had second jobs, and our wage take was minimal. With hindsight, it's hard to imagine how we managed to fund our publications. The idea to produce a series of feminist postcards proved to be a good one financially. The sale of the cards may have underwritten a few publications and paid for the overheads. WCP partner, Liz Harper, was to the fore in producing the postcards since she, more than the rest of us, had a design talent and skills. Liz, with her background in the anti-nuclear movement, brought her ecological and sustainability lens to our collective thinking, being way ahead of her time in that regard. Another talented designer, Catherine McConville, contributed to several books and postcards, and often entertained us after work with her beautiful singing voice.

In 1985, WCP staff were offered the chance to attend the UN End of Decade Women's Conference in Nairobi, Kenya, as part of the Irish NGO delegation, funded by an International Trade allocation for women to promote our message and publications. The delegation was diverse and eclectic, including Irish women from the media, IT, publishing, and the arts. It was a once-in-a-lifetime experience, and gave us a sense of connection with the global feminist movement. Valuable alliances were forged and, for WCP, the conference provided a chance to pitch our postcards, in particular to a US audience, an exciting though not massively lucrative opportunity as we recall.

WCP also played a significant role in training and skill-sharing, especially in disadvantaged communities, by documenting and recording lived experiences hitherto ignored. This was exemplified in our collaboration with community-based groups such as the Kilbarrack Local Education for Adult Renewal (KLEAR), vocational education programmes at Mountjoy and Arbour Hill Prisons, as well as Focus Point homelessness service, in order to document life-experience publications.

Strong links were forged with the National Adult Literacy Agency (NALA), as well as the burgeoning community of writing groups around the country, leading to publications, such as the innovative WICP book *If You Can Talk You Can Write*, published in conjunction with the Women's Writing Group in Kilbarrack in 1983.[13] These collections of short stories, poems, local history, and autobiography demonstrated the creativity that comes to the fore when people gain traction and confidence from each other through supportive writing groups. *Write Up Your Street*[14] was the first independent collection of material from the burgeoning writing groups. Its publication was not to be seen in isolation, but rather as a part of the ongoing development of community writing, literacy, and local publishing, and as a complement to public readings and other events. At the time, we were working with such groups with a view towards skill-sharing and empowerment.

WCP had a number of firsts that still have relevance today. While Attic Press was busy producing a series of new women's fiction, including works by such notables as Evelyn Conlon and Melissa Murray, WCP was embarking on a book of stories by children for children titled *I Hate Mustard*.[15] The idea came from a retired teacher, Ann McCabe, and she worked with us to produce this ground-breaking volume. We received sponsorship from an unlikely source, supermarket chain owner and later Senator Fergal Quinn, and it captured the media's attention and the public's imagination when the call for stories went out on The Gay Byrne Show on RTÉ Radio 1.

WCP was always open to new ideas, especially if they involved elevating marginalised voices and experiences. Our challenge was to overcome the lack of means to pursue more of them. We embarked on a project to document stories in the oral tradition of women Travellers, going around the country tape-recording vital and vivid reflections and memories, which sadly never got to print. We explored a series around working lives and trade union recent history with Bríd Smith, featuring struggles including the Dunnes Stores strike led by Karen Gearon. Again, these did not proceed due to a lack of financial backing.

In a world where women were denied basic human rights and were invisible in so many spheres of public life, where to be gay was a criminal offence, where working-class communities were ravaged by heroin use and unemployment, where Mother and Baby Homes continued to exist, where contraception was illegal and unavailable, as was any access to abortion bar the lonely and illegal boat to England, we sought to give voice and legitimacy to the perspectives and lived experiences of those directly involved.

In a sense, WCP operated in a zone between public and private sectors, attempting to operate and, indeed, compete in a commercial sphere. The concepts of not-for-profit businesses and social enterprise were not the norm, not well understood or supported. It was highly important to us that our company structure reflected our ethos and way of working. We aligned ourselves with and learned from the resurgent Irish co-operative movement, adopting models from West Cork and Donegal, and receiving help and advice from the Centre for Co-operative Studies, University College Cork (UCC) in the person of Mary Linehan. Accountant Peter O'Duffy, brother of friend and *IFR* contributor Molly O'Duffy, was generous with his advice, especially on an ethical approach to winding down. WCP adopted a model of a not-for-profit, workers' co-operative with limited company status. It served us well at the time, and still has value as an alternative way of structuring work.

We reflect on the significance of IFI, the WICP Course, and WCP for today's world and wonder why it all matters. This project aimed to integrate values and beliefs into a model for working life where our labour had meaning and relevance, and to some extent it succeeded. What was not at all obvious to us back then was the relevance to the present day of the works produced and the processes involved. The change movements of the 1970s and 80s existed during both a bleak and yet extraordinarily dynamic time. These days, equity is acknowledged as a fundamental principle of social justice and progressive social change effort. The concept and principles of intersectionality are more widely understood, discrimination is multilayered and hierarchical. Privilege, by virtue of race, ethnicity, class, sexuality, or gender cannot be ignored. Those most disadvantaged by structural and systemic inequality – be it racism, sexism, homophobia, classism – must have their voices and experiences brought to the forefront, listened to, respected, and enabled to lead change efforts. We finish our reflection in the hope that WCP contributed in some small way to the importance of giving voice to all those who need to be heard and included.

Mary Flanagan was involved in feminist and community publishing in Dublin in the 1980s. Since then, she has worked as a community worker, social worker, educator, and art writer. She has two grown-up children and lives in Roscommon, where, along with her husband, she keeps animals and a garden.

Marianne Hendron is from Portadown, County Armagh, and attended university in Dublin before becoming involved with community publishing. She travelled to Australia in 1987, returned to Ireland in the early 1990s, and eventually left again with her Australian partner and their two sons to settle in regional Victoria. She has spent the last 30 years in social work, community development, and senior health roles.

CHAPTER 12

Children Have Equal Rights in Society Here (Cherish)

Mary Higgins

Cherish was established in 1972 by a group of four single mothers in Dublin. The group had come together in response to a small advertisement in a number of Irish newspapers in March 1973, placed by Maura O'Dea, herself a single mother who wanted to get in touch with others in the same situation, and to make it known publicly that such a thing as unmarried mothers actually existed, that they and their children experienced particular disadvantages, and that they had ideas on how these should be addressed. Her ideas and ambition were immediately shared and supported by the other women, and Cherish, the self-help group for single mothers, was born.

The name Cherish was taken from the 1916 Irish Proclamation of Independence, which committed to 'cherish all of the nation's children equally'. It is also a seldom-used acronym for 'Children Have Equal Rights in Society Here'. The small self-help women's group grew quickly into a credible and effective service for single mothers and their children, an authoritative voice on their experiences and needs, a successful champion for improvements in their rights, opportunities, status and futures, and an enduring presence in Ireland. Cherish rebranded in 2004 as One Family, and continues to work on behalf of single-parent families.

This essay reviews the context, work, challenges, and achievements of Cherish and reflects on its impact and success. In doing so, it draws on my own personal experience as a young, single, pregnant woman who joined Cherish as a member in 1973, became actively involved as a committee member, and worked as Information Officer from 1979–87. It also draws on the personal experiences of two former Cherish colleagues.[1]

In 1972, single mothers were largely unheard of. Pregnancies outside marriage obviously did occur, couples in second relationships, for example, had children (there was no divorce), and while these might not have been approved of, they were tolerated. But for women on their own to be pregnant was shocking and shameful, because it was a major offence against the patriarchal and Catholic societal norms of the time. We joined a long list of unpalatable human realities that were hidden, as quickly and effectively as possible, in specially-provided residential institutions, including orphanages, industrial schools, county homes, psychiatric hospitals, and Magdalene Laundries. For women and girls who were pregnant and unmarried, there were specially designed Mother and Baby Homes, which date back to the mid-1900s and, like other institutions, were funded by the State and run by religious orders, in this case Catholic nuns, although there were also a small number of Protestant-run homes. It was in these homes that the majority of unmarried pregnant girls and women at this time spent their pregnancies; some went to them voluntarily to conceal their condition and shame from their families, but most were likely to have been placed there by their families, often with the assistance of the local priest. Some also travelled to England to relatives or to similar institutions there. In 1971, the non-denominational ALLY had been established, offering an alternative to institutions through a scheme of placing pregnant, unmarried women and girls in families, in exchange for housework and childminding.

Whatever the pregnancy accommodation arrangement, the regimes were similar, with an emphasis on concealment and adoption. Women changed their names, false scenarios of work overseas or in Dublin were constructed and arrangements made for correspondence to be posted from the corresponding locations to families to support the stories. Babies were adopted by families in Ireland and overseas, arranged through the Catholic and Protestant adoption societies, most of which were attached to the Homes. Following the emotion of childbirth and the tragic loss of their babies, women generally left Mother and Baby Homes, some returning to their families (to continue the story of where they had been), but many were not allowed back and had to create new lives elsewhere, while some moved on to Magdalene Laundries and other institutions, where they remained indefinitely. Little was known about the operation of these institutions at the time, but their full horrors have now been revealed and highlighted through the work of a number of organisations and individuals, and formally investigated.[2]

As far as the Church, the State, and most of the population was concerned at the time that Cherish was established, there were no alternatives to adoption for children born outside marriage in Ireland, and none were needed; there simply were no options and no choices. Against this backdrop, the founders of Cherish demonstrated significant courage, and a certain audacity, firstly to decide to raise their own children, secondly to speak out about doing so, and thirdly to set up an organisation to ensure that they could continue doing it. They were neither the first nor the only group of women to stand up in this way. Other women activists were also coming together to highlight and lobby for the long-standing unmet needs of women and injustices against them and the traditional notion of family was slowly becoming more diffuse through an increase in separation and cohabitation, which helped indirectly to support the establishment and work of Cherish.

None of the Cherish women had any prior experience of doing what they were setting out to do, but they did have their own sense of outrage at the position of single mothers and their children in Ireland and their own experiences of isolation, fear, and shame that accompanied a lone pregnancy then, and some vision of what needed to be done to fix the situation. What they lacked in experience they more than made up for in drive, determination, mettle, and ambition. Their key priorities were to offer support to other single mothers, to improve conditions for them and their children and to create choices for women and girls who were pregnant outside marriage. They identified two immediate key aims: the introduction of a social welfare payment for single mothers and the abolition of the legal status of illegitimacy through which our children were stigmatised and discriminated against, legally regarded as 'Filius Nullius' (child of no one), 'illegitimate', and 'bastard'.[3] An 'Unmarried Mother's Allowance' was introduced in the Budget of 1973,[4] but it was 1987 before the abolition of illegitimacy was finally achieved.

They also knew enough to understood that these ambitions would not be achieved just by hoping they would be, and set about making links and alliances with other organisations and individuals who could provide support, advice, and guidance. A key and early supporter was Mary Robinson, who took on the role of Cherish president.[5] Professor Robinson was unfailing in her legal and political advice as well as moral support and attendance at fundraising, Christmas parties, and other events. Bishop Eamon Casey[6] was another early champion, opening doors to fundraising and other opportunities, including contact with some helpful individuals in the Catholic Church. The National Council for One Parent Families (NCOPF)[7] in England was also an early and important ally, particularly given that the two organisations were on the same path of challenge and change.

A wide number of other individuals in public life and positions of influence, as well as others with specific expertise, provided advice and connections to other relevant individuals and agencies which supported us in our operations, service delivery, and campaigning; this continued and diversified over the life of the organisation. Law firms made themselves available for pro bono advice, input to Cherish meetings, and representation to members in maintenance cases, while medical, financial, and other professionals provided similar advice and support related to their particular competencies. The media was obviously key to raising awareness of Cherish, challenges facing single mothers, and what needed to be done to address them. None of us had any knowledge or understanding of how it worked, but were able to tap into the skills and experience of those that had. At the time, women journalists, many of whom were active in campaigning for women's rights, were to the fore in both print and broadcast media and this really helped with both access and coverage. Coverage was usually positive, but not always. There was a tendency to depict 'unmarried mothers' as victims and poor unfortunates who should be pitied, and to focus on individual stories rather than policy issues. This was not the image we wanted to project, although the alternative of harridans, fallen women, and cheeky bitches wasn't quite it either, but, at different times in our history, were the dominant terms which contributed, at least to some extent, to the opposition to us from conservative Catholic bodies, such as The League Of Decency, the Society for the Protection of Unborn Children (SPUC), Mná Na Eireann (Women of Ireland), and a couple of Father's Rights organisations.

The Cherish founders, who all had careers prior to their pregnancies, were smart when it came to organisational structure, funding, and staffing. In less than a year, they had secured funding from the then Eastern Health Board to employ a social worker. This enabled the provision of a professional service, assured the quality of the service, provided credibility with other organisations and professionals, and strengthened links with university schools of Social Work, which in turn provided access to research, practice development, and to enthusiastic final-year students who did their placements with us. Alongside the social worker came the employment of a Fundraiser or Administrator, who recruited a fundraising committee that was both well-connected and bold, organising original events, helping to raise our profile, and building up support for Cherish among the business and arts sectors. Office systems were impeccably designed, organised, and maintained, and we all learned about record-keeping, filing, office management, and administration from a real expert.

A key practical success was the acquisition of accommodation in Pembroke Street, Dublin, for one pound a week through a Caretakers Agreement, which provided a base and headquarters for Cherish for four decades. A three-story Georgian-style house, it was huge and had potential, but when we moved in it was in a terrible state of decay. The top floor was unusable, there were holes in the roof and buckets to catch the rain coming in, and it was infested with mice, which often emerged during meetings to the horror of all present. The roof was repaired in 1977, through an exceptional grant from the Department of Health, and when the building came up for sale a year later, Cherish managed to raise the funds to buy it. In 1979, FÁS,[8] using apprentices, carried out a complete renovation, during which we remained in situ, and all services continued. As a result, we had a weatherproof building, two flats on the top floor for single mothers and children, and plenty of meeting and office space, which we rented to and shared with the Rape Crisis Centre for a number of years.

Service delivery in Cherish always followed the principles of being non-directive, focusing on supporting individuals to reach their own decisions, and covered a wide range of situations, including contraception, pre- and post-adoption and abortion, and referrals to more expert or appropriate services, which also expanded as needs and service availability changed. It was a very busy service with callers to the office, attendance at meetings, and phone and written communication, certainly in the thousands annually; as demand increased, more funding was secured to employ two additional social workers (and an Information Officer) to secure its continuation and appropriate development. Open meetings were a key offering and provided opportunities for peer supports, discussion, exchange of information, expert input, identification of issues of concern, and subjects for future meetings and other activities. These expanded as time went on and facilities developed, allowing more variety in content, timing, and topics, adjusting as needs, preferences, and opportunities expanded, including the provision of certified training courses and onsite childcare. Finding somewhere to live, living on a low income, and accessing childcare in the event that paid work became available were key concerns for the majority of Cherish users. Public housing was not readily available to single-parent families, private landlords generally would not accept children, and child care was mostly dependent on informal arrangements rather than any coherent system, although the Eastern Health Board did fund some subsidised services for which single mothers were eligible, but these were few and far between.

Cherish offered practical help in a number of ways: maternity and baby clothes, as well as equipment and furniture were donated and accessed by callers; we brokered sharing, live-in, and other accommodation solutions; passed on information on vacant flats where children were permitted; provided advice and information on tenants' rights, making applications to local authorities, and claiming social welfare. We were given use of a house by the Eastern Health Board and another that was made available to us by a member of the public which, together with two flats in Pembroke Street, enabled us to offer some accommodation. All of this was helpful to the women and children who benefited, but did not obliterate the challenges.

The issues of housing, income, childcare, and the challenges attached to lone parenting were ones that Cherish continually highlighted and sought to have addressed through advocacy with senior officials in various government departments and local authorities in individual cases, and on a wider scale through written submissions and broader lobbying and campaigning. Relationships with officials were positive in general, we had good access and were often successful in securing appropriate interventions in individual cases, and even changes in practice. Much of our broader campaigning took place as part of wider movements since many of the issues affecting single mothers were common to other groups – a shared underlying cause being poverty. Cherish was very active in movements working against poverty and homelessness, for civil legal aid, better welfare rights and information about them, as well as improvements in the situation for children in general, including those in residential care.

Cherish was not the only organisation working for and on behalf of single (unmarried) mothers and their children. ALLY was active beyond family placement services, as were community-based and hospital-based social work services, and Cherish worked closely with these in relation to individuals and on wider issues too. In 1976, The Federation of Services for Unmarried Parents and their Children (FSUPC)[9] was established, bringing together service providers and practitioners to improve, develop, and coordinate services, providing a platform for discussion and joint policy-making.

A number of women's organisations were also active, and Cherish collaborated with them on issues of shared concern and interest. Action, Information, Motivation (AIM) and Women's Aid were close associates, with a number of overlapping areas of activity, as was the Irish Family Planning Association (IFPA). We were active members of the Council for the Status of Women (CSW), involved in organising International Women's Day celebrations every year, we worked with Attic Press on projects, took part in Reclaim the Night marches, supported the Contraception Action Programme (CAP), were members of the Anti-Amendment Campaign Steering Group, and participated in a wide range of public meetings, demonstrations, and other activities on women's rights. However, we were primarily focused on our commitment to single mothers and their children and, if a cause did not contribute to achieving this, we did not participate; playing tennis or swimming in the Forty Foot, for example, would not be high priorities for our service users.

One issue that was a high priority for Cherish was the abolition of the status of illegitimacy, and this was eventually achieved through the Status of Children Act, which came into effect in 1988. This must count as one of the main achievements of Cherish and it was 'hard won', as they say. Mary Robinson attempted a few times early on to introduce amendments to the Constitution that were not successful, but did raise awareness of the issue and the need to address it, and at the same time, raised the hackles of many policy-makers and activists, who regarded such a move as an attack on the very fabric of society. But we were not deterred, we developed policy documents and proposals, held public meetings, addressed political parties, lawyers, and other worthies, and kept going. We made many enemies during this lengthy campaign and lost the support of some of our allies because of our stance on the issue.

We disagreed with the majority on the way in which illegitimacy should be abolished. Many supported the equalisation of children's rights (to paternal identification and inheritance), but contended that this could only apply if fathers also had equal and automatic rights of guardianship. Based on the experience of Cherish, we did not agree with this, believing the rights of the two were entirely separate and that any rights for fathers, such as guardianship, access, and custody, should be based on the exercise of responsibilities. Our proposals were for the automatic equalisation of the rights of children, and for a more accessible process through a Statutory Declaration, rather than Court proceedings, where parents agreed on the father's rights. This is what is contained in the Status of Children Act, 1987. There were many people who supported this position, key among them: Trinity College Dublin (TCD) Law Professor William Duncan; Young Fine Gael, at the time, who lobbied their own party members; and others, including the late Nuala Fennell who, as Minister for State for Women's Affairs and Family Law Reform, effectively shepherded the Bill through the Seanad, ensuring it was on the agenda for the incoming Dáil following the imminent General Election.

Looking back at Cherish over 50 years on leaves me somewhat in awe of those founding women – at their vision, ambition, and capacity to create a body that was so simple in its structure, yet so powerful in its execution. I don't remember ever seeing an organisational chart, a vision, strategy, or set of values, and I doubt that these ever existed, but all of these were clear, shared, and lived. Decisions were made by the committee through a process of review of current presenting needs, clarification of purposes, development of goals, and agreement on a way forward. Its clarity of purpose drove its achievements. Cherish survived and thrived because it maintained a focus on what the founders had set out to achieve, which was to improve life for single mothers and their children. They achieved what they did by keeping the needs of the target group at the centre, constantly responding to the changing needs they presented, maintaining relationships with colleagues and policy makers, and by presenting evidence-based and coherent proposals. Unfortunately, many of the problems faced by single-parent families were beyond our influence, and the key issues of poverty, lack of housing, and access to other opportunities persist.

Mary Higgins was born in London to parents who emigrated from Leitrim. She left London in 1969 and has lived in Dublin since 1972. Following her time in Cherish, Mary held a number of leadership positions in voluntary and statutory bodies, mostly in the areas of housing and homelessness, and as an independent management and social policy consultant to voluntary, statutory, and philanthropic bodies.

CHAPTER 13

Attic Press: A Reflection

Mary Paul Keane

Attic Press came into being in the autumn of 1984, a time when the Catholic Church still had a stranglehold on the Irish people, recession was deep, unemployment was high, and migration was significant. The Kerry Babies[1] case and the death of Ann Lovett[2] were soon to become part of the Irish narrative. The first divorce referendum in 1986 was defeated, but the Family Planning legislation had been relaxed in 1985. It might be considered extremely brave, or even a little stupid, for a group of feminist activists to consider launching a feminist publishing house in the dark, depressing Ireland of the 1980s. Attic was a slow burner; its origins lie in Irish Feminist Information (IFI) and in the embryonic Women in Publishing Network (WIPN). IFI had produced a number of feminist posters and the annual *Irish Women's Diary* for a number of years; WIPN was a group of women, working in mainstream publishing, who came together to run a series of training workshops for women working in the industry. We also undertook research, and one of the significant findings was that, in 1982, only 11 per cent of books published in Ireland were by women, and of that 11 per cent, nine per cent were published by Arlen House.[3]

WIPN and other informal groups of women across the spectrum of industry, media, and the arts who came together to support and mentor each other are unsung heroes who played a significant role in challenging the pervasive patriarchy, a well-worn term loved by feminists of the day. It was clear to all of us that the metaphorical invisible barriers, more commonly known as the 'glass ceiling', were pervasive in Irish publishing at every level; not in a passive unknowing way, but in a negative proactive way. The prevailing Irish culture was a marriage of convenience between the State and the Catholic Church, both profoundly anti-woman.

I was at the heart of WIPN and Róisín Conroy, a woman I had yet to meet, was the face of IFI. The coming together of two women from different backgrounds and with different skills became the driving force behind Attic Press. Publishing, training expertise, and feminist activism were its backbone. I left Wolfhound Press and joined IFI. Róisín was an expert strategist and conceptualist, and she and I understood that my expertise lay in an understanding of the publishing process, distribution, and editing, with a sprinkling of conceptualism and creativity. I was both in awe and a little challenged by Róisín, which brought an energy to our collaboration, but also provided the foundation for many of the future battles we would have. In a nutshell, Róisín thrived on confrontation and, by contrast, I was more passive. I had other means of achieving and surviving, but that belies both our strengths and our unique dynamic. At the heart of our relationship, we liked and admired each other.

In the first two years of my time with IFI, we applied to AnCo, the Government Training and Funding Agency, for funds to run a full-time, nine-month long Women in Community Publishing (WICP) programme. For two years, we were successful and trained up to 40 women in the art and skills of community publishing. Róisín was the funding strategist, but she also did some mentoring to the participants, and I did most of the training, alongside invited speakers. I think we would have been happy to continue this for another few years, but the funding ceased after two programmes. We had supported women to establish small community presses, many graduates of the programme got work utilising their publishing skills. For example, the Women's Community Press evolved from the programme and worked upstairs in the Irish Women's Workers Union (IWWU) building.

On reflection, and after much consideration, we decided the best way forward was for us to establish a radical women's press that would challenge the prevailing status quo and lead to transformative change for women. Attic Press was born with Róisín and I at the helm. Róisín and I were responsible to the IFI board and, as such, Attic was an imprint of IFI. The board was made up of seven academic, artistic, and brave women. Personally, I found great advice and support there. It's important to acknowledge the influence of both Catherine Rose of Arlen House, *Spare Rib*, and Virago Press in London. These companies, and other organisations, were key figures in our network, and were essential to us. Róisín was the archetypical networker, it was in her DNA. IFI and Attic Press had a full floor, with a training room in the IWWU building in Fleet Street, Dublin 2, for minimal rent. Women always found ways to support each other, and I'll be eternally grateful to Padraigín Ni Mhurchú, head of the IWWU and a great trade unionist, for her presence and for her support.

Lots of discussion, planning, and strategising was central to the evolution and articulation of our values, culture, aims, and objectives, as well as key strategies that would ensure our sustainability. We clearly understood, and Róisín and I both agreed on this: IFI and Attic would have achieved its primary goal when mainstream publishing had erased its negative bias towards women, and women were given equal opportunity to access publishing opportunities.

In the first year, we published *The Best of Nell*, a collection of Nell McCafferty's articles from *The Irish Times*. The introduction was written by Eavan Boland, who evoked a deep appreciation and understanding of Nell. This book sold extremely well for us and ensured the successful establishment of Attic as a force to be considered. As editor, I worked very closely with Nell, which was both challenging and rewarding.

We also published *Smashing Times* by Rosemary Cullen Owens, a history of the Irish women's suffrage movement, a significant contribution to writing women back into history, as well as a handbook on women's health, and for several years we published the *Irish Women's Diary* under the Attic imprint, which sold well. We received a lot of publicity in that first year, which supported sales and increased our profile.

Róisín and I had defined roles; I was the editor, but as I had experience with distribution, I shared that with Róisín, while she managed finance, networking, and publicity. I wish I could say these roles were fully respected, but they were not, and this lack of boundaries became one of our key battle grounds. We had very different styles in managing conflict, and I learned significant lessons in conflict resolution. However, we carried on for a considerable number of years, approximate to the seven-year itch.

In 1985, we travelled to the International Book Fair in London; Nell and Eavan were also there. This was important as it introduced us to the concept of rights, sales, and distribution. It was also invaluable to see what other international women's publishing houses were producing, and to discuss shared challenges. It was both stimulating and beneficial. We also attended the mid-decade conference in Kenya to mark the progress of International Women's Decade, where we met several Irish academic women, out of which came the *Women's Studies Handbook*, a series of academic articles on women's history, sociology, and literature. We also met politicians and artists. It was an exciting year and gave great energy to both of us. Women's Community Press had grown from the publishing training programme we had delivered previously. In 1987, we launched Evelyn Conlon's *My Head is Opening* at the London Book Fair.

We published Ursula Barry's *Lifting the Lid: Handbook of Facts and Information on Ireland*. This book succinctly detailed key facts about Ireland and women's position within the economy. A key focus was the difference in pay for women doing the same jobs as men, as well as many other challenges women had to face in accessing work and or promotion. Ursula also commented on and provided key facts that highlighted Ireland's excessive dependency on foreign investment, a debate which continues today. There is a strong argument that suggests this dependency is a result of internalised oppression, a result of our experience of colonisation. And, in 1989, we published the seminal work *The Serpent and the Goddess* by Mary Condren, which is an account of the decline of matriarchal power in western civilisation and an analysis of its implications for today's women, and today's Catholic Church. This book became a classic in Irish studies.

As mentioned previously, a minuscule number of books by women were published, and significantly less fiction by women. I felt it important for Attic to take up this mantel and set about publishing contemporary women's fiction. This became yet another battle to be had. Róisín had little or no interest in the importance or greatness of fiction. Discussion was had between us, and at board level where there was support, but it was only when I brought the newly found information that the Arts Council would give significant financial support to publishing houses for fiction, that it then became possible, and Róisín relented. We advertised and networked for submissions, and manuscripts began to come through the letterbox. I remember opening the envelope of collected short stories from Éilís Ní Dhuibhne, and was stopped in my tracks by its brilliance. We published her first collected short stories, *Blood and Water* (1988), and later *The Bray House* (1990). Éilís became a unique and widely recognised voice in Irish Literature. Other new Irish fiction writers published by Attic included Evelyn Conlon's *My Head is Opening* (1987) and *Stars in the Daytime* (1989), Melissa Murray's *Changeling (*1989), and Linda Cullen's *The Kiss* (1990). We had book launches for all of our books, and generally had a good press attendance as well as other interested people. I well remember Fintan O'Toole of *The Irish Times*, who, when we initially met him, was quite flippant and sarcastic, but as the years passed, he mellowed, as did we.

I left Attic Press in the early 1990s. The relationship between Róisín and I had become difficult, and my leaving was a long, painful negotiation in which the Board was heavily involved. In the end, I left satisfied, although the relationship between Róisín and I had become fraught to the point where she did not come to my leaving party. I moved to Galway, opened a bookshop called Sheela Na Gig, and happily sold Attic Press books. Attic Press became a driving force in an eclectic mix of feminist, social, political, historical, and other publications, and importantly, fiction written by women. It was a voice respected nationally and internationally, and I was proud to have played a part in its success.

As a postscript, I feel that it is important that I talk about Róisín in her final journey. I reconnected with her when she came to my father's funeral. I was surprised to see her there, but glad. We didn't see a lot of each other as I was in Galway, but I clearly remember the day we met and she told me about her recent diagnosis of motor neurone disease. I was so sad for her, and held her hand for a long time. We talked, and that began a whole other conversation. Róisín faced her journey with the same strength and control she had always brought to her life. She fought for, and succeeded in achieving, her last desire to die at home on 21 April 2007. She embraced acceptance, and the love of the friends and family around her in a gentle and loving way. Following her diagnosis, Róisín, the natural archivist, donated all of the archives of Attic Press to Cork University Press in 1997, ensuring its lasting availability to future scholars and historians. I aways thought Attic Press would become a mere footnote to any future historians on women's history, but due to Róisín's generous donation, we may remain or become much more significant than expected.

Mary Paul Keane was born on the Northside of Dublin. Her sense of empathy and life experience led her towards working, through education, with women who wanted or needed a second educational opportunity. She has been an educator and an activist throughout her life. Mary Paul was a co-founder of Attic Press, which forged the way for women academic and literary writers in the early 1980s. She was also the co-founder of the highly successful bookshop Sheela na Gig in Galway, where she has lived for 20 years.

Chapter 14

Space for Radical Change

Ger Moane

In the 1970s, even University College Dublin (UCD), then a bastion of conservative Catholicism, could not be immune as the women's movement began to rock Ireland. By 1975, Betty Purcell had formed a women's liberation group on campus, and I encountered them when a group that I was part of, studying computer science, decided to raise funds by organising computer dating. In preparation, we had gathered posters of pop stars and made fliers, but then one of the students drew a cartoon of a woman with three breasts. The two or three women in the group, myself included, were very uneasy with this, and tried to protest, but we had neither the language nor the solidarity of the women's movement to draw on. The male students dismissed our concerns, told us we were ridiculous, and that it was just a bit of fun. We were silenced, yet somehow we went along with the plan, and hovered around the table we had set up in the Belfield restaurant with posters of John Travolta and Olivia Newton-John – and the cartoon of the three-breasted woman. Suddenly, a group of about 20 women came storming in. Betty Purcell stood at the front with her hands on her hips and insisted that the cartoon be removed immediately, that it was outrageous and unacceptable. The same students who had dismissed us, jumped up, with no argument, and immediately removed the offending image. It was an assertion of women's power that opened my path to Irishwomen United (IWU).

A while later, I was sitting with a friend in the Belfield bar on a Friday night when two women came around selling a magazine called *Banshee*. The title intrigued and intimidated us, but the women encouraged us to be bold. They laughed and joked and told us about a great meeting on a Sunday afternoon in Dublin. We bought the magazine and our interest was piqued by the graphics, as well as by words and phrases like 'women's rights', 'patriarchy', and 'contraception'. We didn't have to read it to know that we were going to the next meeting.

When the time came, we caught the bus into town and climbed the stairs of a Georgian house in Pembroke Street. We could hear the buzz before we entered the room. It was packed with women – sitting on chairs, on the ground, on the windowsills. My stomach heaved as I stood at the threshold: *could I slink along the wall and sit at the back?*, I wondered. And that's what I did, all while holding the arm of my friend. We were quickly immersed in a heated discussion about contraception, all forms of which, including condoms, were illegal at the time. The idea that contraception was a woman's right was totally new to me. Stories of unwanted pregnancies and forced intercourse in marriage unfolded. If there was no contraception that meant enforced motherhood. That phrase took the breath out of me, and set my heart pumping as a flush rose through my face and my mind raced with questions and counter-arguments. I slipped out at the end with my friend and headed for home. She'd heard enough and wasn't going back. But the heady atmosphere, and the passion of the women, lured me back and I was soon immersed in IWU.

The meetings were packed a lot of the time. If there were chairs, they were all occupied, so women perched on window ledges or sat on the floor. I always made sure to get there in time to get into the room and avoid making my way through the group. The meetings were heated and full of new ideas about politics and women's rights. Women presented well-thought-out views that were immediately challenged in heated exchanges, or welcomed in excited discussion. Plans were made for direct actions, campaigns, and workshops. I heard the phrase 'consciousness-raising' for the first time at one of the meetings, but I didn't open my mouth for months, until I joined a smaller group responsible for the production of *Banshee*.

The meetings crackled, and afterwards we went to the pub. That was when I fell in love with a woman. Even though many of the women in IWU were lesbian, their lives were still hidden to me, hinted at, ghostly, apparitional. They were in the ether but, while they were right in front of me, I didn't really see them, and I didn't have a category: lesbian or gay. I had special feelings for this woman, but I didn't even think of it as a sexual thing to begin with. I just knew I wanted to spend as much time with her as possible, and that I loved being around her, but we never got one-to-one time. She was always surrounded by other women, always in a group, like many of us, always busy organising, and involved in direct action campaigns.

IWU meetings were intensely exciting. Every Sunday I got on the bus in the early afternoon for the meeting at 4pm, and went to the pub after, and ran out hours later, barely making it to the last bus. And, of course, in addition to the meetings, there were actions that were already legendary when I joined in 1976. I travelled with a group out to the Forty Foot in Sandycove for what became a regular challenge to the men who felt they owned the bathing spot. We met close-by with banners and slogans, ready to make noise. It was exhilarating to be part of a bunch of feisty women who chanted and shouted and brought mayhem and disruption to the easy entitlement of the naked men.

As I spent more time in the group, of course, I realised that there were strong personalities who influenced the agenda, and fiercely held and clashing views over priorities around feminism, socialism, republicanism, contraception, violence, and sexuality. Women in IWU made the powerful argument that contraception was essential to women's labour force participation, linking what appeared to be a radical feminist 'women's issue' of reproductive choice to socialist feminist concerns about material conditions in the economy. Many lesbian women were outspoken and centrally involved in discussions and direct actions, and although 'the right to sexual self-determination' was in the IWU charter, sexuality was not given the political analysis that other issues received. Homosexuality was still largely viewed, in the wider society, as a perversion, a disorder, a mental illness, and so my private feelings of sexual attraction to women remained unexamined until much later.

(above) 'Fifties Fashion' placard at a demonstration. Unidentified photographer.

(right) Letter from Maura O'Dea calling for contact with unmarried mothers. *Irish Independent*, 6 March; *Evening Herald*, 13 March 1973.

Calling unmarried mothers

Sir,—We are a group of unmarried mothers who have mostly kept our babies. We meet regularly and our aim is to make representation to the Government on behalf of all women in our position to obtain recognition of this very serious social problem.

We are very anxious to contact other unmarried mothers, who have either kept their children or given them up for adoption. Anyone interested, please write or 'phone 902327 or 974160 (both after 7 p.m.).

MAURA O'DEA,
335 Lr. Kimmage Road,
Dublin 6.

Women's Charter Convention, 8 June 1975. Private Archive.

(above) 'Join Irishwomen United' poster. Private Archive.

(below): Contraception Action Programme Banner. Private Archive.

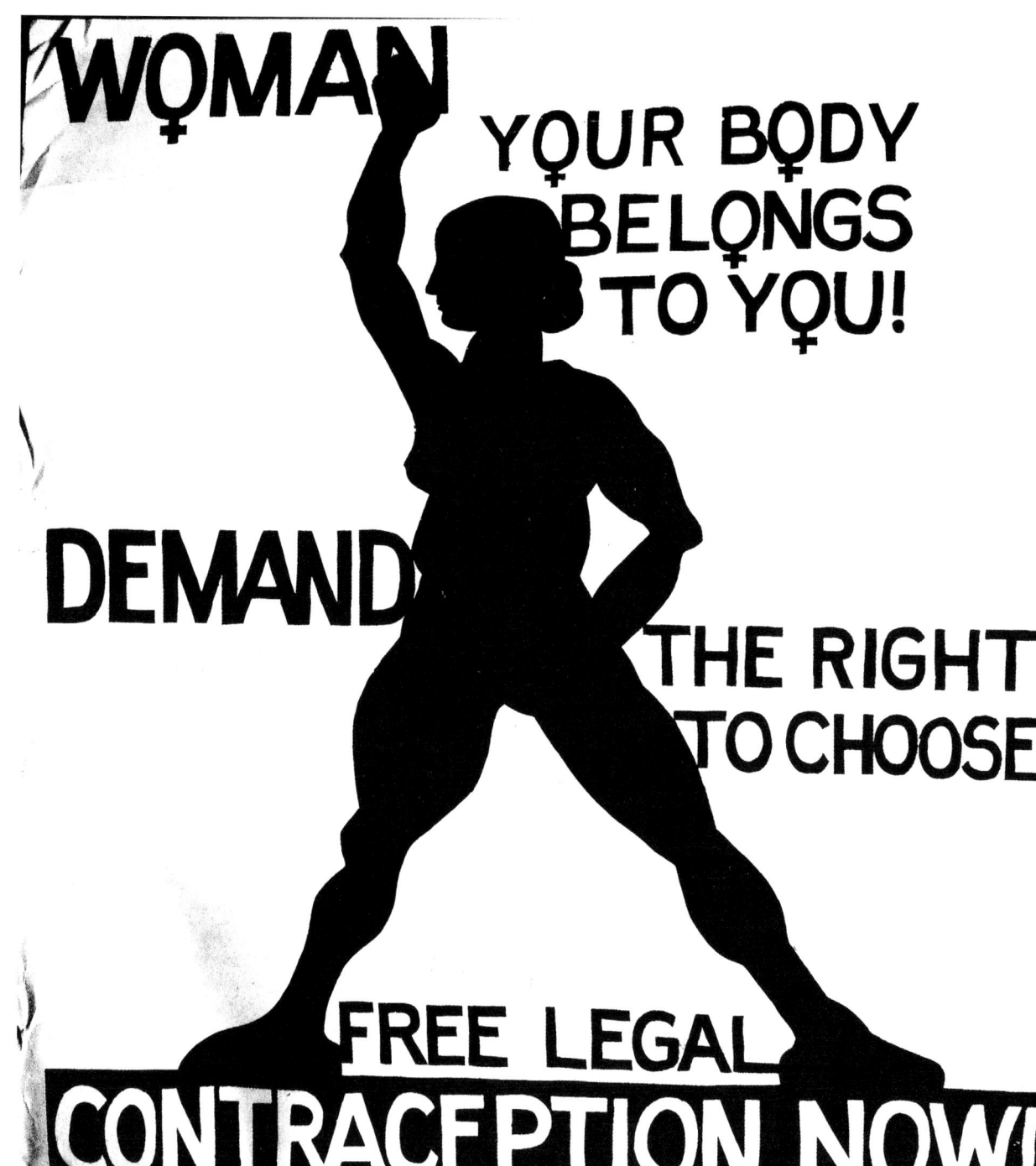

Contraception Action Programme poster. Private Archive.

Poster for Women's Disco. Private Archive.

Postage stamp issued in Ireland to mark International Women's Year, 1975.

Selection of *Banshee* magazine covers. Private Archive.

Public meeting on rape leaflet. Private Archive.

OIFIG AN AIRE SLÁINTE AGUS AN AIRE LEASA SHÓISIALAIGH
(OFFICE OF THE MINISTER FOR HEALTH AND THE MINISTER FOR SOCIAL WELFARE)

BAILE ÁTHA CLIATH 1
(DUBLIN 1)

September 1978

Evelyn Conlon
758 Collins Avenue Extension
Santry
Dublin 9.

Dear Evelyn Conlon

Thank you for your recent letter regarding the Rape Crisis Centre which you have established.

I will be glad to assist you in obtaining a telephone service and if you let me have the address of the Centre I will get in touch with the Minister of State at the Department of Posts and Telegraphs on your behalf.

With kindest regards.

Yours sincerely

CHARLES J. HAUGHEY, T.D.

Letter from Charles J. Haughey, TD to Evelyn Conlon. Evelyn Conlon Papers; Department of Special Collections, Princeton University Library.

Spare Rib Mansion House meeting poster. Private Archive.

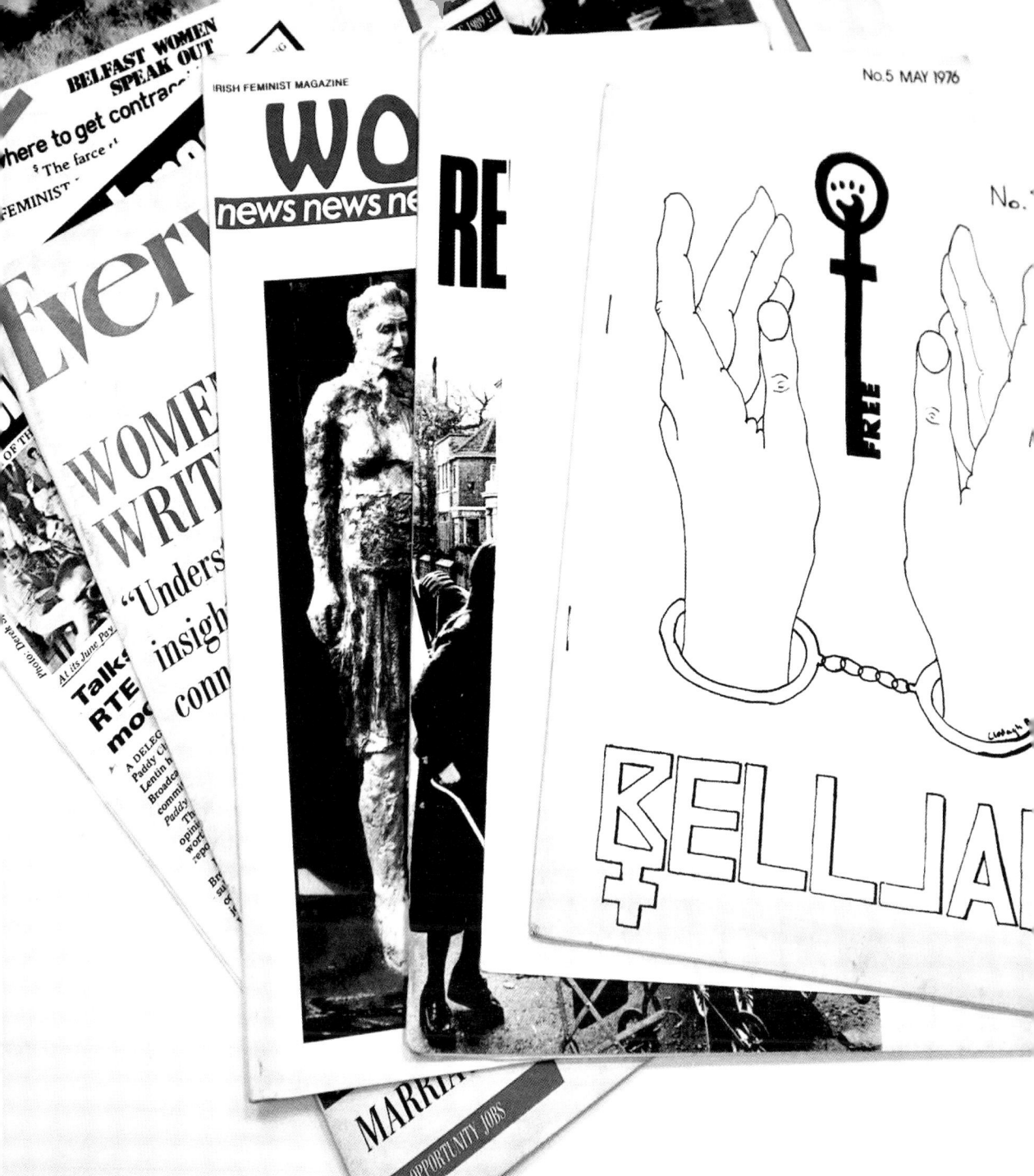

'Bell Jar' and women's studies magazines. Private Archive.

WOMEN WRITERS IN CONVERSATION

AT
THE LILIAN BAYLIS THEATRE
Saturday March 10th at 7.30

Are Irish Women still
"....dogged by visions of the Virgin Mary"?

Maureen O'Neill to Nora Barnacle

a discussion with

FRANCES MOLLOY

EVELYN CONLON

BRIGID McCONVILLE

chaired by

NORA CONOLLY

FRANCES MOLLOY has been a skivvy, a nun and a mortuary attendant: her first novel "No Mate for a Magpie" was published by Virago.

EVELYN CONLON is an active feminist. Her latest novel, "Stars in the Daytime", is published by the Women's Press. She has recently completed an award-winning script for the film "Fire in the Concrete Block".

BRIGID McCONVILLE is a freelance journalist and author of books on women and sexuality. Her works include "Sisters" and "Married to be a Mother", published by Pan.

NORA CONNOLLY is a well known Irish actress. She has worked extensively on stage and in film and television.

THE LILIAN BAYLIS THEATRE
Arlington Way N1 (Angel tube)

Admission: £2 and £1 concs. Information and bookings: 607 8940.
THIS IS AN INVISIBLE IRISH EVENT SUPPORTED BY ISLINGTON ARTS & ENTERTAINMENTS

(above) Irish Writers Discussion, London. Evelyn Conlon Papers; Department of Special Collections, Princeton University Library.

(right) Slogan painted on papal cross. Pat Langan, *Irish Press* (permission for use granted to Evelyn Conlon). Conlon Private archive.

Anti-Amendment March, 13 Nov. 1982. From left: Jacky Ardagh, Mary Holland, Ann-Marie Hourihane, Evelyn Conlon, Unidentified activist, and Inez McCormack. Photo by Derek Speirs.

Pro-choice demonstration placard. Private Archive.

Anti-Amendment Constitution poster 1. Design Fintan Vallely. Private Archive.

WOMEN ARTISTS AGAINST THE AMENDMENT

COME CELEBRATE
THE CONTINUING
CHAOS WITH US.
Poetry, Painting
Film, Song
Music, Food
AND Beverage
ALL UNDER THE ONE ROOF IN
WOMEN WORKERS UNION HALL
FLEET ST. (next door to ESB)
SATURDAY 7th May 6–11 pm.
Come early.

ARTISTS INCLUDE:—
PATSY BRODERICK
EILEANN NI CHUILLEANAIN
LELAND BARDWELL,
NOLLAIG CASEY, ROMA CASEY
EVELYN CONLON, MARY DORCEY
MARY DUFFY, MAUREEN FAHY
MIL FLEMING, HONOR HEFFERNAN
SUZIE KENNEDY, GERaldINE KING
MARY LALOR, CATHERINE McEVOY
EDEL McWEENEY, AILISH MOORE
MARIE MULHOLLAND,
MAIREAD NI DHOMHNAILL,
FIONA REID.

Compere — Nell McCAFFERTY
FILM — PAT MURPHY

Unwaged £2. Waged £3

(Pregnancy testing optional extra.)

HANDS OFF THE CONSTITUTION !!
THE ANTI-AMENDMENT CAMPAIGN P.O. BOX 1285 DUBLIN 7

SAT MAY 7th
5pm–11pm

Airport picket r/e X Case. Photograph by Evelyn Conlon. Private Archive.

(above) Attic press flyer for *Ms Muffet and Others*.

(top left previous page) Painting of slogans for airport picket r/e X Case at Castlewood Terrace, Rathmines, Dublin. Private Archive.

(bottom left previous page) Anti Amendment 'Hands Off!' poster 2. Design Fintan Vallely. Conlon Private Archive.

(right, previous page) 'Women Artists Against The Amendment' poster. Design Fintan Vallely. Private Archive.

A History of the Irish Suffrage Movement 1876-1922

Did your granny have a hammer ???

Mary had a little bag / And in it was a hammer,
Mary was a suffragette / For votes she used to clamour.
She broke a pane of glass one day / Like any naughty boy,
A constable came along / And now she's in Mountjoy

A History of the Irish Suffrage Movement pack: Attic Press 1985

Has your Granny got a hammer? Attic Press information pack. Personal Library.

IWU held to the feminist ideals of collective organising, which involved a lot of discussion and also rotation of responsibility, including for the production of *Banshee* magazine. I joined the group after a few months, and was soon meeting regularly in a flat in Merrion Square, seeking or writing contributions and filling the regular columns. The magazine featured the topics discussed at meetings – contraception, work and equal pay, the Church, prostitution, censorship, women writers, violence, body image. It called for direct action in order to challenge established views on several fronts. Putting it together was more practical than the discussions at meetings, which tended to be more analytical and theoretical. They ranged from pitching different perspectives about patriarchy and colonialism and capitalism to arguments about priorities, themselves embedded in political analysis.

Selling *Banshee* in Dublin pubs was a mixture of defiant fun and sheer embarrassment. We'd arrive in with a handful of magazines and approach a group, focusing on one of the women. As soon as we said the words 'banshee' and 'feminist', the temperature shot up. Women and men would laugh, but men also shouted and closed ranks, joked or patted us condescendingly, tried to flirt or push us away. We would stay shoulder to shoulder and make a beeline for a more friendly pub later in the evening where we could shake off the insults and revel in the sales to a few friendly women.

I'm not quite sure if or how IWU ended. From my perspective, it dissolved into the world of radical activism that was erupting in Dublin and around the country in the mid-to-late 1970s. I spent most evenings and weekends huddled in groups of radical women, determined to blow open the taboos, restrictions, inequalities, discriminations, exclusions, violence, and coercion that dogged our lives. In the midst of activities, I was vaguely aware that things were changing in IWU. At a meeting on 'where do we go' in Spring 1977, we did our best to keep the passion alive. I wasn't aware of, or involved in, the more personal conflicts that resulted in some women leaving IWU, but it was clear that the energy was either flagging or moving in different directions. The last issue of *Banshee* came out in 1977, around the same time as the last conference.

I went with the flow of lesbians and radical feminists, joining a group to produce a new magazine, *WICCA*, that would continue the radical politics of *Banshee*. A group of women, including Joni Sheeran (now Crone), wanted to organise a conference for lesbian women, but there was still too much fear about being out at a time when women would lose custody of their children on the grounds of being an unfit mother if they were known to be lesbian, and sex between men was criminalised. So the conference was advertised as 'a women's conference on lesbianism'. It was the first time I had been in a room of out lesbians talking about lesbian sexuality and politics, enjoying lesbian culture and, of course, a disco. In a later move, some of the IWU lesbian woman and others formed a group to campaign for a women's centre in Dublin, and also created Liberation for Irish Lesbians (LIL) and the Dublin Lesbian Line.

Sometime in 1978, Linda (now Zelda) Hall invited me to join a group who were aiming to set up a rape crisis centre in Dublin. These meetings were very different from IWU Sunday meetings. The topic of rape and sexual violence was intensely emotional: upsetting, challenging, enraging. It was hard to face the reality of rape, and especially the violence of it. We learned to frame rape and sexual assault as a form of violence and control, challenging the prevailing view that it was linked to men's sexuality and was the fault of women. We heard horrific stories when the phone line opened. What kept us going was our belief in the importance of what we were doing, and the solidarity of the group. There were uplifting times as well: a workshop on body image, a weekend away to learn listening skills.

The disco on Thursday nights was a highlight of that time. It was open to all women and attracted many from different parts of the women's movement. We didn't have the language for what we now call the sexuality spectrum and sexual fluidity, but at the time, it provided a space for straight and gay women to socialise together without being presumed to be lesbian, and provided a cover for women to meet other gay women. And it was wild. We danced in the packed room to the sounds of Donna Summer, Blondie, and Chic, and shared a sense of rebellion, of taking on the system, of sensing a different way of being. A Reclaim the Night march in 1978 brought huge numbers of women onto the streets of Dublin, and I revelled in the courage and passion of women marching together full of determination and outrage.

I left Ireland for the USA in September 1979 on a student visa to complete a PhD in psychology in Berkeley, California. I was convinced that a revolution had started and Ireland would be transformed: the monolith of church and state would fall apart, the hypocrisy of the collective will to punish 'fallen women' and incarcerate them in Magdalene laundries, Mother and Baby Homes, and what we then called mental hospitals, which co-existed with a determination to turn a blind eye to family and institutional abuse, would all be exposed. The relentless oppression around sexuality would shrivel, and poverty and class inequality would disappear. The dark gloom of oppression would lift and we would have an equal society, where parenting was fully supported, everyone had access to housing, health, and education, and we would be free to love as we wished.

Like many Irish people, it was only when I left Ireland that I felt able to fully embrace my lesbian identity. Before I left, I had taken to spending more time with lesbian women, hanging out in a lesbian group house with Mary Dorcey and others from IWU and elsewhere. I was still fearful and unaware about my lesbian sexuality, and told myself and others that I was only there for the heated debates. It was there that I met a woman who lived close to Berkeley and who urged me to contact her when I arrived in the States, but even with this open door, I put off calling her until months after, and when I finally did, I approached her house full of trepidation. We went to a local gay bar, and towards the end of the evening she turned and told me she was heterosexual. We lost touch until several years later, when I bumped into her at a Holly Near concert in Berkeley, dressed in dungarees with her arm around a woman, and we laughed as I introduced her to my then lover Mary O'Sullivan, who I had met in IWU. A journey that started in IWU has continued since through LG, LGB, LGBT, LGBTQ+, and on into contemporary queer culture and politics.

While living in Berkeley, a local store opened as a pornography shop. I visited the store with a friend and at first we saw magazines that looked like *Playboy*, and plenty of sex toys, but then I noticed an 'entrance by permission' sign, and I asked the shop assistant to let us through. It was 'the back room' where the violent pornography was on display. We both gasped, shocked by the onslaught of sadistic, misogynist images, and we left full of determination to take action. I joined Women Against Violence in Pornography and Media (WAVPM) and was relieved to be in a familiar space with a group of women organised as a collective with a feminist analysis of violence against women that clearly linked the violence of pornography with rape and sexual assault. Of course, there were disagreements, even in this small group, as befits a feminist collective. The group was very oriented towards developing the skills to facilitate discussion, and it was here that I first learned to use a flipchart, amongst other things.

Returning to Ireland just over five years later, in late 1984, I found a country in the grip of gloom. There had been a massive backlash against feminist and progressive movements, orchestrated by church and state, in the form of a referendum in 1983 to place a ban on abortion, the Eighth Amendment, into the constitution. Women and progressives were absolutely shattered, still wounded, pale and shaking from the vitriol and divisiveness that the campaign unleashed. There was a litany of tragedies: Joanne Hayes,[1] Ann Lovett,[2] and Declan Flynn,[3] to name the most prominent, along with massive unemployment and emigration. Even so, the stalwarts from IWU and the women's movement had managed to establish the Dublin Rape Crisis Centre, campaigns for contraception had gathered pace, and the Dublin Lesbian Line had kept the vital phone line open. But I felt adrift. I had got my first job after completing the PhD in 1985 as a lecturer in University College Galway, and I spent that first term trying to keep ahead of students in hours of lecturing.

In early 1986, I received a feminist lifeline in the form of an invitation from Sylvia Meehan and Mary Cullen from Maynooth to join the Organising Committee of what was officially called the Third International Interdisciplinary Congress on Women, but in practice was called Women's Worlds. It was a conference based on feminism and women's studies, would involve up to 1,000 academics from around the world, and required funding and professional conference organising. Ailbhe Smyth of UCD and Margret Fine Davis of Trinity College Dublin (TCD) had managed to secure the Congress for Ireland, and the aim was to bring the energy of international feminism and women's studies together with the growing movement of community women's education and activism. This was reflected in the theme of 'Visions and Revisions' adopted for the Irish congress, which took place in Dublin in July 1987.

Once again, I was working with women I had met in IWU, as well as many others, as feminist activists, educators, and artists pushed the Congress boundaries and mobilised to organise a programme of workshops and cultural events. The overall result was a week of over 1,000 women from around the world mixing with about 600 women from Ireland in conference sessions, workshops, and cultural events. The intense preparation, involving outreach, fundraising, and mutual education, was highly energising. During the Congress, the Mansion House was packed out on several days of keynote speeches and cultural and community events, resonating with the early days of the women's movement. Workshops, such as Evelyn Conlon's on women's writing, Pauline Beegan's on women and madness, and Joni Crone's on lesbian issues, were packed out. Unfortunately, owing to a family tragedy that occurred just before the Congress, I wasn't able to fully appreciate all this, and only later heard from activists, writers, educators and lesbian women, who had all made new connections and were immensely invigorated by the Congress.

One impact of the Congress was to give credibility and support to the establishment of women's studies programmes in universities. I found myself back in UCD, this time as a lecturer, involved in setting up an MA/Diploma in Women's Studies, which was first offered in 1990. Even UCD was now the ground for feminist activism. I was involved with

Ailbhe Smyth and other colleagues in teaching a core course on feminist theory, which was quite a challenge. Skidding around the Arts Block trying to figure out just what feminist theory was felt exhilarating, and I was grateful for the analyses that had been so profound in IWU. I published a book on the topic of gender and colonialism, which provided a feminist and postcolonial analysis of oppression and liberation, and I had to laugh when a women's studies student met me in the Arts Building and, forgetting my name, said 'oh, you're gender and colonialism'. We had always hoped to develop an outreach programme, and against much opposition, launched the Certificate in Women's Studies in the late 1990s. Going out to community women's groups brought alive the passion and politics of IWU as we grappled collectively, and against the odds of academic demands, to co-create feminist approaches to experiences of violence, poverty, and political exclusions.

The women's movement in Ireland was on the march throughout the 1990s, galvanised by the election of Mary Robinson as President, and her call for women to rock the system. And in 1992 the horrific X case mobilised another outpouring onto the streets when a 14-year-old girl known as 'X' was denied access to an abortion after being raped by a neighbour.[4] Although no longer existing as a cohesive group, activists from IWU and other groups were meeting and working in collectives, such as the Women's Coalition, and taking to the streets. There were small victories at the time, but it took the tragic death of Savita Halappanavar[5] in 2012 to shift the establishment, and a full mobilisation of the women's movement and allies in 2018 to remove the anti-abortion amendment.

In the 1990s, lesbian issues were not always a priority either for the women's movement or for LGBT campaigns. I joined with several other lesbian women in Dublin to form Lesbians Organizing Together (LOT), which, through most of the 1990s, aimed to provide support, resources, visibility, education and legislative protection for lesbian women. I remained active in community politics in the 2000s, and I took to the streets again for the two referenda: to place marriage equality in the constitution in 2015, and to remove the Eighth Amendment in 2018, which seemed to mark a culmination of progressive politics.

IWU had a profound influence on me. It set me on an emotional, as well as intellectual, journey that continues to this day. The passion of the politics, combined with theoretical analysis and emphasis on direct action, were core elements that have stayed with me. IWU was intensely critical of 'the system', which helped me in my academic job as well as in my political life. The solidarity and excitement of direct action meant I always wanted to be involved in grassroots politics, and this gave me an important focus, as well as a buffer against the vagaries of academia. The analysis in IWU of systems, such as patriarchy, capitalism and colonialism, convinced me of the importance of a structural analysis. In my teaching and in my activism, I used and developed a structural approach that emphasised society as a hierarchy with modes of control that maintain hierarchy. When I applied this to psychological aspects of oppression and liberation, I became part of a global movement in psychology (feminist liberation psychology). The structural model helped to raise awareness in students of psychology about societal issues, and to work towards practices for liberation with activist and community groups.

In addition, I think IWU has left a legacy of hope and vision through its ideals of collective organisation, women's rights, and a radically different society. Over the last ten years, Ireland has been commemorating the centennial of what is now referred to as the revolutionary decade of 1913–23, when women and men mobilised for freedom from colonial oppression. I think the 1970s can also be seen as a revolutionary decade, when women and men erupted and mobilised to overcome the rule of church and state, which was established in post-independent Ireland. At both times, there were backlashes and resurgences, threats from conservative and oppressive forces, victories and defeats. We have made enormous, progressive gains in the last 50 years, but we still have violence, poverty, discrimination, and the mounting threat of climate catastrophe. Perhaps there will be another decade in which new visions and forms of activism will erupt and again create space for radical change.

Ger Moane, PhD, grew up in Dublin in a family of eight children. She taught in the School of Psychology, University College Dublin, for many years and is a long-time activist in feminist and LGBTQ+ politics and communities. She is author of *Gender and Colonialism: A Psychological Analysis of Oppression and Liberation* (Palgrave, 1999/2011). Her forthcoming book, *Winter Sun* (Tribes Press), is a novel about Newgrange.

CHAPTER 15

I Just Wanted To Do Something Practical

Anne O'Donnell

When I think about Irishwomen United (IWU), it feels like it was part of my life for a long time. In fact, it only existed for a few years – but a lot happened in those years which completely changed my life, and I imagine changed the lives of many other women who were involved. This essay tells some of the stories I most strongly remember about my time in IWU.

I don't remember where I heard about IWU and the Sunday meetings, but I do remember how I became interested in feminism and the issues that motivated me to go to that meeting. It was the early 1970s and, like lots of Irish graduates just out of college, I went to London and got a job as a Primary School teacher in Tower Hamlets. At that time, Tower Hamlets was a very deprived area and most of the teachers were left wing and committed to social equality. I became friendly with a teacher called Carole who was a feminist and a lesbian. I knew almost nothing about feminism, despite having been involved in several left groups and organisations while I was in University College Dublin (UCD). Carole was an avid reader of *Spare Rib*, a feminist magazine founded in Britain in 1972. I too became a fan of that magazine, and began to realise the extent of women's inequality in almost every aspect of life across the world. I became very aware of the rights enjoyed by women in Britain, such as contraception, divorce, and abortion, and the lack of those rights for women in Ireland.

I came back to Ireland in 1975, and the absence of those rights fired my anger and led me to my first IWU meeting one Sunday afternoon in Pembroke Street. The meeting was like no other I had ever attended. It was in a big room on the upper floor of a Georgian house and was packed with women of all ages from their early 20s to their 50s. There were some couches and armchairs around the room, but most women were standing or sitting on the floor. It was hard to follow what was going on because there didn't seem to be an agenda and women kept standing up, raising issues, and arguing with each other. Despite not really understanding what was going on, I was fascinated by the issues being discussed and started to attend meetings every Sunday. For a very long time, I never opened my mouth and was terrified at the idea of speaking up. I was in awe of and intimidated by how outspoken, articulate, and confident many of the women were.

Gradually, I began to understand that IWU saw itself as a collective with no structured leadership and that any woman at the meetings could raise whatever issue she wanted. I vividly remember how some women would just walk in and start talking angrily about situations where they encountered sexism, demanding to know what we were all going to do about it. Other women seemed more focused and identified as lesbian feminists, republican feminists, or radical feminists. They used the meetings to raise issues relevant to their political beliefs or sexual orientation, and to seek the approval of the meeting to act on these issues. I didn't want to align myself with any specific aspect of feminism and began to feel disillusioned. I just wanted to do something practical that would make a difference for women and girls.

Then an opportunity arose to work on a project. A small workshop group was set up to explore inequality in education and I volunteered to get involved. As a primary school teacher, I felt that I might have something to contribute to this group and found it much easier to talk in the small group environment. We developed and published a booklet in 1975 called *Education Widens the Gap Between the Sexes*. I still have a copy on my bookshelf at home and read it recently for the first time in years. The introduction to the booklet notes that:

> Education, far from being an influential factor in helping to create a new consciousness of equal status for women and men or girls and boys, is in fact a major influence in maintaining and re-enforcing existing sexual inequalities. Through our research and discussion, we have come to the realisation that education widens the gap between the sexes and discriminates severely against girls both in the actual availability of subjects and courses, and in the oppressive attitudes it portrays concerning women and the role of women and girls in society.

50 years later, it is heartening to be able to say that our campaigning and awareness-raising, and that of others who came after us, has resulted in significant progress for girls on educational equality, although some challenges remain for women in all parts of the education system in Ireland.

The experience of working with a small group on the education booklet helped me to begin to overcome my fear of speaking out, but I still said nothing at the big Sunday meetings. I continued to turn up every week, but my main interest was in joining workshop groups on specific issues or actions. I volunteered to get involved in the editorial group that was working on IWU's magazine, *Banshee*, which was the first feminist magazine in Ireland and was published between 1975–77. I worked with them on several issues of the magazine, which carried articles on issues such as equal pay, adoption, women's health, crimes against women, body image, among many others. Working on *Banshee* was both an opportunity to become better informed about the extent of discrimination against women in Ireland and a platform to highlight those inequalities and demand equality and change. The experience also helped me to build writing and editing skills.

I have great memories of the many IWU protests, such as at the Forty Foot bathing area in Sandycove, Dublin, which, at the time, was 'men only'. I remember a group of us deciding that we would go to the area for a swim and make a day of it by bringing a picnic and a tablecloth, which we hoped would be a touch that would really annoy the men. The laying out of the tablecloth, sandwiches, and drinks had the desired effect and seemed to anger the men as much, if not more, than the fact that some of the women got in for a swim.

Another protest I was involved in, in January 1976, was when we decided to picket and occupy the offices of the Federated Union of Employers (FUE) in Fitzwilliam Street to protest about discrimination against women in the workplace, particularly on equal pay. The protest started in the late afternoon with a large group of IWU members carrying placards outside the building. Suddenly, we all started to go into the building. I recall Nell McCafferty and other women asking the very stunned employees to leave since we intended to occupy the building and hold a meeting in the boardroom. Most of the women employees quickly left, but some of the men tried to object and stop the occupation. They failed. The next thing I remember is that we were in the boardroom, with Nell at the top of the table asking if someone would phone RTÉ and other media to come in and film us conducting a board meeting. We waited for the media to arrive, after which Nell chaired a meeting decrying FUE's policy, which discriminated against women in the workplace, and demanding equality for women workers.

In 1977, *Spare Rib* magazine was banned in Ireland as 'obscene' by the Censorship of Publications Board, following a complaint by a member of the public to the Board. Not surprisingly, everyone in IWU was appalled and angry. It was decided, at an IWU meeting, that a group of women would go to Belfast, collect copies of *Spare Rib*, and defy the ban by selling them in Dublin. I was determined to be involved in this action because the magazine had played such a big part in raising my feminist consciousness when I lived in London. On Saturday, 12 February 1977, twenty of us from IWU got the train to Belfast where we met with women from the Northern Ireland Women's Movement (NIWM), and collected 22 copies of *Spare Rib*. We arrived back to Connolly Station in Dublin that evening and walked off the train chanting *Lift the ban on Spare Rib*. In defiance of the ban, we offered the magazine for sale to people on the station platform. We were greeted by a troop of Gardaí who attempted to seize the magazine copies from us. I had some of the magazines in a briefcase and one of the Garda tried, unsuccessfully, to take it from me. The tug of war between me and the Garda was photographed by an *Irish Times* photographer. The Gardaí eventually gave up and we left the station with the magazines, and we were delighted that we succeeded in publicly flouting the ban on the sale of the magazine, but I was worried sick that if the photo was published in *The Irish Times*, I could lose my job as a primary school teacher. The following day was a Sunday, and I went into *The Irish Times* office and spoke to the photographer, who said that they intended to use the photo on the Monday. I begged him not to use it because of my fear of losing my job. I don't know how he did it, but he persuaded the editor not to use the photo. I was recently reminded of this experience when I was taking part in a national demonstration to protest about the brutal war in Gaza. My friends and I found ourselves marching behind a big group of primary school teachers representing the Irish National Teachers Organisation (INTO). Each teacher was carrying a small yellow children's chair to represent children who had been killed in Gaza. I thought how much Ireland has changed, that these teachers can speak publicly and act on their beliefs without fear of repercussions. I felt a sense of pride that the women of IWU and the actions we took, such as defying the ban on *Spare Rib*, were part of a movement to create an Ireland where freedom of speech and belief is possible.

Despite having been involved in so many workshop groups, protests, and actions, I still had a huge fear of speaking out. I remember why and how and that changed. During 1981, I attended a very large meeting in Liberty Hall on the issue of abortion. It was an issue on which I was well informed, and I remember realising that no one had raised an important aspect of that issue. I was completely terrified, but said to myself, *this is not about you or how you look or sound. This is a really important issue about the lives of women, and someone needs to raise it – why not you?* I put up my hand and raised the issue. It was a realisation that I have tried to stick to for the rest of my life. There are times when you need to get yourself and your baggage out of the way and speak up on important issues.

Anne O'Donnell was born and lives in Dublin. She has worked as a primary school teacher, in the National Women's Council of Ireland, and in the Department of Children and Youth Affairs. During the Irishwomen United days, Anne worked on equality in education, which led to an interest in children's rights. For the last 25 years she has worked at strategic, policy, and practice levels on the right for children and young people to have a voice in decision-making. Anne was a founder member and the first Administrator of the Dublin Rape Crisis Centre.

CHAPTER 16

The Feminist Way

Mary O'Donnell

The influence of feminism on my life is derived from a number of sources: reading, personal experience, and conversations with many women (and a few men). These elements formed trilateral waves of information and adaptation, witnessing, and sometimes immersion into other ways of seeing, but also reflection. For writers, the study of life is our business, even if sometimes unconsciously so, and for reasons that are beyond the remit of this essay, I believe I had an exceptionally strong recall of events that occurred in my far past, the result of which was to make me a keen and often anxious observer of the world around me and how it worked, especially in relation to women's lives and the agency they have or do not have.

As a schoolgirl, I had already decided that I must be a feminist, ever since seeing the triumphant members of the Irish Women's Liberation Movement (IWLM) emerge from the 'contraceptive train' on the evening television news on 22 May 1971. I watched admiringly as they charged back into Connolly Station, waving what was believed to be contraceptive pills and condoms in the faces of the Customs Officers who met them. These women had bright, good-humoured faces as they challenged the patriarchy. Before that, every time I heard Bernadette Devlin speak sense about the North of Ireland, its war, and its sectarian inequalities – so misunderstood in the Republic – I was impressed. When she was elected as an MP to Westminster in the mid-Ulster by-election of April 1969, I was astounded and excited. A woman speaking to and about the people in that beleaguered part of our island. A woman and a young, fighting politician who wanted to change the world.

In those years, I sometimes felt imprisoned by illness, and many long-term hospital stays. I didn't just want to read, I wanted to *do*. Nonetheless, when I was 18, my mother, Maureen, arrived to the Dublin hospital where I was having tests waving a copy of Germaine Greer's *The Female Eunuch*[1] in her hand, triumphant about the reading matter she offered. From the age of 11 or so, Maureen had gifted me some of the jewels of Irish censorship laws: *Tarry Flynn*,[2] *The Country Girls*,[3] *The Lonely Girl*,[4] *Mary Lavelle*,[5] *The Dark*.[6] Her own oppositional nature drove her to help me on my way, as she had not been helped on her way when she was young. But reading the right books at the right age and attending the right marches does not automatically make feminists of us. Gradually, thought *and* action were essential when it came to understanding equality and how it might exist in Ireland between men and women. For me, the apex of all inequalities that affected women and working-class men came during the 1970s – in other words, when I grew to fuller consciousness.

Other women leaned in on my life in a formative way while I was still a pupil in the St Louis Convent secondary school in Monaghan. I realised early on that social justice, the twin of feminism, concerned me. Having spent a lot of time in hospitals between the age of 16 to 18, thus having had a disrupted education and a lot of time to make up for, I burned to enter the adult world to do something, change something, make things better. For whom, I wasn't quite sure. And as for *how*, I wasn't sure at all. At that age, I didn't even understand myself or where the roots of my own thoughts lay, but knowing that I wanted to change something in the world was a given; that I wanted to be part of those women who I observed kicking up a riot as they attempted to create change in terms of female equality was also a given. I could hardly wait to leave school, to become engaged, go to Dublin – where I believed everything happened – and to meet my sisters-in-arms. Naturally, it didn't quite work out like that. I went on to read Arianna Stassinopoulos's *The Female Woman*[7] in 1973, and was disenchanted by its attack on feminism and, especially, its vitriol for Germaine Greer. Then I read Betty Friedan[8] and, of course, a little later, Marilyn French's best-selling novel *The Women's Room*.[9] A jumble of new perspectives, you might say, in feminism's new and varied marketplace.

Paradoxically, after university, I had also gone on to do what I sometimes later believed was the worst thing a young Irish woman could do, which was to get married and take on the strain of a mortgage in a small town I regarded as the end of the earth. That town was Maynooth, then a rural village outpost dominated by a Catholic university, a disused canal, a mill, which exuded the odour of grain, and a string of small shops up its main street.

I kept reading widely, from Betty Friedan to Wilhelm Reich. This was a time in which I developed more than I ever could have done at university, because I was ranging far and wide in my reading habits and needs. I connected with other women who were also trying to work something out for themselves. The women who were married seemed to have a different battle on their hands, because they – we – were still in the 'flirting with the enemy' camp by having set ourselves right within a system of oppressive structures where, for example, a day's battle for the sisterhood might involve trying to get a stranger or a relative to understand why you were not taking your husband's name in marriage. I was also struck by the character Val's comment in *The Women's Room*, which shocked me a little at the time, yet always remained with me: 'Whatever they may be in public life, whatever their relationships with men, in their relationships with women, all men are rapists, and that's all they are. They rape us with their eyes, their laws, and their codes'.[10] Surely this couldn't be true, I mused. I knew men who were not remotely like that, certainly not rapists, as far as I could tell.

Later again, I read Andrea Dworkin's *Right-Wing Women*, and found her insistence on this very point compelled me to acknowledge certain things. She wrote, among other things:

> The intelligence of women is not out in the world, acting on its own behalf; it is kept small,

inside the home, acting on behalf of another. This is true even when the woman works outside the home, because she is segregated into women's work, and *her intelligence does not have the same importance as the lay of her ass.* [my italics][11]

Dworkin also regarded the act of penetration by any male, no matter whether he was an unhostile lover, husband, or boyfriend, as an act of rape. I did not agree with that, although the idea holds an undeniable symbolic value. Yet, through that observation, I learned also that those who bring the 'good news' of whatever the desired new world is to be, are sometimes themselves as imperfect, unfinished, and probably traumatised as the rest of us. You accept the positive news and hold some distance (in my case) from what seems unsound, unreasonable, or rooted in that person's private pain.

Whatever about this observation by Dworkin, the stream of words as I read and researched made absolute sense to me, seemed to pour towards me. It was a time in which many of the women I got to know were speaking this new language, babbling in feminist-speak, *Babel*-ing, if you like, because once the grammars of feminism were half-mastered, it was only a matter of time until the vocabularies of real change would become enriched and transformative within our society.

In my practical, day-to-day life, and parallel to private study, I was unemployed for a while, but seeking work. Many of the administration jobs I applied for became an unrelenting series of disappointments. Reliably, in the late 1970s, the question of being married arose during the course of an interview, followed then by a cautious remark, 'you'll be thinking of having a family, I suppose', something I could neither confirm nor deny at the time, but which was clearly an impediment. Roughly translated, I now know for certain that a woman living in Ireland during that period was at a disadvantage if she had married. It didn't matter whether or not the marriage was a happy one, she was still enslaved, in a golden cage, a canary left to sing on its own or, to put it another way, her job was to domesticate herself, have babies, and to assume responsibility for joint domestic harmony. *Was that me?*, I worried and gnawed. No, it wasn't, but to all outside appearances, it might have been. *What would Andrea Dworkin say*, I wondered, *were I to find myself in her company, unlikely as that was?* What would our own local city feminists say if they knew that I'd sold out and was letting myself be raped by someone pretty regularly, even if I enjoyed it? Hard as it may be to acknowledge, this was one model of doctrinaire feminism that prevailed in Ireland at the time, and it wasn't always helpful.

In certain ways, feminism in Ireland in the 1980s sometimes seemed disingenuous and narrow, applying only to women who were single, or single parents, or working class, or lesbian. I would never be seen as a 'real' feminist if this was what feminism meant. Then there was the question of 'class' and feminism. When commentators look back from today, they sometimes imply or say directly that feminism in the 1970s and 80s served the needs of middle-class, white females only. This is not true, although I acknowledge how important it is to have the time and money available to study, to protest, to act with other feminists. However, class did not seem to be an impediment, but the movement did help middle-class women to articulate important issues about equality; in other words, to get started in that work of personal and social transformation.

I attended two very different courses in 1983 that exerted a practical bearing on my life and thinking. One of these was an eight-week course held in the Milltown's Jesuit-run College of Industrial Relations, and was called 'Women At Work'. The title alone is interesting as it signifies how, at the time, so many of us thought that gender equality had more to do with work (as in equal pay and opportunity outside the home), than it did with broader concerns, such as marriage equality and childcare, and the connection between the two. In practice, the course covered things that interested me and developed my appetite for helping to create change. It heightened my awareness of questions to do with sexuality, orientation, and androgyny. Looking back, I find it comical of how proudly I emerged in one of the course surveys as a pretty 'androgynous' type. Of interest to me today is how the word 'androgyny' does appear, historically, to relate to the desire of some men to change gender, rather than the other way around. However, back in 1983 it was viewed in a much more tepid light, a sign of both male and female characteristics in one's psychological makeup. I emerged from the 'Women at Work' course more informed about the bizarre state of inequality in the world, and spoke more fluently and confidently about the things that concerned me, especially in the kind of blundering encounters that developed when men – who understood feminism in terms of bra-burning and 'wimmins libbers' – would counter-attack in a simplified and threatened version of world order as they perceived it.

The second learning experience occurred when I met some of the new women poets of my generation through the Women's Studies Forum at University College Dublin (UCD) in September 1983, set up by Ailbhe Smyth, who remembers the beginning of the Forum:

> I was increasingly involved in the development of Women's Studies in Ireland, and also just back from an inspiring year on Sabbatical at the University of Aix-Marseille and full of determination that we were going to do something about that in Ireland. And of course, it was immediately following the awful 8th Amendment campaign which was so depressing – it seemed vital to start something quite radical and positive! Radical, because the UCD hierarchy had nothing but contempt for Women's Studies (and women generally were not well viewed at all). Anyway, I thought we needed something that was both academic and activist and put up notices for a meeting of the WSF inviting all women staff to attend! We quickly became a group of about seven or eight staff – academics, librarians, admin staff etc [sic] and set about holding seminars on Tuesdays at lunchtime.

She goes on:

> I was very keen to have women writers come to UCD to do readings – and everyone agreed. So that's what we did (and later included women artists too). I'm not sure precisely what year we started – probably 1984. Eavan did come to read – magnificently – but of course so did many others too ... I do remember Nuala Ni Dhomhnaill saying it was the first time she'd ever been asked to read in a university.[12]

The then well-established poet, Eavan Boland, invited several of the younger, emerging poets to read from their work there. Apart from a workshop under Derek Mahon at Trinity College Dublin (TCD), where I had briefly encountered Paula Meehan's and Sara Berkeley's work, this forum offered the opportunity to hear the former luminous poet read her work. Paula seemed worldly-wise and well-travelled, a solo traveller, in fact, who had undertaken much wandering and wayfaring that, clearly, had advanced both her knowledge and self-knowledge, as well as inspired her poetry. Others took part, among them: Glenda Cimino, who was running Beaver Row Press and mothering her newly-born infant, Gaia; Anne le Marquand Hartigan; the experimental poet Susan Connolly; Nuala

Ní Dhomhnaill; and, of course, me. It was bracing to read my own work in Eavan Boland's presence, but conversation and dialogue flowed regarding what was then still referred to as 'women's poetry' rather than 'poetry'. These were courage-giving encounters, that gradually released me to be the person I wanted to be.

Boland, who was kind and enlightening in equal parts, reminded us that, even then, there was only one poetry in Ireland, a male one, and that she – and the rest of us women – were at odds with it. This became my wake-up call. At that time, I had little sense of just how unequal the state of poetry publishing was in our country. Naïvely, I believed that talent would out, cream would rise, and that all was fair and square in matters of literature. It doesn't, it didn't, and it still isn't, although today for quite different reasons, often to do with official identity politics.

Eavan Boland was an early influence in the creation of some of my poems. Having read her poem 'In Her Own Image', I realised the free, untravelled terrain that lay there to be explored, which was never discussed in Ireland, but which writing about seemed, suddenly, to be like breaking through the invisible wall that decreed what was 'permitted' and what was not. Until then, the body had certainly not been permitted space in poetry or literature. So those of us who included aspects of feminine experience in our writing were really like frontier-women heading into the unknown, with suspicious male voices assailing us or ignoring us as fitted their agenda at the time. I have continued to explore the body as a subject threaded throughout my poetry – the body in infertility, the body in abortion, the body in menstruation, the body in childbirth, the body in physical sickness, in old age, being cared for, used, abused, loved, unloved and, of course, the spirit body and the animal body.

The third learning experience that influenced me was my attendance at some of the Women's Education Research and Resource Centre (WERRC) talks – sometimes lectures, sometimes poetry readings – which took place in UCD, again under the astute guidance of Ailbhe Smyth. WERRC formed a significant belt of information, of accrued and accruing knowledge regarding women's lives and female possibility, and thanks to it and to Ailbhe, a Master's degree in Women's Studies got underway and thrived.

One might also observe that I was a creature of my generation – an educated, intelligent woman, who was also a writer and an intense reader. Could I have avoided feminism? Certainly. Many women did, accidentally and deliberately. But practice and ideology were unavoidable for me. The latter was a lot easier than the former, and I was not confident about what I could bring to the public debates of the time in the face of the presence of the more vocal voices, among them Nell McCafferty, and what appeared to sometimes be a hegemony of female journalists who, despite their justice-oriented intentions, seemed deaf to the nuance of how most women lived outside Dublin. Beyond the city 40 years ago, there were few Rape Crisis Centres, there was no Well Woman Clinic, Women's Aid was a vision for the future, and for women who adopted outwardly conventional lives, there was always a risk of being dismissed. But, if the feminist agenda then sometimes lacked inclusiveness, in recent decades it has become a more refined and discriminating movement that has metamorphosed into practical legislative outcomes that are of benefit to the lives of most women and, by association, men.

Yet, without the feminist programme and those who shaped it – the major global movement for change that has shaped most western societies seeking justice, equality, and the basic living rights of a group that comprises half of the population – women and their lives would be rendered silent, static, lesser, and unjust. All equality movements seek urgent change and oppose stasis, and have built on one another in varying degrees. Had Rosa Parks not resisted bus segregation by refusing to sit at the back of the bus in Montgomery, Alabama in December 1951, had the Irish former dentist Lydia Foy not fought for twenty years to have her birth certificate reflect her gender identity after receiving sex reassignment surgery in 1992, had ten young Dunnes Stores workers not refused to handle South African goods because of the way that government treated black people, had Bernadette Devlin not rejected the traditional Irish republican principle of abstentionism in the British parliament, feminism as a movement would be lesser. President Mary Robinson's statement that she 'was elected by the women of Ireland who, instead of rocking the cradle rocked the system', became another stable shoulder that Irish women built upon, contributing significantly to a consciousness of the movement to transform Ireland's feminist evolution. All such movements have built alliances, and have (even unconsciously) inspired different sectors and groups to believe in strength in numbers.

For this reason, a sense of urgency about helping to push back against the obstacles that still prevail in the lives of women is essential. As a lay person, the more I examine International Labour laws, the more I realise how exploited women were, and are, worldwide, the more I realise that wife-beating is seen as a necessity in some cultures (and sometimes in our own), that the brutalisation of the vulvas of little girls through female genital mutilation still exists. I may not have been one of the women on all the marches, although I took part in some, and I was not publicly vocal except through my writing, but gender equality is embedded in my life, and has wandered by default into my writing, including my fiction and poetry. I don't often explicitly use words such as 'patriarchy' and 'feminism', but the concepts are embedded in me and influence how I think and write in as spontaneous a way as it is for me to breathe. The truth is, feminism is like an intelligent giant octopus with tentacles that reach towards women everywhere, without condescension, but with empathy and urgency. Why else would we write, march, urge for change in countries that deny their female populations a basic education, that marry girls off at the age of nine, that insist that men come first? It is our duty to do these things, because we are empowered by decades of movement-building and a layering of knowledge and how-to that aims to support women's lives everywhere.

But death happens by a thousand cuts. If women are to continue (as they must) with confronting and even suppressing patriarchy – it will never be eradicated as a standpoint – there is work to be done. My sense that (some) men truly are threatened by (most) women continues; women who, to them, occupy too much space in the world. An important question centres on what we can do to counter the manner in which patriarchy continually regroups after each 'defeat,' after every advance in legislation that favours equality. I believe certain lines have been drawn in the sand in recent years, as a result of the bravery of women who have waived their anonymity, and brought us closer to a fairer collective social response to gender-based violence.

There's still a way to travel to the finishing line of gender equality. Today, it takes more than a train journey from one jurisdiction to another and back. Perhaps the way forward is best travelled by constant dialogue, again and again as necessary, and to hope that less complacent men might also work authentically in the push for greater global equality. To quote the feminist writer and teacher Cynthia Enloe in *The Big Push:*

> Patriarchy is at work when anything that is deemed feminine is positioned either on a pedestal, to be admired but not to wield authority, or on the lower rungs of the international system's ranked order, where it can be controlled and/or exploited for the benefit of those deemed less feminized.[13]

Dr Mary O'Donnell's work includes poetry, novels, short fiction collections, essays and lectures. Her poetry collection *Massacre of the Birds* has been published in Brazil, where her work forms part of the Irish Studies programme. In 2023, Mary received an AnPost/Irish Book Award for her political poem 'Vectors in Kabul'. Her ninth poetry collection, *Jakkurpa* will be published by Wake Forest University Press (USA), and her new short fiction collection, *Walking Ghosts*, comes from Mercier Press. She is a member of Aosdána.

CHAPTER 17

The Personal Really Was Political

Betty Purcell

The excitement of heading to the 4pm Sunday meetings of Irishwomen United (IWU) in Pembroke Street, Dublin, was an enormous thing. Butterflies in the tummy; a sense of mission. The world was really changing, and we were the makers of that change. *Who would be there? Would I speak well enough? What surprise agenda items would appear?* The Sunday meetings did not always follow the agenda points set out by the organisers. One of the wonderful benefits of such a mixed group of articulate and outraged women was the ability to take a worthwhile diversion.

And, most of all, the energy of all those women crammed into a room, buzzing with needs, perspectives, and eloquence. I was 19 years of age. As the organisers of those early meetings, we had agendas to pursue, and for me, a big one was contraception. I had been elected to UCD Students Union on a platform of 'Contraception on Campus', and it was a key demand of the movement. I remember reporting back on a meeting a group of us had with then Senator Mary Robinson about her Bill, which had failed in the Senate.[1] She was about to reintroduce it, and we were keen to have a say in the form legal contraception should take. We wanted it free at point of delivery in the health service, and for no more than cost price in private clinics and pharmacies. Our thinking was radical, and Mary Robinson spoke to us about the importance of legalisation. The debate the following Sunday was on how far we should insist, publicly, on free access. It was one of many reform versus radical debates we had in those months.

The mistreatment of women in Armagh Jail was another issue I felt very strongly about. These were Republican prisoners who requested, but were denied, political status. Some of us had visited them in jail, and they were anxious that the women's movement take up their cause. On one of the visits, I met Mairéad Farrell,[2] the leader of the female political prisoners, and she told us about the degrading treatment of strip searching, as well as the women's desire to organise their own affairs, and to pursue educational programmes. Within a few years, these issues would become the main requirements of the H-Block prisoners,[3] leading to the hunger strikes, and the transformation of politics in the North of Ireland. But, at the time, these debates in the IWU Sunday meetings were tough and hard fought. In time, they would become one factor leading to the fraying of IWU's unity as an organisation.

I was there from the inception of IWU, but to tell the story of my involvement I have to go back a bit. My mother and father separated in 1958, when I was only two years old. It was a defining moment of my life, because, in those years, unhappy couples stayed together because of convention, and because, for women, there was no other possibility. My father was a gambler and an alcoholic, and when my mother gave him an ultimatum to change, they went together to London to see if they could start over. We three children moved in with our grandmother for what was supposed to be a few months. With my mother away, and us children relocated, my father connived with his mother to sell the house without my mother knowing in the hope that, with nowhere to come back to, she would be forced to stay in London, where he could get back to his old ways. My mother was not inclined to go along with this plan. Incensed by the sale of the home she had invested her own savings in, she came back to Dublin and started her life as a single provider for three children. She refused to apply for the newly minted Deserted Wives Allowance on the basis that she was separated and not deserted. Through a woman TD in Fianna Fáil, my mother got an interview with Mrs Guiney of Clerys Department Store, and began her new working life. It was doggedly hard work, but we lacked for neither love nor care. My mother was a vivid, theatrical storyteller who loved to tell us stories of her mainly American customers, to whom she sold Aran hand knits, evenings spent reciting Shakespeare to us, supervising homework, and yearly trips to the Pantomime, as well as her favourite Gilbert and Sullivan operettas. John McCormack's songs were her soundtrack, along with the passionate music of Chopin. Her moments of 'escape' included sung mass in the pro-Cathedral, or Benediction on a Sunday morning, the incense and chants revitalising her soul. Her life was always busy and full. She was active in the Clerys Trade Union, collected Easter Eggs for the children in Dublin orphanages, and taught us to stand for justice not power, something she felt very strongly about.

By the time I was 15, I was involved politically with the Labour Party working with TD Noel Browne. I was reading about feminism and the women's movement in the US too. In 1972, I became involved with Nuala Fennell's Action, Information, Motivation (AIM) movement. Her determination to pass a bill, as a Fine Gael TD, called The Family Home Protection Act, meant that the family home could no longer be sold over a woman's head, and ensured that no woman would face what my mother had. It was one of the first real reforms of the early women's movement, and I was exhilarated by its passing. The possibility of real change seemed to be everywhere.

In 1974, I went to University College Dublin (UCD) on a Dublin City Council grant, and was a founder member of UCD Women's Group. My politics had moved steadily left, and I was now a member of the Movement for a Socialist Republic. It was Anne Speed, one of the group's leading members, who raised the idea of a new radical women's movement, based around a Charter of Demands,[4] to be called Irishwomen United. Although we (the Movement for a Socialist Republic) were a small, far-left organisation, the idea was ambitious. The call for a conference to agree the Charter went out in April 1975. It was signed by Anne Speed, Anne O'Brien (one of the movement's key activists, who died very young), and me. The conference took place in June 1975.

It is important to acknowledge the work of the Council for the Status of Women (CSW), whose report was issued in 1972. While focused on attainable reforms, and working with mainstream politics, it had spotlighted all the deprivations suffered by

Irish women societally. The Irish Women's Liberation Movement (IWLM) of 1970–71 had demonstrated the activist agenda that we hoped to reconstitute, and although the initiative for IWU came from left activists, the traffic wasn't all one way, or top down from political women. We argued hard in our own movement for the autonomy of the women's movement, and for it to shape itself organically. There would not be a group of male leftists in the background shaping our agenda. We would learn from other women and their experiences, as part of our personal growth in the movement.

The movement, as it emerged, was a coalition of activists, some from the left, some from radical feminism, and a key grouping of lesbian activists. For me, one of the things I got from the radical feminist and lesbian women in IWU was the place of organised consciousness-raising in meetings as a way for women to share experiences and insights. At 19, I thought I knew it all, and certainly I had a definite idea of what issues we should be campaigning on, but through the consciousness-raising that took place in the meetings, I came to know so much about those women's lives, as well as poignant tales of battles with male violence, vocal struggles with employers and Trade Union leaders, the search for a meaningful sexuality, and, everywhere, the screaming need for reproductive rights. The personal really was political, in a way I'd never seen it before.

The excitement generated by the call for a Charter Conference was palpable. Women convened from the colleges, the unions, from local women's organisations, including those fighting for specific reforms. And political women too. We women from the Movement for a Socialist Republic were joined by women from Revolutionary Struggle and the Labour Women's Group. The Charter demands now read as very reasonable, and many, but not all, have since been achieved. For us, the battle was to insist on the inclusion of free access to services.

The Charter was what united all of the members of IWU. Campaigns and organised action immediately followed the Charter Conference in June 1975. Equal pay was a key demand, and was due to be enforced, by European directive, in January 1976, but already the campaign for derogation was being led by the employer organisations. The under-developed shoe industry was used as the excuse. The employers argued that the implementation of equal pay there would lead to job losses in the industry. The campaign to stop the implementation was waged over 18 months, from mid-1974 to the end of 1975. Massive job losses in textiles and clothing, in sugar confectionery, and in light assembly were predicted. What all of these industries had in common was substantial under-development and an inability to compete with international competitors. Women were being forced to pay the price for management inertia, and the government started to talk about sectoral derogations.

In December 1975, Government Ministers Liam Cosgrave and Michael O'Leary announced that they were applying to the EU for a derogation from the January implementation date, to examine the 'vulnerable' industries. IWU took the radical action of occupying the offices of the Federated Union of Employers (FUE), an action proposed by Nell McCafferty at our Sunday meeting. We were surprised to find how easy it was to walk in, and take over the FUE Boardroom. We were accompanied by members of the Irish press. At first, the employer organisation refused to meet us, and the Gardaí were called. We made it clear we would not be leaving until the Executive Directors answered our questions. Finally, after several hours sitting in, two vice presidents of the FUE came into the Boardroom and began negotiating with us. We made clear our demand for full, equal pay for similar work, and work of equal value; in other words, the male rate for the job. They admitted that the industries being talked about had not formally submitted a plan for derogation, with the one exception of the shoe industry, and they further revealed that the Trade Unions at national level had made no submission demanding the implementation of equal pay. After several hours of discussion, we left the building, pleased that we had highlighted our case. That night our protest was covered on the news, and the Government announced that equal pay would be implemented throughout the civil service in January 1976.

The glorious summer weather of 1976 had us packing our swimming togs and heading in another direction, to the so-called 'gentleman's bathing place' at the Forty Foot in Sandycove. That stunning spot, immortalised in James Joyce's *Ulysses*, was appropriated for their sole use by a bunch of middle-aged men, who walked naked in the environs and refused entry to women bathers. Around the corner, the small, crowded beach was home to women and children, and even serious swimmers were excluded from the beauty of the Forty Foot and its diving points. About 50 of us descended on the spot, and jumped in the beautiful blue water of the cove. We painted over the 'Gentlemen Only' sign, and our glee was noisy and palpable. I was among the swimmers. I didn't realise how turbulent the sea was at that spot, and soon found myself in trouble. Thankfully, I was pulled ashore by one of our group, Elaine McWilliam. It would have been truly humiliating if I'd had to be rescued by one of the hostile, angry men, who stood on the shore shouting vile abuse at us. We came regularly from then on, and won the opening of the Sandycove bathing space to women. It is now one of the most popular swimming and diving spots in South Dublin, with free access to all.

We also had fun invading men-only pubs, and those that refused to serve pints to women. I remember such an action in the historic old Dublin pub Neary's of Chatham Street. We came in as a group and ordered 14 drinks, gin and tonics, vodka and orange, etc., and when the drinks were all mixed, we added, 'and 14 pints of lager'. The barman said he couldn't serve pints to females, but looking at our large order, he went to phone the manager'. We got our pints, and the rule began to change. It seems outrageous that this went on in the mid-1970s, but we also had no access to contraception and divorce, the major campaigning issues of our organisation.

I was on the editorial Board of IWU's monthly magazine, *Banshee*. We rotated editors, in line with our emphasis on democratic decision-making and the fundamental principle of empowering and up-skilling members. Our Education sub-committee produced a pamphlet, *Education Widens the Gap Between the Sexes*. We found it noteworthy that girls, who out-performed boys at Leaving Certificate level, found themselves in less well-paid professions after graduating. The concentration of women in teaching and the caring professions contributed to this outcome.

We worked with women's groups in the colleges, demanding crèches on campuses and in work-places. We believed that access to childcare was vital to women staying in work, and to their career development and promotion in their jobs. IWU's whole *modus operandi* was activism. At every Sunday meeting, we decided on our activities and tactics, and on which element of the Charter would be our focus. Those of us who were focused on our sisters North of the border argued their case, and many actions happened around women prisoners North and South. It might be argued, as Linda Connolly has done,[5] that such a level of activism has a life span, as it had with the IWLM. The differences around the North certainly contributed to an exhaustion that eventually saw the depletion of IWU as a cohesive group.

Women started to move towards the objectives and single issues they individually felt strongly about. For me, the critical change that we needed was contraception. It is no coincidence that the strongest grouping that emerged from IWU in 1976 was the Contraception Action Programme (CAP), which continued its work right through until 1978. The laser focus on campaigning for free and legal contraception available to all led us to campaign in local communities in Dublin and around the country. This was where the need was greatest, as middle-class women were beginning to find avenues of availability.

IWU had set up mobile contraceptive 'shops' in the Dandelion Market, in Cathal Brugha Street, and in Harcourt Road, Dublin. We brought our van and petitions to Ballymun, while other activists made the (un)availability of contraception in rural Ireland their priority. I remember knocking on the door of a flat in Ballymun with a petition for contraception. The door was opened by the singing priest, Father Michael Cleary, who told us to 'fuck off' out of his locality. As a young person from a Catholic background, I was shocked by his invective as he roared down the corridor after us, that what we needed was 'a good fuck'. His anger was vile in the extreme.[6]

It became clear that mainstream politics was about to implement reform, and we wanted to minimise the limitations on availability. We were resistant to control being tightly held by the Minister for Health, to limit family planning to what Charlie Haughey's Bill would soon call bona fide family planning, an 'Irish solution to an Irish problem'. We proposed an amendment to the Government's Bill under discussion, insisting on state-financed clinics in every regional health board area. We argued that contraceptives should be free, and education on all methods be provided, including in schools, and that censorship of information should be repealed, with wider sex education provided through the birth control clinics.

IWU had its moment in the sun from June 1975 to late 1977. As the organisation began to dissipate, through the parallel forces of exhaustion, political conflict, and individual reinvention, there was a sense of loss but also of transformation. As Connolly observes:

> For those activists who actively participated in the small groups in the women's liberation sector, after a short period of time a gradual organic process of redirecting their involvement, or dropping out of activism altogether, occurred. The majority ... transferred their activism to direct action through the provision of services and campaigns connected to male violence, in particular (such as women's refuge, rape crisis services, and anti-pornography campaigning.) This process ensured that the movement survived and continued to evolve.[7]

I began to imagine ways that my work could assist in the principles I believed in: equality, fairness, and the creation of safe spaces to empower women. Others took their campaigning into specific service provision, to campaigning for a Woman's Right to Choose, or to the path of reform offered by the mainstream political parties. For me, the path where I could be of most use was in journalism, a path trod earlier by influential and important feminist leaders like Nell McCafferty, June Levine, Mary Anderson, and my personal hero, Mary Holland. I applied for a job as a Producer in RTÉ Radio. At my interview, I argued for a daily women's programme, which would represent the huge number of issues facing women, from birth control to childbirth, equal pay and fairness in training, legal equality in mortgages and bank lending, maternity leave, violence against women, to the smaller social issues that said so much, like women not being allowed full membership of golf clubs. I didn't know that the main interviewer on the Board, Michael Littleton, had such a programme in preparation at the time. I started in RTÉ Radio in Spring 1979, and we went on air with *Women Today* in May of that year. Marian Finucane was the presenter, a woman of talent, insight, and empathy. Over the next seven years, women opened their hearts, speaking with great honesty to Marian, and their voices began to be heard. *Women Today* became an incredibly important piece of broadcasting history.

The first programme I produced was on what now seems such an arcane topic: Sylvia Meehan, then head of the Employment Equality Agency (EEA), debated Dr Cyril Daly, an old-fashioned doctor who I knew from my days in the *Irish Medical Times*, on whether women should continue working after marriage. The marriage bar was a reality throughout the civil service, and even in RTÉ, women lost their staff positions on marriage, to be brought back on temporary contracts at the whim of management. It was a great opener. A serious subject, affecting so many women. Yet Sylvia applied a gentle and humorous technique against the Neanderthal ideas the doctor argued. The phone lines were jammed, and we had to add staff to handle the massive number of calls. And so it continued, every day from then on.

Women Today was a real outgrowth of the women's movement. Some of the colleagues working on it had been very active feminists, reporters such as Róisín Boyd and Hilary Orpen. Over the next number of years we covered so much: the debates on divorce, the insertion of the anti-abortion Amendment into the Constitution, 'men-only' pubs, women and social security, lesbian mothers, childbirth, adoption, women's struggles for housing, especially after marital breakdown. We were very busy, and had the most tremendous fun. Although the programme was recognised as groundbreaking and historic in giving voice to women's needs, only one tape of a *Women Today* programme survives in the RTÉ Archives. All the other programmes were taped over in a cost-saving re-use of tapes in the 1980s and 1990s. As some of my sisters from IWU might have wryly commented: plus ça change!

IWU played a significant role in the changing landscape for women's rights in the 1970s. We made a contribution to the shaping of legislation, to the normalisation of equality in public discourse, and to the development of women's leadership in different sectors of reform. Our intense activism meant our significance far outweighed our numbers. We were in the right place at the right time. The door was beginning to open, and we pushed it wide. Personally, I met many lifelong friends through the movement. We were able to campaign, analyse, and develop in that exciting time of our young lives. We didn't realise then we were laying down memories for life. We were too busy at the time to notice them happening.

Betty Purcell was born and lives in Dublin. She is an author and journalist, a founder member of Irishwomen United, and mother to two daughters. Betty worked with RTÉ in radio and television current affairs for over 33 years. She was a producer of the *Women Today* programme, which ran from 1979 until 1983. A book on Betty's experience of living in Sandinista, Nicaragua, *Light After Darkness*, was an Attic Press publication; a memoir of her life in RTÉ, *Inside RTÉ*, was published by New Island Press. She has contributed to several anthologies.

CHAPTER 18

Reflections from Another Country: Irish Pregnancy Counselling Centre (IPCC)

Ruth Riddick

The past is a foreign country; they do things differently there.
L. P. Hartley, *The Go Between*

If you were to be born in a Dublin maternity hospital in the mid-twentieth century, your mother had two options: the Catholic-majority hospital (Holles Street) or the Protestant-minority hospital (the Rotunda). According to women's secret knowledge, saving the baby came first in the former, while saving the mother came first in the latter. I was born in Holles Street: my mother survived. We were lucky: several decades and a tortuous 'pro-life' constitutional amendment later, Savita Halappanavar did not.[1]

The Ireland into which I was born thought nothing of such scandals as entertaining the Roman Catholic Archbishop's opinion of proposed legislation before introducing it in the Dáil. It was inevitable that this hegemony, characterised by an all-pervasive misogyny, couldn't last. The fabulously media-friendly stunt known as the 'contraceptive train' lingers, not least because it was so perfectly of its time. Long festering grievances in the North (the 'fourth green field' of Republican song) had recently erupted in violence, highlighting the contested politics of a hard border on the relatively small island, something that is still an issue post-Brexit. Cross that border and different standards applied, certainly with respect to the condoms available for purchase there.

Abortion, despite legalisation in Britain in 1967, some four years before 'the train', was another matter entirely. Curtailing women's options was a cause that both sides of the male-dominated Troubles could get behind, and the British legislation was not extended to the North of Ireland, despite its status as part of the United Kingdom. I wrote about the problems for local women that inevitably arose.[2]

The 1970s saw Irish women naming – and shaming – the institutions of misogyny, and setting up our own services in response. Counselling, the feminist response to crisis pregnancy, came at the end of the decade. Initiated by a typically 1970s advocacy collective – the Women's Right to Choose Group – the Irish Pregnancy Counselling Centre (IPCC), established in 1979, was explicitly feminist. That is, we believed in the individual woman's right to choose (parenting, adoption, abortion – all equally valid options), and that women have the moral authority to make such weighty decisions. This belief was not new in political philosophy, but it remains radical, even as access to abortion in Ireland has been established in law. I was invited to join the staff of IPCC after my spontaneous intervention at the Women's Right to Choose Group meeting in Liberty Hall, where I became the second woman in Ireland – after Mary Holland – to publicly acknowledge having had an abortion. This intervention was widely reported at the time.

Our non-directive practice is summarised nicely by the International Coaching Federation as: 'partnering with clients in a creative and thought-provoking process that inspires clients to maximize their personal and professional potential'.[3] Decades later, I'm still promoting self-efficacy and moral authority, the very basis of feminism, in my role as an addiction recovery coach and trainer. Advocacy for abortion anywhere is rarely based on this belief, encoded in the *right to choose* slogan. Ann Furedi, a colleague from the 1980s, is one important exception, and she makes this philosophical argument in her 2021 book, *The Moral Case for Abortion*.[4] Ann served as a long-term, lightning-rod Executive Director of the British Pregnancy Advisory Service (BPAS), a legal abortion provider.

Predictably, IPCC went bust within three years. Business models weren't high on the early feminist agenda, and service providers were more likely to be repurposed activists than business managers. Although IPCC received fees-for-service, and professionals were paid, the service was not financially viable, nor could it have been. For all we supplemented our income with sporadic fundraising, it became prudent to shut up shop. This was problematic for two reasons: the abandonment of clients and the timing. There was no service alternative in place, and a proposal to amend the Irish Constitution, aimed at safeguarding the current anti-abortion provisions, was already underway.

I am a realist, and even as I painted the walls of the replacement Open Door Counselling, adopted Neil Harkin's logo design, and drafted intake forms on neighbour Pat Murphy's spanking electric typewriter,[5] I knew that our days were numbered. My personal resources couldn't last, and we needed to be adopted by an established organisation, one that was aligned with our ethos. The obvious candidate was the Irish Family Planning Association (IFPA), established in the early 1970s from within the liberal professional class, privately wary of feminists, notwithstanding that we shared a service ethic and a hostile ideological environment. It would be some ten years before then CEO Tony O'Brien established a national non-directive pregnancy counselling service at IFPA and, on my recommendation, hired the late Sherie de Burgh to run it. 'What are her qualifications?' he asked me. 'In our friendship of a quarter century, no matter what's been going on, I've always felt better about myself after spending time with her', I replied. It's to Tony's credit that he took my word. Sherie was a natural, and later advised government and taught college. Her 2017 funeral was an extraordinary display of community respect and deep love.

Irish abortion law famously dates from the 1860s as part of a series of multi-dimensional provisions known collectively as the Offenses Against the Person Acts. In the context of a rapidly urbanising industrial society, these laws may have been welcome as much needed governance of unprecedented social relations. This period was also the heyday of the British Empire, with colonial Ireland still recuperating from the predations of what is now termed the Great (man-made) Hunger of 20 years prior.

During this busy century, the Catholic Church in Ireland positioned itself to take a leadership role once Ireland successfully detached from Britain in the first half of the 20th century, with no need to jettison those old imperial laws that suited the new Catholic Nationalist project. Thus, all laws then in effect were seamlessly adopted by the Irish Free State, as long as they could not be shown to be in breach of later Irish constitutional guarantees. Swathes of the Offences Against the Person Acts passed unnoticed into domestic Irish law; unnoticed, that is, until they were, indeed, challenged under the 1937 Constitution, by which time new and higher authorities had entered the scene.

Ireland joined the then European Economic Community, now the European Union, at the beginning of 1973. Previously, Ireland had signed the European Convention on Human Rights, effective from 1953. Generally poorly understood, these supranational allegiances take precedence where conflict arises with domestic law, as happened in respect of the homosexuality and abortion provisions of the Offences Against the Person Acts, Irish law (homosexuality) and the Constitution's Article 40.3.3 (abortion, particularly information about extra-jurisdictional legal abortion services).

Historically, illegal abortion was known (and prosecuted) in Ireland. For the most part, Irish women went to England following its legalization there in 1967, often to addresses gleaned from magazine advertisements in the likes of trendy *Cosmopolitan*. Under British law, statistics were kept, the first official data confirming instances of Irish women's abortions. On their return, women might seek out the informal network of priests who would offer post-abortion solace in the confessional, forgiving this 'reserved' sin.[6] I had a list of phone numbers in my desk.

Arising from the provision of pregnancy counselling, two issues emerged for consideration by the courts: 'referral' and 'information'. The immediate charge against pregnancy counselling was that its work amounted to no more than abortion referral, contrary to the extant Offenses Against the Person Acts and, after the referendum of 1983, the constitution itself. This charge was, of course, nonsense. 'Abortion referral' is a precise term defined in the 1967 British Abortion Act, which limits authority to refer for legal abortion to two qualified medical doctors in Britain under specific conditions stipulated in the Act. No practitioner in the Republic of Ireland – a foreign jurisdiction – could possibly satisfy these stipulations.

Service providers in Ireland could, and did, give information about lawful abortion services abroad as well as services at home supportive of parenting and adoption. It was our practice to offer letters of introduction to our colleagues in any service that we had previously investigated as legitimate, including feminists in England offering free accommodation and, possibly, some financial aid. The status of these letters was wholly informal, but they offered useful information and, perhaps, some comfort. I detailed this practice in a formal interview with Garda Deputy Commissioner, Tomas O'Reilly,[7] at his office. He asked, in the words of the 1861 Act, if we were administering 'noxious potions' or otherwise interfering physically with pregnant women. I informed him that we existed precisely to avoid any such behaviour. As we chatted, I expressed incredulity that my complainants would bother the police to settle a matter of political or ideological difference, something that wouldn't occur to me. I'd go the activist route instead. His response floored me: 'That's because you believe you belong, Ruth', he said. 'Your opponents don't. They feel under siege and from the likes of you, and when you're attacked in this way, you send for the Guards'. These considerations were barely understood beyond the walls of our office in Belvedere Place, a Georgian terrace off Mountjoy Square in North Dublin city. If we weren't being denounced as 'encouraging whoredom in Kimmage',[8] we were dismissed as silly bitches with bourgeois concerns.

So, if we weren't an 'abortion-referral' agency, what were we doing? In the years between 1980 and the mid-1990s, I published several monographs detailing the principles and procedures of non-directive pregnancy counselling. One of these, published by the feminist Attic Press in the *LIP* pamphlet series, appears to be still in circulation.[9]

The legitimacy of this practice was noted by the President of the High Court, Mr Justice Liam Hamilton, who referred to us in his judgement as professionals providing 'much needed services'. The effect of his 1986 anti-information judgment was, of course, to shut down those very services to avoid exposing clients to contempt-of-court charges. We immediately instituted a helpline (Open Line), coordinated through my home phone, where I gave the controversial information while referring to on-call counsellors. *The Irish Times* front page report gave full details about how to contact Open Line – 'the only Riddick in the telephone directory'. Acting on my behalf in the subsequent appeal, the late Paul Carney, SC, read these principles and procedures verbatim into the record of the Irish Supreme Court.

The 1980s, a long decade in Irish reproductive politics, had everything: abortion and repeating divorce referenda ('the second partitioning'), pickets on our service, volunteers to walk clients to and from their counselling appointments, days and days and days in the Four Courts (High Court, 1986; Supreme Court, 1988) and, subsequently, in Strasbourg (European Court of Human Rights, 1992), endless pre-social media column inches, lots of insults and threats of jail (I never believed I would serve time), scary untrue rhetoric (abortion gives you breast cancer), closure of our counselling rooms, the pivot to phone help, and the ongoing informational notices posted to the walls of women's toilets. And all the blood: avoidable maternal death from Ann Lovett (1990, grotesquely in a religious grotto dedicated to 'virgin birth')[10] to Savita Halappanavar (2012, antiseptically, in a religious-run national hospital).[11]

At the core of the decade-long Open Door Counselling case was the interpretation of the constitutional guarantee of the 'right to life of the unborn', a provision that was added, by referendum, in 1983. However, nobody ever paid attention to then Taoiseach Dr Garret Fitzgerald's addition of the significant phrase, 'with due regard to the equal right to life of the mother'. This circus was a legal inanity since the original Offenses Against the Person Act (Sections 58 & 59, 1861) has always allowed for instances where abortion might be deemed legal by either the legislature or the courts. Direct political action might have closed off this legislative potential, but, in thrall to their American advisors, the anti-choice movement was fixated on the constitution where women existed only as 'wives' and 'mothers' with 'lives and duties in the home'. Ironically, women's right to life, to information, and to travel only came courtesy of this movement's ill-considered constitutional initiative. The 'right to life' clause added to the constitution (Article 40.3.3) clearly envisions situations where abortion might be lawful, having due regard to the equal right to life of the mother. It's a travesty, as well as a tragedy, that this right wasn't invoked to save Savita Halappanavar's life.

The litigation against Open Door Counselling took place in its entirety in a period when the primary supranational authority of both European trading and human rights law was already well established. The foreseeable outcome of domestic litigation was that

Europe would put the kibosh on it, as it did in the case of both travel (European Court of Justice) and information (European Court of Human Rights). There had to be legislation, a further referendum, more legislation, and yet another referendum and more legislation to *maybe* straighten out the mess.

Beyond all these factors was the one consideration I believed rendered the whole exercise preposterous: we were engaged in a Victorian-era censorship argument having entered the lawless digital information age. Already, satellites were beaming images and experiences in real time across time zones. How can you control or censor the digital transmission of information? We're still grappling with that live question more than 20 years into a new century.

I won't comment on how Ireland has weathered its adventures, since I relocated abroad in 1997, but I do know and accept that Irish society is changed beyond recognition, and I'm grateful that Open Door Counselling played a role in those changes. Irish women born anywhere around mid-century got angry. Before the turn of the millennium, and despite our many differences, we had irrevocably changed Irish society and elected one of our own as a Head of State 'for all the people'.[12] I leave reproductive advocacy and service provision to younger generations where these matters belong. In one of my final public appearances at a University College Cork (UCC) women's studies class, I concluded that the Irish feminist agenda of the 1970s was unfinished. One bright student asked what I intended to do about it. 'Nothing', I replied. 'It's your turn. Figure out what matters to you and go for it!'

Dubliner Ruth Riddick lived Southside and went to school Northside, passing the rubble of Nelson's Pillar on the number 3 bus. Radicalised by Germaine Greer's *The Female Eunuch* (the author graciously replied to her fan letter on exotic Japanese notepaper), she is a lifelong advocate for women's moral authority.

CHAPTER 19

And Sisters, We Were Controlled: Ireland in the 1970s

Anne Speed

It's a challenge today to remember or understand what Ireland was like in the 1970s. We had lived through the promise of the 1960s, the rise of the women's movement for the second time that century, the campaign to get the USA out of Vietnam, the struggle against white rule in South Africa, and the colonial revolution that rejected European power in Africa and Asia. All of this, combined with the general rebelliousness of young people, including more and more women, influenced what we thought was possible on the island of Ireland.

In the North of Ireland, influenced by the African American civil rights struggle, civil unrest erupted against many years of sectarian repression, leading to the Troubles, which affected the whole island, much to the alarm of the powers that be. In the South, we measured what had been achieved 50 years after the 1916 uprising, which women had fought in, only to find that progress had been pushed back, through a conservative political alliance with the churches, in order to socially control the population. The more conservative a society is, the more it will try to control women. And sisters, we were controlled.

By the early 1970s, we had won the right to vote and not much else: a wife was officially the property of her husband; rape was legal in marriage; contraceptives were banned since 1935; divorce was unconstitutional; women could not sit on juries[1]; by law, children's allowances were paid to the husband, and it was legal to pay women less than men for the same job. In some cases, women who married lost their jobs, under the so-called 'marriage bar'. Most women were destined for domestic invisibility and child bearing. But something was changing. Young women emerging from schools and colleges, who had taken advantage of increased educational opportunities in the 1960s, didn't like what they saw and wanted to rebel. And, being women, they wanted to rebel practically.

As a young, working-class woman, I was the product of migrant workers. My mother, from Lambay Road, Glasnevin, met and married her future husband, from Scotland, in Birmingham. They brought me, aged three, to live in Dublin. My dad, James, worked in the Lucas battery factory off North Circular Road. My Mam, Maureen, worked in the home. Tragically, she died of heart disease when I was 12. I lost interest in school. I emerged with my Leaving Certificate aged 17 and started a quality-control job in Williams and Woods, a Protestant firm that produced confectionary. Class and status (snobbery) infested the management of the workforce. I was instructed not to talk to assembly line workers or cleaners. I found egalitarianism in the trade union movement and began a life of rebellion against the status quo.[2] I became involved in left politics, inspired by the writings of Leon Trotsky, absorbing all the international and national influences I could. I spent some years in socialist organisations, including the Revolutionary Marxist Group, which became the Movement for a Socialist Republic in 1975, and joined with People's Democracy in 1978. As a woman, my mindset tends to turn ideas into action, to think and act strategically, to work out how to achieve goals.

In Britain, women in the Dagenham Ford car factory were agitating for equal rights and calling on the Trades Union Congress (TUC) to formulate a Working Women's Charter. Here, with Derry McDermott, we got the willing agreement of John Carroll of the Irish Transport and General Workers' Union (ITGWU) to develop an Irish Charter for Women's Rights. However, in spite of strong support from a liberal and far-seeing union General President, Carroll refused point-blank to include a right to contraception. We argued, how could women control their working lives if they could not control fertility? Bodily autonomy was central to women's liberation. Undaunted, I spoke on the subject at the 1973 ITGWU conference. I noted in my remarks a sea of grey-haired, grey-faced men facing me, and said that the trade union movement needed to look like, as well as talk about, a movement for equality. Afterwards, in a sign of the times, some male delegates considered my topic a basis for amorous, as distinct from political, discussion. I spent the rest of my time fending off their misguided advances.

I had been in Connolly station Dublin when the women of the Irish Women's Liberation Movement (IWLM) returned from Belfast on the 'contraceptive train' in 1971, and had attended the subsequent, large women's liberation meeting in the Mansion House. That was consciousness-raising at work. Afterwards, the Fownes Street Group decided to set up area-based groups to agitate on contraception, and I worked with the Dublin 7 group as I lived in Phibsborough. By 1974, I was continuing to have conversations about a women's charter that would represent the real interests of women. These discussions attracted activists interested in agitation in a democratic movement without hierarchy, a place where women could not only express, but also act out their autonomy. It was the genesis of Irishwomen United (IWU).

It is important to understand the mid-1970s. After 16 years of Fianna Fáil being in power, a seemingly more 'modern' Fine Gael-Labour coalition took over in 1973, but it was far from modern or forward-thinking, ushering in, instead, an era of censorship and repression in reaction to the expanding revolt taking place in the North. Repressive laws, including a non-jury Special Criminal Court, and Gardaí beating confessions out of suspects, were part of the political background. As a participant in Shop Stewards Against Internment (SSAI), I opposed incarceration without trial in the North. I retained a continuing involvement in opposing repression and also opposed the southern government's attempt to reframe the subject through censorship.

I became aware of women in nationalist communities with sons and daughters imprisoned or interned, increasingly mobilising in Relatives Action Committees (RACs). These activities became the foundation for the All-Ireland H-Block-Armagh campaign, demanding rights for political prisoners; and for the women's rights groups that emerged in Belfast and Derry, led by working-class women like Maura McCrory and Mary Nellis. The Coalition's liberal veneer was undermined by two events in 1974, directly affecting women: contraception and equal pay. The issue of strip searching of women prisoners was emerging as a deeply disturbing and cruel treatment, and many feminists became enraged.

In 1973, the McGee Case established the right of married couples to privately import contraceptives, and after the coalition defeated Senator Mary Robinson's bill to legalise their sale in 1974, the Minister for Justice, Patrick Cooney, introduced a farcical bill. Single people had no right to contraception he said in the Dáil, because there was no such natural right as a right to fornicate. He explained that, 'the provision in the Bill is quite simple and unambiguous; it makes it unlawful for an unmarried person to purchase a contraceptive'.[3] Feminist activists were dismissive of this pretence at 'reform' and became outraged when Liam Cosgrave, as Taoiseach, voted against the measure as too 'liberal' and, thereby, with the opposition, defeated the measure. Just like their suffragette forebears, IWU separated itself from parliamentary hypocrisy by engaging in direct action. IWU later launched the Contraception Action Programme (CAP), which distributed contraceptives openly, illegally.

Equal pay became a legal requirement after EEC entry in 1973. The 'marriage bar', which affected many women in private industry, including shops, banks and insurance companies, as well as the civil service, had already ended. Irish employers immediately whinged that paying women the same as men would threaten their businesses (meaning their profits). The government listened and asked Brussels for a derogation until they worked out how to reconcile the interests of a large majority of women versus a small bunch of wealthy businessmen. Women voiced their opposition and rage in well-attended public meetings.

The newly formed IWU took direct action. We occupied the Federated Union of Employers (FUE) HQ until they met us to explain to women how industry was undermined by equal pay for women. They appeared, eventually, and delivered some mealy-mouthed rationalisations. Nell McCafferty wanted to stay overnight, but I said our point was made and we left. We were plastered all over the evening newspapers that existed then, and we were on television and radio. We could leave with our activists' confidence sky high.

Simultaneously, RTÉ's *Late Late Show*, with its finger on the pulse of Irish Society, did a long segment on the issue. The FUE's John Dunne spoke to Gay Byrne of the sad plight of low-paid men, whose precarious employment was threatened by women demanding equality. IWU women were in the audience. I responded to Dunne by saying I knew and worked with low-paid men, but pointed out that I had never met a low-paid man lower paid than a low-paid woman. I got an immediate response that resonated across the country (repeated to me for years afterwards). We were part of a growing consciousness among women who knew they were oppressed by church and state, and IWU become a vehicle for expressing their opposition to the power that ruled over them. The government did not get its derogation, and its 'liberal' credentials were further severely dented. Women workers did not go silent. Women telephonists launched a campaign for equal pay in 1976 and gained their union's support for a series of two-day strikes. They eventually secured equal payment a couple of years later. That is a story that deserves to be told.

IWU continued radical direct action against social bastions of male power. The Forty Foot, an exclusively male bathing spot in Sandycove, was invaded by IWU women, taking to the water in droves. The late Anne O'Brien had a bag of flower dumped over her by some of the men who objected. IWU activists scrawled a women's liberation sign on the tennis courts of the then exclusively male Fitzwilliam Tennis Club.

IWU highlighted misogyny and patriarchy that resulted in extreme violence against individual women. We fought the Catholic Church as an instrument of male and state power. We protested outside Archbishop Dermot Ryan's palace, and attracted rebels from an equally stultifying Protestant background. The Church of Ireland had a relatively 'liberal' persona, but demanded, in agreement with Patrick Cooney, that the law should allow contraceptives for married couples only (whose 'conscience' permitted it). They also warned of the 'danger' of young, single people using contraceptives and wanted the coil outlawed as an 'abortifacient'. We recognised that patriarchal power used all religion as an instrument, but also existed independently of it. Gay rights were articulated by lesbian women in IWU, and they found a supportive movement of autonomous women who practiced what we preached. They became the direct action champions of all of our campaigns.

It was at this time that I made a decision that would change my life. I left my job without having another to go to, and the next three months on the dole gave me a life experience that has never left me. Then another door opened and I went to work in the Bray Family Planning Clinic for some months, followed by two years with the late Dr Jim Loughran in his independent Merrion Square clinic, where medical assistance and advice was provided on all forms of birth control.

Whilst IWU had an official Charter, our activities and consciousness-raising focused on three key areas:

- women's bodily autonomy;
- defence against misogyny, domestic and sexual violence;
- challenging trade unions to defend and strengthen women's economic rights.

In the early 1970s, a more middle-class section of the women's movement had emerged, and whilst motivated by the fact that patriarchy oppresses all women, in the mid-1970s they began to express class-prejudice in response to a key IWU and then Contraception Action Programme (CAP) demand for free, legal contraception. *Sex on the rates?*[4] was a no-no, said Gemma Hussey, who went on to forge a ministerial career in Fine Gael. Ironically, 55 years later, Fine Gael's Simon Harris brought in exactly that measure. Some retreated further as they went forward. Another Fine Gael feminist betrayed women when she sported The Society for the Protection of Unborn Children (SPUC)'s little-feet anti-abortion symbol on her lapel in the early 1980s, whose defence to an astonished political colleague, was 'unlike you, I want to be re-elected'.

The 1970s came to an end with Charles Haughey's 'Irish solution to an Irish problem' contraception law in 1979. The Health (Family Planning) Act, designed to regulate contraception by restricting the supply of contraceptives to authorised channels for family planning purposes only. Ludicrous as it was in requiring a prescription for condoms, and requiring their use for 'bona fide family planning purposes' (what else?), it took the sting out of the issue. My recollections, as a founding member of CAP, and of its five years campaign existence, are recorded in Laura Kelly's *Contraception and Modern Ireland,* and in Therese Caherty, Pauline Conroy, and Derek Speirs' collection, *The Road to Repeal.*[5]

We broke the law on contraception, in a shop, in market places, and in a caravan in working-class areas. We opened a shop called Contraceptives Unlimited in Dublin, which became a well-publicised success. The state did not interfere with these popular initiatives, and we remained open for a number of months and had many customers.

Our bodies, ourselves. Women were prepared also to break unjust laws on abortion. Decriminalising abortion was discussed by IWU in *Banshee*. The 1967 British Abortion Act, necessitating a trip to England, leavened its Irish illegality. Some of us would go on to establish an abortion rights group in 1979, and the Open Door non-directive counselling service. We aided women who sought information on how to access abortion in Britain.

Abortion was also on the right's agenda, with awareness of IWU and CAP's initiatives in the 1970s. They wanted a reactionary, in place of a liberal, agenda. In a pincer movement after the 1979 contraception law passed, conservative doctors and barristers bombarded ministers and civil servants with lurid tales of a tide of abortion sweeping Europe and, eventually, Ireland. Garret Fitzgerald was initially taken in and set off an anti-abortion amendment momentum that culminated in the notorious 1983 amendment. Consciousness-raising, writing, and agitation steadily grew a pro-choice minority that, after 1983, became a majority. It took so long to reverse the abortion ban because ministers were too afraid for too long to confront their own innate-conservatism and disregard for women's rights. The late Savita Halappanavar[6] was a victim of that delay in 2012.

IWU members were passionate, committed, intelligent, and brave. We spoke, stepped out, stood up, and refused to back down. We had among our ranks some of the best of our generation. Besides the previously mentioned Gaye Cunningham, we had future writers like Evelyn Conlon, poet Mary Dorcey, radio and television producer Betty Purcell, IT wizard Marie Redmond, campaigning activists like Anne O'Donnell and Maura Molloy, plus my dearly beloved friend Anne O'Brien, rest in peace, as well as leading academics Pauline Conroy and Ursula Barry. I have gone on to work at a senior level in the Irish trade union movement.

The story of IWU is the story of Irish women's lives throughout that decade. It is also the story of the formative years of my political life. They were influenced by encounters with republicans, trade unionists, socialists and, most profoundly, feminists. Some of the most exhilarating days of my earlier life were spent in the company of IWU activists. It was on those days that I forged my belief that a better life for women is the basis of a better life for all and that it is not merely desirable, but also entirely possible.

Anne Speed was born to an Irish catholic mother and a Scottish protestant father. She first worked in industry, family planning services, and, subsequently, became a full-time trade union official. Anne has spent over 30 years in the Service Industry and Professional Technical Union (SIPTU), and a further 13 years in UNISON (Belfast). She is a member of the Irish Congress of Trade Unions (ICTU) Executive Council, and was a founder member of Irishwomen United.

Chapter 20

Fabulously Blasphemous: Finding Myself in Irishwomen United

Saundra Stephen

The 'contraceptive train' to Belfast in 1971, organised and carried out by members of the Irish Women's Liberation Movement (IWLM), awakened a lot of women and men to the imbalances in Irish society at the time, but perhaps more importantly, it set in motion a movement for change that was to alter forever the living conditions of women in this country. For me, however, and for many women like me, it was IWLM's successor, Irishwomen United (IWU), that had the most significant, long-term influence on my life. My own awareness of the need for women's liberation and equality, as well as an individual battle with Irish censorship, led me to feminist activism and membership in IWU.

As a secondary school teacher in a comprehensive school in Ballymun, Dublin, I brought my feminism and my belief in social justice into my teaching at every opportunity. I asked the students to call me 'Ms', which they obligingly did; young people are much more willing to change once they understand why the change is important to someone. Occasionally, I had to laugh when they were trying to respect my wishes, but called me 'Mrs Ms' instead.

Before joining IWU, I and a few friends had independently organised a protest campaign against the tabloid newspaper *The Sunday World's* huge billboard advertisement, which we felt objectified and exploited women. The offensive advertisement depicted a woman sitting in a sexualised pose, salaciously asking the viewer, 'Are you getting it every Sunday?' We printed out posters with *This Ad Insults Women*, and climbed about inner-city Dublin with a ladder, a large paintbrush and a quart of wallpaper paste, sticking our slogan posters over the billboard advertisements. Ironically, *The Sunday World* was the only paper that covered our protest campaign, but we had chosen high-visibility, drive-by locations, so thousands of commuters saw both the advertisements and our posters. Our intention was to make people think about the objectification of women's bodies. In the absence of CCTV cameras, we were never able to be identified.

Throughout the 1970s, I had also read every feminist book I could find. Betty Friedan's *Feminine Mystique*[1] and Germaine Greer's *Female Eunuch*[2] had initially opened my eyes, raised my awareness, and influenced my feminist politics. I ordered a copy of *Our Bodies, Ourselves*,[3] which remains something of an international manifesto on women's health and sexuality, produced by women for women. I had ordered it from the Boston Women's Health Book Collective, but instead of getting the book in the post, I received the original envelope with a note from the Customs and Excise Department of the Irish Government telling me the book had been confiscated under a 1929 Act prohibiting lewd material. I was incensed. I made many phone calls to the relevant Department about the absurdity of their confiscation, and wrote several letters demanding the return of my property. Eventually, someone decided that I should be 'allowed' to have the book, and it was posted to me. This incident strengthened my resolve to fight for social justice and against the petty tyranny of censorship.

A couple of years after my customs protest, and while I was still teaching, my path somehow brought me to an IWU Sunday meeting at 12 Lower Pembroke Street, Dublin. I instantly felt the power and intention of the group and knew that I had found my community. I became a regular attendee from that day on.

The meetings were exciting, intense, and the energy in the crowded room was electric. The atmosphere was filled with hope and charged with purpose. Women of all ages, with diverse viewpoints, political persuasions, and levels of political involvement, joined together to effect positive change. Some women came from trade union backgrounds, others from a socialist or republican backgrounds; there were lesbian separatists and radical feminists and women from all professions, and none. Those who seemed to have already thrashed out their ideas were very articulate and fiery with their politics, and this led to many lively and meaningful discussions. Although there were arguments, clashes and debates, no perspective was left unexplored or unchallenged. Everyone had their say, and we always came to a consensus in the end – no matter how high the passions were or how long it took – because we were united in the larger purpose of political change for women. The issues facing the women of Ireland were so grievous, serious, and pressing that we knew we had to come together to change things for our sisters, our daughters, and their children.

Our Charter of Demands was our guide and it kept us on track. Sometimes, different women would prepare their positions in advance of our Sunday meeting, and have them typed up for discussion purposes. Whatever the issue we were working on, we would plan to initiate an action to bring it into the public eye and into a wider conversation.

I attended each meeting, demonstration, and activity with gusto, and felt completely in tune with the purpose of our Charter and with these amazing women from whom I learned so much. I was most impressed by and felt more aligned with the socialist feminists, and did, for many years, call myself a socialist feminist. I have since slightly shifted politically, but have always considered myself a feminist, first and foremost. Because we were a small enough group, IWU women were asked to stretch beyond their comfort zones and participate in whatever way they could. On occasions, I found myself at fundraisers in various pubs, with my five string banjo, belting out Peggy Seeger's *I Wanna Be an Engineer* and *What Did You Learn in School Today, Dear Little Girl of Mine?* to cheering, rousing crowds of supporters.

The first all-Ireland women's meeting, which I was involved in organising, meant that women from North and South came together to discuss solutions to our shared oppression as Irish women. We met in the Elizabethan Rooms, just under the arch in Trinity College. The meeting was brilliantly attended, and the room was absolutely packed. Yet, there were tensions. The women from the North felt that we didn't include them, or really understand their situation. As I recall, they felt that they were dealing with life or death daily struggles while we, in the Republic, were dealing with bourgeois issues. Nevertheless, all agreed that, whatever our differences and approaches, a historic solidarity had taken place that day in the centre of Dublin.

The mid-1970s was a time of great change for Irish women, both personally and politically. Not only was Ireland coming out of the dull days of economic depression, but women – and especially those of us who were politically active – were seeing the possibilities of freedom from the oppressive stranglehold of the Catholic Church on Irish life and on women in particular. Before social media became a dominant platform for circulating information, pamphlets, booklets, and magazines were the way to communicate with the general public, as well as fellow political organisers, and like-minded friends.

We sold IWU's magazine, *Banshee*, in the pubs around Ballsbridge, where I lived at the time. This was a great way to start conversations with the general public, and with men who were, at the time, the majority of pub-goers, to raise awareness of inequality and the need for change. In general, those we spoke to in the pubs were very sympathetic and supportive.

Banshee was Ireland's first feminist magazine and a copy of our Charter appeared on the back of every issue. Apart from being on the editorial board, I learned how to do layout for the magazine, a skill that became incredibly useful to me. In those days, before computers, layout was laboriously done by hand, using rulers and glue. The headings had to be manually created with Letraset, a time-consuming, dry-transfer lettering method. In addition to laying out the boards, I also did photography and drew cartoons. We weren't a low-budget magazine, we were a no-budget magazine that still managed to sell out eight highly informative issues.

'Gentlemen Only' was the sign that met us at the Forty Foot bathing area in Sandycove, Dublin. This bathing area is the only place on the Dublin Bay coastline where it's possible to swim at low tide, and men, some of them naked, had been swimming and sunbathing there for almost a century, to the exclusion of women and girls. In the past, they had even attacked females who dared to go there for a swim. Some women told us that the sign used to say 'No Women or Dogs Allowed', but that it had been recently changed. When members of IWU arrived to claim our right to swim – there had been a previous demonstration by local women swimmers in 1974 – we were met with a hostile reception, in the form of very angry older men shouting at us to 'get the hell out' of their space. They were pre-warned of our arrival, and one old misogynist was so incensed, he had come prepared with bags of flour and a plan of attack. There were lots of nude men stretched out on the concrete steps, hoping to intimidate us, but we ignored them and took up a place on the rocks to one side of the swimming area. We were 30 strong, determined women and carried signs that read *Stop Bathing Apartheid*, *Forty Foot Gentlemen Attack Women*, and *In Ireland, Private Property means Men's Property*.

All of us were prepared to stand up for our rights, but only a few of us had come prepared to swim. I was the first to dive into the sea from the rocks above, and was followed by five others, while our supporters cheered and chanted the slogans on our placards. The angriest of the men had by now enlisted the aid of some young boys and had given them bags filled with flour to throw on us. One of the bags hit me in the face as I was changing after my swim, and I chased after the little scut. As I did, one of the men deliberately stuck out his foot and sent me sprawling on the concrete steps. I was hurt and had a big bruise on my arm. I was lucky that I didn't break all my teeth, but he was even luckier that I didn't. I reported him anyway to the local Garda station for his deliberate assault. The Forty Foot protests raised awareness of discrimination against women in a way that grabbed public attention. The event was reported by the evening television news and appeared in all the Irish papers. The photograph of me diving into the water and news of the attack on me was in *The Irish Times*, and everyone seemed to be talking about it and our protest. It took a few more years and other local women defying the 'Gentlemen Only' sign to establish women's right, once and for all, to swim at the Forty Foot.

It beggars belief, but back then, some pubs refused to serve women pints, while others like Fagan Brothers in Drumcondra, refused to serve women in the large, comfortable bar and would only serve them in the snug, a tiny toilet-sized area in the front of the establishment. Needless to say, this had to be challenged and changed. IWU made regular ventures into these establishments. We were always refused service. The Fagan Brothers pub saw protests on a regular basis with demands such as *Women Must Be Served*. We used to go in just to defy them. While you'd get the odd, grumbling curmudgeon, most of the male customers used to cheer us on. Other pubs were determined to keep women in their place too. I remember once going to Neary's pub in Chatham Street with a group of about seven IWU members, led by Nell McCafferty, a well-known and beloved journalist. We sat up at the bar and ordered seven hot whiskeys. As soon as the bartender had the hot whiskeys with the boiling water, slice of lemon, and cloves lined up before us on the counter, Nell told him that we'd also like 'seven pints of Guinness' as the rest of our order. The barman refused to serve us pints so Nell told him we were refusing to pay for the hot whiskeys, which were steaming on the bar in front of us. The barman told us he would call the police, but Nell challenged him to 'go right ahead'. A big sergeant duly arrived, agreed that the bartender had not, in fact, filled our order, but there was nothing he could do. Round one to IWU. We left Neary's in fits of laughter, without a drop of alcohol in us, yet glad that the pub had to bear the cost of the whiskeys. I believe women were carrying out this effective protest all around Dublin in the many pubs and bars that discriminated against women. Gradually, these establishments realised that they had to change as our protests were costing them money and women were not going to put up with their rubbish any longer.

IWU certainly knew how to organise a newsworthy protest and, though the group had begun to diversify by the late 1970s, campaigns and feminist activism continued through to the end of the decade. One glorious protest took place outside the Archbishop's palace in leafy Drumcondra – the 'Holy Ground' of Dublin, so called because most of the land for miles around was owned by the Catholic Church. My father dropped me to the protest with a load of home-made placards in the boot of the car: *Contraception Now* and *Church and State Must Separate* were just a couple of the slogans. The demonstrators marched in a circle outside the big gates of the 'palace', and someone started singing a hymn that we had all learned in school and everyone joined in:

> Faith of our Fathers only faith, we will be true to thee 'til death. Oh how our hearts beat high with joy, when 'ere we hear that glorious word – CONTRACEPTION for our mothers, we will fight for thee 'til death.

The audacity of us, to be singing so fabulously blasphemously for contraception outside the bastion of patriarchal, misogynistic, religious power in Ireland.

IWU's Charter supported the basic human right of a woman to control her own body. However, not only was contraception illegal in Ireland, but disseminating information about it was too. In 1977, when the British feminist magazine *Spare Rib* published an issue educating women about various types of contraception and abortion, the Irish Government, which had previously banned the family planning booklet published by the Irish Family Planning Association, promptly banned the importation of *Spare Rib* magazine. Inspired by our sisters in the earlier IWLM 'contraceptive train', a whole train carriage of feminists, united in intention and fired with purpose, went to Belfast to collect copies of *Spare Rib* magazine, which our British sisters had shipped over for us. There was an atmosphere of rebellious hope on the train going up and coming home with our 'contraband' – this time, a banned, dangerous feminist magazine. We arrived back at Connolly station where lots of our supporters, the press, and Guards were waiting for us. Our supporters cheered as we defiantly declared our act of civil disobedience and held our *Spare Rib*s aloft. No one was arrested. It seems the Gardaí were deterred by the huge crowd and the presence of the press. Defiant and determined as always, our next issue of *Banshee* featured a three-page illustrated guide to contraceptives.

Taking photographs for *Banshee* magazine inspired me to get a good camera and to learn photography and documentary filmmaking. The documentary *The Battle of Algiers*[4] had a profound impact on me, and I came to believe in the potential of image and documentary film to change the world. At the time, there was nowhere in Ireland to study documentary filmmaking. A scholarship from Goddard College, in their Master's Degree in Social and Cultural Issues/Film and Video, saw me give up my good, pensionable teaching job and head off to Cambridge, Massachusetts, and eventually land in Santa Fe, New Mexico at The Anthropology Film Centre. The influence of IWU travelled with me all the way across the Atlantic, not just in the delivery of the feminist message, but also in choosing the right kind of innovative protest to catch the eye of the press and engage the interest of the public.

My favourite protest, in the eye-catching style of IWU, was one called 'Ladies Against Women'. This was a parody protest in Cambridge, Massachusetts, against Phyllis Chaffley, who had been invited to speak at the Massachusetts Institute of Technology (MIT). Phyllis, who believed that a woman's place was in the home, had a huge following of conservative women throughout America. We wanted her to know that her regressive ideology wasn't universally welcome, so we dressed in formal ball gowns, white gloves and head dresses, and one of our number was barefoot and pregnant. My placard read *59 Cents is Too Much*, referring to the inequality in pay for American women at that time where, for equal work, a woman earned only 59 cents for every dollar earned by a man. Some of the other signs included *CLAP* (Christian Ladies Against Promiscuity), *My Home is His Castle*, and *Tupperware Not Welfare*. The protest was so successful that we were invited on *Five All Night Live*, a popular talk show on one of the major TV stations. They thought we were a real 'ladies' group until we showed up at the studio with our signs and some bright-spark producer figured out that we were a bunch of radicals. I remembered learning in IWU that no matter what limiting question you were asked by the media, you answered with what you wanted to say. We managed to get our message across on air despite the very careful questions asked by the presenter.

In an essay about my memories of and involvement in IWU, I have been impelled to include my political activity in America in order to emphasise just how important and influential, both personally and professionally, IWU has been on my life. I learned valuable skills through IWU, but perhaps more importantly, I learned about how a small, eye-catching, newsworthy protest can be very effective in raising awareness, reaching people and changing hearts and minds. In our recent (2018) Repeal the Eighth campaign in Ireland, we defeated that Eighth Amendment, which denied women their bodily autonomy. We came *Together for Yes* and instituted constitutional change in the 36th Amendment. In celebration and true IWU style, I brought a few boxes of After Eights (chocolate mints) to the Dublin Castle celebration of our win and handed them out to much laughter and high-fives. This action went viral on social media, reaching a wide audience, a far cry away from the hawking of magazines around pubs.

IWU taught me about collective action, about consciousness-raising, about equality, and social justice, and these are things that I have carried with me, in body and soul, wherever I go. And though I do sometimes feel a hint of despair these days – at the state of women's rights now, the erasure of female-specific language and definition of woman – I retain hope in the future and in the potential of women, individually and collectively, to pick up where Irishwomen United left off, and to continue to change the world for the benefit of us all.

Saundra Stephen, PhD, is a Dubliner, a therapist, and a lifelong educator. She spent many years in the USA where she was actively involved in arts and human rights issues. Concerned that women are losing their rights globally, she believes it is time for Irish banshees to re-organise and let their voices be heard again.

Notes

Chapter 1: The Untold Spark

1. Evelyn Conlon, *Reading Rites* (The Blackstaff Press, 2023).
2. Ibid., p. 150.
3. Colleen McCullough, *The Thorn Birds* (Harper & Row, 1977).
4. Dworkin, Andrea, *Right-Wing Women* (The Women's Press, 1983).
5. Conlon, *Reading Rites*, p. 74.
6. Conlon, 'The Park', in *Taking Scarlet as a Real Colour* (The Blackstaff Press, 1993), pp. 58–72.
7. Conlon, 'The Last Confession', in *Taking Scarlet as a Real Colour* (The Blackstaff Press, 1993), pp. 135–45.
8. Conlon, 'Escaping the Celtic Tiger, World Music and the Millennium', in *Telling* (The Blackstaff Press, 2000), pp. 212–18.

Chapter 2: After the Train: Irishwomen United and a Network of Change

1. The cost of *Banshee* was 15 pence per issue, or £1.50 for six issues within Ireland and Britain, and £2 elsewhere. Ailbhe Smyth, *The Irish Women's Studies Reader* (Attic Press, 1993), p. 261.
2. Bean (pronounced 'ban') is Irish for 'woman'.
3. See Appendix 1. Charter of Irishwomen United.
4. Smyth, *The Irish Women's Studies Reader*, p. 260.
5. See Mary McCauliffe, 'Irish feminisms: Past, present and future: 100 years and beyond', in Clara Fischer and Mary McAuliffe, *Irish Feminism Past, Present and Future: Essays in Honour of Mary Cullen and Margaret MacCurtain* (Arlen House, 2015), pp. 329–36.
6. *The Irish Times*, 2 Aug. 1976.
7. Appendix 2. Chronology of Women's achievements in Ireland 1861–2024.
8. Irish women were excluded from jury duty until 1976 when Máirín de Burca and Mary Anderson took the State to the Supreme Court and won. The exclusion of women from the jury lists was found to be unconstitutional, and the Juries Act 1976 was passed. As a comparison, in Australia, women were not able to serve on juries until a few years later: 1977 in New South Wales and Victoria, 1979 in the Australian Capital Territory, and 1985 in Western Australia. This can be taken as a good indication of the effectiveness of women's activism in Ireland at the time. It is easy to assume that because Ireland was behind many other countries in some sectors that it was behind in all, when, in fact, this isn't the case.
9. The Irish Civil Service (currently 40,000) is a small part of the larger Public Service (currently 350,000). The Civil Service carries out the work of the government and is responsible for delivering a range of public services.
10. See Laura Bambrick, https://publications.inmo.ie/view November 2019: pp. 48–72.
11. Linda Connolly, *The Irish Women's Movement: From Revolution to Devolution* (Lilliput Press, 2002).
12. Ibid., p. xvi.
13. Office of the Minister of State for Women's Affairs, *Irishwomen in Focus 1: The Road to Equal Opportunity: A Narrative History* (1987), p. 11.
14. Yvonne Galligan, *Women and Politics in Contemporary Ireland* (Routledge, 1998), p. 49.
15. The Joint Committee of Women's Societies and Social Workers, was made up of representatives from a number of women's organisations, which met initially to discuss a response to the proposed

amendments to the Criminal Law Amendment Act. The Joint Committee dealt with many issues relating to women and children, and influenced many of the changes that occurred in Irish society. The Committee was especially angry at the wording of the 1937 Constitution, and members were determined to have their voices heard. A letter, dated 10 October 1936, to Éamon de Valera, demanded a meeting (they had already been refused once), which resulted in some (minor) changes to the wording of the Constitution. See, National Archives Dublin, The Joint Committee of Women's Societies and Social Workers, General Correspondence, 98/14/4. This was also covered in Episode 1 of *The Records*, RTÉ 1, 15 Oct. 2023.

16. Hilda Tweedy, *A Link in the Chain: The Story of the Irish Housewives Association 1942–1992* (Attic Press, 1992), p. 49.

17. The EEC was the precursor to the European Union (EU).

18. Irish Women's Liberation Movement, *Chains or Change? The Civil Wrongs of Irish Women* (Kevin Clear Ltd., 1971).

19. Tweedy, *A Link in the Chain*, p. 43.

20. For a personal reflection on the establishment of the IWLM and the 'contraceptive train', see Chapter 9 'Making a show', in June Levine, *Sisters: The Personal Story of an Irish Feminist* (Ward River Press, 1982).

21. An important aim of the event was to expose the hypocrisy in women being able to cross the border and obtain the contraceptive pill legally.

22. In one of life's extraordinary coincidences, both Merle Thornton and Nell McCafferty died within five days of each other in August 2024. As far as I know, the two women didn't know each other, but they were central figures in the women's movements of Australia and Ireland, respectively.

23. Carole Ferrier and Raymond Evans (eds), *Radical Brisbane: An Unruly History* (Vulgar Press, 2004), p. 225.

24. Ibid.

25. Maria Luddy, *Women in Ireland 1800–1918: A Documentary History* (Cork University Press, 1995), p. xxvi.

26. Smyth, *The Women's Studies Reader*, p. 267.

27. Ibid., p. 264.

28. Rebecca Pelan, *Two Irelands: Literary Feminisms North and South* (Syracuse University Press, 2005).

29. The Women's Political Association (formerly the Women's Progressive Association, 1970) campaigned for greater participation of women in politics; ALLY (1971) provided a placement service for single pregnant women; the Family Planning Service (later, the Irish Family Planning Association, IFPA) provided non-medical contraceptive devices; AIM (Action, Information, Motivation, 1972), provided information and legal advice for women, and lobbied for the improved protection of women and children in law; CHERISH (1972) provided advice and support to single parents; ADAPT (Association for Deserted and Alone Parents, 1973); Women's Aid (1974) began and continues its work in the field of domestic violence.

30. Laura Kelly, 'A basic issue of women's liberation: The feminist campaign to legalise contraception in 1970s Ireland', in *Nursing Clio* (online) www.nursingclio.org

31. *SPUC: A Threat to Irish Women*. Factsheet. Socialist Workers Movement, 1989. The Factsheet was sold at a price of 5 pence, and included the Abortion Helpline number, 794700. National Library of Ireland.

32. In Ireland, a Citizens' Assembly brings citizens together, selected by lottery, to discuss and consider legal and policy issues in Ireland. The Assembly then makes recommendations and reports back to the Irish Government. See 'Citizens' Assembly', in Citizens Information. www.citizensinformation.ie.

33. Bicameral Parliament of Ireland, made up of the President of Ireland and the two houses of the Oireachtas: the House of Representatives (Dáil Éireann) and the Senate (Seanad Éireann).

34. https://citizensassembly.ie/overview-previous-assemblies/assembly-on-gender-equality/

35. Mary Cullen, 'Rational creatures and free citizens: Republicanism, feminism and the writing of history', in Cullen, *Telling It Our Way: Essays in Gender History* (Arlen House, 2013), pp. 249–66; p. 261.

36. Connolly, *The Irish Women's Movement*, p. 141.

37. Smyth, *The Irish Women's Studies Reader*, p. 249.

38. Laura Kelly, 'A basic issue of women's liberation: The feminist campaign to legalise contraception in 1970s Ireland', in *Nursing Clio* (online) www.nursingclio.org Downloaded 17 Jan. 2025.
39. Evelyn Conlon, *Reading Rites* (The Blackstaff Press, 2023).
40. From 1968 until 1987, Queensland, Australia, was governed by the Conservative National Party (formerly the Country Party), led by Sir Johannes (Joh) Bjelke-Petersen, who was associated with jerrymandering, through which his party benefitted, and which allowed him to remain as the longest serving premier in the State's history. Bjelke-Petersen's repeated use of police force against street demonstrations and trade unions, led to Queensland becoming known as a police state. On 4 September 1977, Bjelke-Petersen's government introduced a ban on street protests, and between September 1977 and July 1979, over 3,000 arrests were made, representing the longest period of mass civil disobedience in Australia's history. Women who were arrested were strip-searched in the Brisbane Watchhouse in the presence of male police.

CHAPTER 3: IRISHWOMEN UNITED: NOTHING WAS OFF LIMITS

1. Brehon Law is an early form of Irish law comprised of the statutes that governed life in early Medieval Ireland, based on customs handed-down, orally, from generation to generation.
2. Margaret Mead, *Male and Female: A Study of the Sexes in a Changing World* (William Morrow, 1949).
3. *Our Bodies, Ourselves: A Book By and For Women* (Boston Women's Health Book Collective, 1970).
4. Linda Connolly, *The Irish Women's Movement: From Revolution to Devolution* (Lilliput Press, 2002), p. 113.
5. Laura Kelly, 'Irishwomen United, the Contraception Action Programme, and the feminist campaign for free, safe and legal contraception in Ireland, c1975–1981', in *Irish Historical Studies* 43:164 (Nov. 2019), pp. 269–97.
6. Máiréad Enright and Emilie Cloatre (eds), 'On the perimeter of the lawful: Enduring illegality in the Irish Family Planning Movement, 1972–1985', in *Journal of Law and Society* 44:4 (Dec. 2017), pp. 471–500.
7. Carol Coulter, 'Feminist drive spearheaded change in law on marital rape' in *The Irish Times*, 19 July 2002.
8. Criminal Law Sexual Offences Act 2017.
9. Seosamh Grainseir, 'Irish legal heritage: Marital rape', in *Irish Legal News*, 21 Sept. 2018.
10. The injunction was eventually overturned by the Supreme Court in Ireland following massive public outcry and huge demonstrations, which took place all over the country.
11. European Commission. European Care Strategy https://ec.europea.eu/commission/presscorner/detail/ip_22_5169.
12. Margaret Mead is believed to have said this during an informal presentation, but it doesn't appear in any of her writings. The quotation is trademarked and held by Sevanne Kassarjian, New York. Cited in Nancy C Lutkehaus, *Margaret Mead: The Making of an American Icon* (Princeton University Press, 2008), p. 261.

CHAPTER 4: Arlen House: A Pioneer of Irish Publishing

1. Colette McAndrew, MA Thesis, Trinity College, Dublin.
2. Arlen was the second name of Catherine's son, Peter.
3. In 2000, Arlen House was relaunched by Alan Hayes, the present publisher, at the suggestion of Catherine Rose. Alan carries on in the spirit of idealism reminiscent of the first Arlen House founders. Over the years, he has built the press into a vibrant company, dedicated to publishing women and men. It has published almost 300 books in the last 24 years.
4. David Marcus was later to have tremendous difficulty with Evelyn Conlon's work, see Conlon, *Reading Rites* (The Blackstaff Press, 2023), pp. 53–6.

Chapter 5: Dublin Rape Crisis Centre

1. Linda Connolly, *The Irish Women's Movement: From Revolution to Devolution* (Lilliput Press, 2002), p. 141. Quotation attributed to 'Founder member Rape Crisis Centre, radical campaigner'.
2. All statements from contributors are via personal email to the editors, December 2024/January 2025.
3. Minutes of Meeting Held on Rape, Tuesday, 26 July 1997. Dublin Rape Crisis Centre (DRCC) Archive.
4. Susan McKay, *Without Fear: 25 Years of the Dublin Rape Crisis Centre* (New Island, 2005).
5. In 1974, a group of 40 women met in London to discuss the problem of sexual violence. Two years later – in May 1976 – Britain's first ever rape crisis centre opened its doors and helpline. The 50th anniversary of rape crisis centres in England and Wales was included in 'Woman's Hour' on BBC4 (Radio) in November 2024.
6. Minutes of Campaign Against Rape meeting, Tuesday 16 August 1977. DRCC Archive.
7. Document in DRCC Archive.
8. McKay, *Without Fear*, p. 76.
9. Anne O'Donnell, cited in ibid., p. 74.
10. Thanks to Shirley Scott, Cliona Woods, and Michelle Grehan from the DRCC, and to Deidre Richardson and Maeve Eogan from SATU, Rotunda Hospital, for their generous help.
11. Anne O'Donnell, personal conversation with Rebecca Pelan, January 2025.
12. In the Republic: Carlow & South Leinster; Cork; Donegal; Dublin; Dundalk; Galway; Kerry; Kilkenny; Limerick; Mayo; Midlands (Athlone); Sligo; Tipperary; Tullamore; Waterford; West Cork; Wexford; and in the North: Nexus NI and Rape Crisis NI. There are currently six sexual assault treatment units: Cork, Donegal, Dublin, Galway, Mullingar, and Waterford.

Chapter 6: The Well Woman Centre

1. Society for the Protection of Unborn Children (SPUC).
2. Laura Kelly, 'Family planning clinics and activism in the 1970s', Ch 6, in *Contraception and Modern Ireland: A Social History 1922–1992* (Cambridge University Press, 2023), pp. 184–221.
3. R. H. Tawney, 'The choice before the Labour Party', in *The Political Quarterly* 3:3 (July–Sept. 1932), pp. 521–34.
4. Sympathetic people in the advertising department of the *Sunday World* often gave free advertising in return for occasional paid ads for the vasectomy clinics.
5. Mary McAleese worked as a part-time journalist for RTÉ in the early 1980s. Her documentary on Irish women travelling to England in order to access abortion services was broadcast on 15 January 1980 for 'Frontline'.
6. An attempt was made to make life difficult for the Well Woman Centre when, in a case that spanned three years and several court mentions, in 1986 they were fined £50 for selling condoms in 1983, but, by then, the Family Planning 1985 Act had been passed.
7. Leinster House is the seat of the Oireachtas (Parliament of Ireland).

Chapter 7: DJ at the Women's Disco

* [No notes].

Chapter 8: Reflections on the Irish Women's Movement

1. The Irish Women's Liberation Movement, *Wikipedia*.
2. June Levine, *Sisters: The Personal Story of an Irish Feminist* (Ward River Press, 1982), p. 136.
3. Anne Stopper, *Monday at Gaj's: The Story of the Irish Women's Liberation Movement* (Liffey Press, 2006).
4. Discussions of the 'marriage bar' often suggest that it was compulsory for all women to leave their jobs once they got married. This isn't quite accurate. Women working as nurses, midwives, and primary school teachers, for example, especially in rural Ireland, did not have to leave their jobs given

that these were traditional women's jobs, and few, if any, men would have been qualified to carry out this work. Equally, clerical workers, in particular typists, consisted mostly of women in the civil and public services, and they also were able to keep working.
5. See Mary Doran's essay, 'We all know where you were on the weekend', in this collection.
6. https://corklgbtarchive.com/exhibits/show/lgbt-workers-rights/ictu-1987-lesbian-and-gay-work. Downloaded 16 Dec. 2024.
7. June Levine and Lynn Madden, *Lynn: A Story of Prostitution* (Attic Press, 1987).
8. Nell McCafferty, *Nell* (Penguin Ireland, 2004), p. 300.

CHAPTER 9: WE ALL KNOW WHERE YOU WERE AT THE WEEKEND

1. *Our Bodies, Ourselves* (Boston Women's Health Book Collective, 1970).
2. 'Conversation', in this context, is an archaic euphemism for sexual intercourse, and, in common law, is a tort relating to adultery. *Criminal Conversations* (Dublin, 1980), directed by Kieran Hickey, is a film about two couples who get together for an evening and disclose adultery.

CHAPTER 10: 'YOU BRING THE GAY SISTERS AND I'LL BRING THE SOCIALISTS'

1. My father grew up in London of Irish stock on both sides. The name O'Dorcaide (the dark people) is a very old, probably Munster name, but we seem to have all left by the time of the Famine. My English grandmother had a story from her mother of taking the 'famine boat' in Youghal. My father met my mother on a walk one morning in Chorca Dhuibhne, Kerry – they were both on holiday in the Gaeltacht, she to polish her Irish for her Civil Service job. In her childhood (the 1920s) she had lived for six years in Gortahorc, where no English was spoken. He was coming towards her and she whispered to her friend 'he would be nice if only he was taller' – she was tall and always needed a tall man. Just then he stepped out of the ditch as he came towards them, and he was six foot! The rest is history. My parents are now dead and there is only one sibling living in Ireland, so the name will very likely soon vanish again.
2. Teachta Dála (TD) is an elected member of the Lower House of the Oireachtas (Parliament), known in English as an MP (Member of Parliament).

CHAPTER 11: REMEMBERING FEMINIST PUBLISHING OF THE 1980S

1. An Chomhairle Oiliúna (AnCo) was the state agency responsible for assisting people seeking employment. In 1988, it was amalgamated with the National Manpower Services and the Youth Employment Agency to become FÁS (Foras Áiseanna Saothair), and in 2013 FÁS became SOLAS (An tSeirbhis Oideachais Leanúnaigh agus Scileanna), the training and education authority.
2. The Irish Women Workers' Union owned a Fleet Street building and 'as further space was available in the building, an agreement was reached with the fledgling feminist publishing company – Irish Feminist Information – to take one floor and to organise courses for Women in Publishing (WIP). This agreement served two purposes: it utilised the building in the interests of the Union and it made facilities available to a small group of women seeking to establish themselves as a feminist publishing concern. From this group, both Attic Press and the Women's Community Press evolved, as did a further disparate group of women equipped, through the original publishing course, with an impressive range of non-traditional skills.' Mary Jones, *These Obstreperous Lassies: A History of the Irish Women Workers' Union* (Gill and Macmillan, 1988), p. 340.
3. Homosexuality was legalised in Ireland in 1993.
4. Declan Flynn was a gay man who was murdered in Fairview Park in Dublin in 1982.
5. The Eighth Amendment to the Irish Constitution took place in 1983 and guaranteed the right to life of the foetus, making abortion illegal unless there was a serious risk to the life of the mother. The Amendment was repealed by landslide vote in 2018.
6. Joanne Hayes was arrested in April 1984, accused of murdering a newborn baby and burying the body on a beach in County Kerry. The case became known as the Kerry Babies Case. Hayes claimed that Gardaí had coerced her confession. After a four-year battle, including an official Tribunal, the

case against Hayes was dropped. In 2020, 36 years after the event, the Irish government formally apologised to Hayes for wrongly accusing her of the baby's murder.
7. Ann Lovett was 15-year-old when she died giving birth near a grotto in County Longford in January 1984.
8. From the mid-1900s, Mother and Baby Homes, mostly run by Catholic nuns, were set up throughout Ireland, as places where unmarried women were sent, often by their families, to deliver their babies. Following the discovery that up to 800 babies and children were interred in an unmarked grave in the Bon Secours Mother and Baby Home in Galway, the Irish Government set up a judicial commission of investigation in 2015.
9. See Mary Higgin's essay in this collection, 'Children have equal rights in society here (Cherish)'.
10. *Singled Out* (Attic Press and Cherish, nd). Camera-ready copy available in University College Cork archive. Reference IE/BL/F/AP/3/7/3/885.
11. The gestetner machine was a type of copying machine, named after its inventor David Gestetner (1854–1939).
12. Sue Richardson and Noreen O'Donohue, eds. *Pure Murder: A Book About Drug Use* (Women's Community Press, 1984).
13. *If You Can Talk You Can Write* (Women's Community Press in conjunction with the Kilbarrack Women's Writing Group, 1983).
14. *Write Up Your Street: An Anthology of Community Writing* (Women's Community Press, 1985).
15. *I Hate Mustard* (Women's Community Press, 1983).

Chapter 12: Children Have Equal Rights in Society Here (Cherish)

1. For anyone wanting to explore the organisation's history and impact further, the Cherish archives are now held in the National Library of Ireland.
2. The Mother and Baby Homes Commission of Investigation was established in 2015 following a number of campaigns by the Adoption Rights Alliance, Justice for the Magdalenes, and the work of Catherine Corless and Anna Corrigan into the Tuam Babies. The Commission Report was published in 2022, and a scheme of compensation introduced.
3. In legal terms, illegitimate meant that a child had no rights of inheritance or maintenance from his or her father, lesser than those of a 'legitimate' child. In practice, at the time, Catholic priests around the country refused to baptise them; they were not allowed to become members of An Garda Síochána. Apparently, unmarried mothers were not allowed to enter the Rose of Tralee contest until recently.
4. Cherish lobbied for this in the lead up to the budget. It had also been proposed by the Irish Women's Liberation Movement (IWLM) in its manifesto, *Chains or Change*, published in 1971, and the European commission adopted a resolution in 1970s, Social Protection of Unmarried Mothers and their Children, which also provided for social welfare support, among other things.
5. A role she retained until her election as the first woman President of Ireland in 1991.
6. Eamon Casey was Bishop of Kerry and, subsequently, Bishop of Galway. It was later revealed that he had had an affair with a woman, with whom he had a son, born in 1974. Casey did make financial contributions to the woman and child from diocesan funds. After his death, Casey was accused of having sexually abused a number of women, including his niece.
7. The National Council for One Parent Families (NCOPF) was formerly known, until 1973, as the National Council for the Unmarried Mother and her Child (established in 1918), and it introduced a new logo (a stylised depiction of an adult and child in a circle), which it permitted Cherish to use as its logo.
8. Foras Áiseanna Saothair (FÁS) was the Irish Training and Employment Authority.
9. Now known as Treoir, the National Information Service for Unmarried Parents.

Chapter 13: Attic Press: A Reflection

1. Joanne Hayes was arrested in April 1984, accused of murdering a newborn baby and burying the body on a beach in County Kerry. The case became known as the Kerry Babies Case. Hayes claimed that Gardaí had coerced her confession. After a four-year battle, including an official Tribunal, the

case against Hayes was dropped. In 2020, 36 years after the event, the Irish government formally apologised to Hayes for wrongly accusing her of the baby's murder.
2. Ann Lovett was 15 years old when she died giving birth near a grotto in County Longford in January 1984.
3. Patricia Ferriera, 'Claiming and transforming an entirely gentlemanly artifact: Ireland's Attic Press', p. 99.

Chapter 14: Space for Radical Change

1. Joanne Hayes was arrested in April 1984, accused of murdering a newborn baby and burying the body on a beach in County Kerry. The case became known as the Kerry Babies Case. Hayes claimed that Gardaí had coerced her confession. After a four-year battle, including an official Tribunal, the case against Hayes was dropped. In 2020, 36 years after the event, the Irish government formally apologised to Hayes for wrongly accusing her of the baby's murder.
2. Ann Lovett was 15 years old when she died giving birth near a grotto in County Longford in January 1984.
3. Declan Flynn was a gay man who was murdered in Fairview Park in Dublin in 1982.
4. What became known as the X Case occurred when a 14-year-old Dublin girl was stopped from travelling to Britain for an abortion by the High Court. She had been made pregnant through rape by a family friend.
5. Savita Halappanavar died from sepsis in University Hospital Galway (2012), following a miscarriage during which she was denied an abortion. Public outcry following her death galvanised the movement for the repeal of the Eighth Amendment.

Chapter 15: I Just Wanted To Do Something Practical

* [No notes].

Chapter 16: The Feminist Way

1. Germaine Greer, *The Female Eunuch* (MacGibbon & Kee, 1970).
2. Patrick Kavanagh, *Tarry Flynn* (The Pilot Press, 1948).
3. Edna O'Brien, *The Country Girls* (Hutchinson, 1960).
4. Edna O'Brien, *The Lonely Girl* (Hutchinson, 1960).
5. Kate O'Brien, *Mary Lavelle* (O'Brien Press, 1936).
6. John McGahern, *The Dark* (Faber and Faber, 1965).
7. Arianna Stassinopoulos Huffington, *The Female Woman* (Random House, 1973).
8. Betty Friedan, *The Feminine Mystique* (Norton, 1963).
9. Marilyn French, *The Women's Room* (Simon & Schuster, 1977).
10. Ibid., p. 630.
11. Andrea Dworkin, *Right-Wing Women* (The Women's Press, 1983), p. 38.
12. Email from Ailbhe Smyth to Mary O'Donnell. Monday, 8 April, 2024. Permission granted.
13. Cynthia Enloe, *'The Big Push': Exposing and Challenging the Persistence of Patriarchy* (Myriad Editions, 2017), p. 55.

Chapter 17: The Personal Really Was Political

1. Senator Mary Robinson went on to become the seventh President in Ireland, and the first female President. She held office from December 1990 until September 1997.
2. Mairéad Farrell was from Belfast, and was a member of the Irish Republican Army (IRA). She was arrested in April 1976 during the failed bombing of a hotel and was sentenced to 14 years in prison for explosives offences, and membership of an illegal terrorist organisation. She was released from prison in 1986 and re-engaged with the IRA. She was shot and killed by the British Army in Gibraltar in March 1988.

3. H-Block was the colloquial name for HM Prison Maze, previously known as Long Kesh Detention Centre. Between 1971 and 2000, it was used to house paramilitary/political prisoners in the North. The name H-Blocks came about as a result of the shape of the prison compounds as seen from above.
4. See Appendix 1, IWU Charter of Demands.
5. Linda Connolly, *The Irish Women's Movement: From Revolution to Devolution* (Lilliput Press, 2002), p. 128.
6. Obviously this was Michael Cleary's go-to insult, he was to repeat that same vulgarity in the green room at RTÉ when Evelyn Conlon and others were speaking about the opening of the Rape Crisis Centre.
7. Linda Connolly, *The Irish Women's Movement: From Revolution to Devolution* (Lilliput Press, 2002), p. 142.

Chapter 18: Reflections from Another Country: Irish Pregnancy Counselling Centre (IPCC)

1. Savita Halappanavar died from sepsis in University Hospital Galway (2012), following a miscarriage during which she was denied an abortion. Public outcry after her death galvanised the movement for the repeal of the Eighth Amendment.
2. Ruth Riddick, *The Right to Choose – Questions of Feminist Morality* (Attic Press, 1990). *LIP* is the overall title of seven pamphlets, published by Attic Press in Dublin, and represent an innovative approach to women's publishing. They are all short, provocative, polemical pamphlets on contemporary issues and controversies.
3. https://coachingfederation.org/
4. Ann Furedi, *The Moral Case for Abortion: A Defence of Reproductive Choice* (Palgrave Macmillan, 2021).
5. In 1983, Irish film director Pat Murphy was living in a shared flat in Marlborough Road, Donnybrook, Dublin. All preparation, pre-production, and casting for her film *Anne Devlin* was done out of her tiny bedroom, in which she had a desk and a typewriter. Corinna Reynolds, who worked at Open Door Counselling, often stayed in the flat, and it seems the typewriter was used, when available. (Email from Pat Murphy to Rebecca Pelan 7 August, 2024).
6. Defined as a sin the priest has no authority to absolve.
7. *The Irish Times* obituary, June 4, 2011, https://www.irishtimes.com/life-and-style/people/garda-whose-input-did-much-to-shape-the-force-1.588836
8. Comment reported by Nell McCafferty during our legal hearings; later the title of a book about Irish women by Rosemary Mahoney (*Whoredom in Kimmage*, Houghton Mifflin, 1993). The reference was to 'those clinics women' and, specifically, my red nail polish, also a fetish of columnist John Waters in *The Irish Times*.
9. Riddick, *The Right to Choose – Questions of Feminist Morality* (Attic Press, 1990).
10. Ann Lovett was 15 years old when she died giving birth near a grotto in County Longford in January 1984.
11. Savita Halappanavar died from sepsis in University Hospital Galway (2012), following a miscarriage during which she was denied an abortion. Public outcry after her death galvanised the movement for the repeal of the Eighth Amendment.
12. Senator Mary Robinson went on to become the seventh President in Ireland, and the first female President. She held office from December 1990 until September 1997.

Chapter 19: And Sisters, We Were Controlled: Ireland in the 1970s

1. Irish women were excluded from jury duty until 1976 when Máirín de Burca and Mary Anderson took the State to the Supreme Court and won on the basis that the exclusion of women from the jury lists was unconstitutional, and the Juries Act 1976 was passed.
2. Gaye Cunningham, a contributor to this collection, used to ask me why I was always talking about trade unions, in the days before she, herself, embarked on a long and successful trade union career, which culminated in her appointment as a rights commissioner.

3. Dáil Éireann debate on the Control of Importation, Sale and Manufacturer of Contraceptives Bill, 1974: Second Stage. Thursday, 4 July 1974. 274:3. www.oireachtas.ie
4. 'Rates' here refers to the local authority levies charged on properties in Ireland. The slogan was associated with those opposed to free contraception, essentially, implying that taxpayers would not be footing the bill.
5. Laura Kelly, *Contraception and Modern Ireland* (Cambridge University Press, 2023); Therese Caherty, Pauline Conroy, and Derek Speirs, *The Road to Repeal* (Lilliput Press, 2022).
6. Savita Halappanavar died from sepsis in University Hospital Galway (2012), following a miscarriage during which she was denied an abortion. Public outcry after her death galvanised the movement for the repeal of the Eighth Amendment.

CHAPTER 20: FABULOUSLY BLASPHEMOUS: FINDING MYSELF IN IRISHWOMEN UNITED

1. Betty Friedan, *The Feminine Mystique* (W. W. Norton, 1963).
2. Germaine Greer, *The Female Eunuch* (MacGibbon & Kee, 1970).
3. Boston Women's Health Book Collective, *Our Bodies, Ourselves* (Boston Women's Health Book Collective, 1970).
4. 'The Battle of Algiers', directed by Gillo Pontecorvo (1966; Venice, Igor Film and Casbah Film).

APPENDIX I

Charter of Irishwomen United

IRISH WOMEN UNITED CHARTER

PREAMBLE:

At this time, the women of Ireland are beginning to see the need for, and are fighting for liberation. This is an inevitable step in the course of full human liberation. Although within the movement, we form diverse groups with variant ways of approaching the problem, we have joined together around these basic issues. We pledge ourselves to challenge and fight sexism in all forms and oppose all forms of exploitation of women which keep them oppressed. These demands are all part of the essential right of women to self-determination of our own lives – equality in education and work; control of our own bodies; an adequate standard of living and freedom from sexist conditioning. We present these demands as the following women's charter.

1 THE REMOVAL OF ALL LEGAL AND BUREAUCRATIC OBSTACLES TO EQUALITY:

1 i.e. with regard to tenancies, mortgages, pension schemes, taxation, jury service, equal responsibility for children, social welfare benefits and hire purchase agreements.

2 The right to divorce.

The Constitution should be reviewed with a view to examining the role of women and updated to eliminate discrimination against women.

2 FREE LEGAL CONTRACEPTION:

1 State financed birth-control clinics.

2 The right to a free, legal and safe abortion.

3 THE RECOGNITION OF MOTHERHOOD AND PARENTHOOD AS A SOCIAL FUNCTION WITH SPECIAL PROVISION FOR:

1 State support for programmes implementing the socialisation of housework, i.e. community laundries, kitchens, eating places etc.

2 State provision of an adequate place to live, irrespective of sex, age, number of children and marital status.

3 The provision of local authority, free of charge, twenty-four-hour nurseries, giving every satisfaction in respect of hygiene and education; to be staffed by trained personnel and under the control of the communities in which they are located.

4 EQUALITY IN EDUCATION – STATE-FINANCED, SECULAR, CO-EDUCATIONAL SCHOOLS WITH FULL COMMUNITY CONTROL AT ALL LEVELS, SPECIFICALLY:

1 An end to enforced conditioning of sex roles through curriculum, teaching methods and materials (i.e. textbooks, games etc.)

2 The provision of local pre-school centres for all desiring to use them

3 An end to segmentation of education, to be replaced by fully comprehensive second and third level schools, incorporating both technical and academic learning.

4 Ending of discriminatory barring from particular courses traditionally relegated to men; encouragement for women to enter these courses through programmes of reserved places, etc.

5 Funding and encouragement of a Women's Studies Programme at second and third level.

6 Provision of free creches on campuses

7 Provision of a women's centre on campuses

8 Equal access to further education for all women, regardless of age or marital status.

5 THE MALE RATE FOR THE JOB WHERE MEN AND WOMEN ARE WORKING TOGETHER:

Where the labour force is wholly female, the jobs done by these women should be upgraded and a national minimum wage implemented, linked to the cost of living increase. We reject the use of job evaluation techniques for the purpose of negotiating pay claims.

The right of women to have access to all types of employment, including all types of skilled, and promotion regardless of marital status, pregnancy or maternity.

The right to training and re-training for all occupations including apprenticeships, and the present system of apprenticeships to be restructured. That it be compulsory for all employers to make readily available day release courses, with pay, for all employees.

Working conditions to be, without deterioration of present conditions, the same for women as for men: in addition, the institution of worker-determined flexible hours. The removal of protective legislation should not be a condition to gaining equal pay, and should be extended to include men.

The right to statutory maternity leave of twenty weeks with full net pay; additional leave with pay in cases of illness connected therewith, the right to attend pre-natal and post-natal clinics as required. Prohibition of dismissal from employment on the grounds of pregnancy or maternity.

Employers to ensure that every effort is made to facilitate employees who are pregnant insofar as the latter's duties are concerned, the guarantee of reintegration into employment without loss of status or service, the right to further training or re-training after statutory or prolonged maternity leave, and the option for equivalent forms of paternity leave.

6 State provision of funds and premises for the establishment of women's centres in major population areas to be controlled by the women themselves.

7 The right of all women to a self-determined sexuality.

SISTERHOOD IS POWERFUL

APPENDIX II

Chronology of Changes Relevant to Women in Ireland 1861–2024

1861 Irish Society for the Training and Employment of Educated Women formed in Dublin
Married women's property campaign began

1870 First public suffrage meeting in Dublin

1879 Campaign to extend the Royal University Act to women and girls

1898 Local Government vote granted to women

1898 First meeting of Inghinidhe na hÉireann (Daughters of Erin)

1908 (May) Irish Women's Franchise League founded

1909 National University of Ireland founded with full access to women

1910 Society of United Irishwomen founded. Renamed, in 1935, the Irish Countrywomen's Association

1911 Irish Women Workers' Union established

1914 Cumann na mBán, the women's branch of the Irish Volunteers, founded

1918 Irishwomen over the age of 30 granted the vote under The Representation of the People Act
Countess Markievicz is the first woman elected to the First Dáil Éireann

1919 Countess Markievicz appointed Minister for Labour in the first Republican government

1921 Suffrage for all adults over the age of 21 introduced under the Free State Constitution

1927 The Juries Act declared that juries in criminal and civil cases would be drawn from ratepayers, effectively excluding women from jury service

1929 Censorship of Publications Act included a mandatory ban on books or periodicals advocating 'the unnatural prevention of conception'

1930	Women's Social and Progressive League founded
1931	Louie Bennett appointed the first woman President of the Irish Trade Union Congress
1935	The Joint Committee of Women's Societies and Social Workers founded
The Criminal Law (Amendment) Act prohibited the sale, advertising, or importation of contraceptives
1937	The 1937 Constitution passed. The Constitution included the role of women in Irish society as being predominantly tied to home and family, and introduced a prohibition on divorce (Article 41.3.2)
1942	The Irish Housewives' Association founded. Responsible for setting up the Consumers' Association
1951	Bill on 'Mother and Child Scheme' proposed by Dr Noel Browne, Minister for Health. The Bill was withdrawn following pressure from the Catholic hierarchy
1953	The Health Act provides for free medical, surgical, midwifery, and hospital maternity services
1957	The Married Women's Status Act passed giving married women control of their own property
1958	Garda Síochána Act provided for the employment of bean Gardaí (female police)
1959	Irish Council of Trade Unionists Women's Advisory Committee established
1964	The Guardianship of Infants Act passed, giving women guardianship rights equal to those of men
1965	The Succession Act passed, which abolished distinctions between the rights of inheritance of males and females, and the rights of widows to a fair share of their husband's estate
Irish Federation of Women's Clubs founded
1967	National Association of Widows founded
1968	*Ad Hoc* Committee representative of women's groups presented a memorandum to the Taoiseach calling for the establishment of a National Commission on the Status of Women
Five women at Trinity College Dublin are made Fellows of the College
1970	Women's Progressive Association founded. This became the Women's Political Association in 1973, established to encourage the participation of women in public and political life. Its first president was Mary Robinson
First meeting of the Irish Women's Liberation Movement in Bewley's Café, Westmoreland Street, Dublin, and later, in Gaj's Restaurant, Baggot Street, Dublin
The Social Welfare Act provided for Deserted Wife's Allowance
Commission on the Status of Women, chaired by Dr Thekla Beere, established by the Fianna Fáil Government
Commission on the Status of Women asked by Minister of Finance to prepare an interim report on equal pay, with particular reference to the public sector

1971 *Chains or Change*, a manifesto by the Irish Women's Liberation Movement published
(March) Aer Lingus became one of the first employers to offer equal pay to women and men
(March) Members of the Irish Women's Liberation Movement appeared on the *Late Late Show*
(March) Irish Women's Liberation Movement protest in the Pro-Cathedral, and picket placed on the Archbishop's residence
(April) First public meeting of Irish Women's Liberation held in Mansion House, Dublin, attracted an audience of 1,000 women and men
(May) Irish Women's Liberation Movement's 'contraceptive train'
(October) Women's Progressive Association formed, later became known as the Women's Political Association

1972 Family Planning Services, later became the Irish Family Planning Association. Set up to provide non-medical and non-pharmaceutical contraceptive devices
ALLY (Friend) formed as the first non-denominational voluntary agency to help unmarried mothers
(October) Senator Mary Robinson's Family Planning Bill (to amend the Criminal Law Amendment Act of 1935) failed to get a first reading in the Senate
(October) Commission on the Status of Women published its interim report on equal pay
(January) AIM (Action, Information, Motivation) formed by Nuala Fennell and others, focussing on Family Law Reform.
(June) Mary McGee brought an action for damages against the Attorney General and the Revenue Commissioners arising from the seizing by customs officials of contraceptive jelly prescribed by her doctors, under the Criminal Law (Amendment) Act 1935. The High Court ruled against her, and the case was referred to the Supreme Court
(November) Widows marched through the streets to Liberty Hall for a mass meeting, the first occasion in the period when women took to the streets to publicise their cause
CHERISH (Children Have Rights in Society Here) founded by six single mothers, led by Maura O'Dea Richards, to improve the quality of life for single parents and their children. Mary Robinson was its first president
(December) Report of the Commission on the Status of Women published, regarded as a charter for women in the modern Irish state

1973 Sexual Liberation Movement had its first meeting
Council for the Status of Women formed, to be the main co-ordinating body for women's organisations
Senator Mary Robinson introduced a Private Member's Bill into the Senate to amend the 1935 Criminal Law (Amendment) Act, and the Censorship of Publications Act 1929 and 1945
The Civil Service (Employment of Married Women) Act removed the ban on the recruitment or employment of married women in the Civil Service, local authorities, and Health Boards
The Social Welfare Act made provision for the payment of a deserted wife's benefit, and for the payment of an unmarried mother's allowance
ADAPT (Association for Deserted and Alone Parents) founded
General Council of County Council elect a woman (Senator Mary Walsh) as Chairperson for the first time
Mary Catherine Tinney appointed the first woman ambassador to Sweden and Finland

1974 AIM opened its first advice centre
The Women's Representative Committee established by the Minister for Labour to implement recommendations contained in the report of the Commission on the Status of Women

The Supreme Court, by a majority of four to one, ruled in favour of Mary McGee and found that the ban on the importation of contraceptives was unconstitutional
(November) Mairín de Burca and Mary Anderson, two journalists who had been founder members of the Irish Women's Liberation Movement, took a case to the Supreme Court claiming that the 1927 Juries Act was unconstitutional
The Anti-Discrimination (Pay) Act passed
The Social Welfare Act gave payment of the Children's Allowance to mothers
The Social Welfare Act made provision for payment of an allowance to single women over 58 years and to wives of prisoners
The Maintenance Orders Act passed, which provided for a reciprocal enforcement of maintenance orders between Ireland and the United Kingdom
(May) Women's Aid founded
(July) Women's Aid opened its first refuge in Harcourt Street, Dublin

1975 International Women's Year
Arlen House established in Galway
Banshee: Journal of Irishwomen United launched
(January) The Irishwomen's Suffrage Movement held an exhibition in Trinity College Dublin
Adoption by Irish Council of Trade Unions of Working Women's Charter
Supplementary Welfare Allowance introduced to provide a standard basic minimum income
(June) Irishwomen United held its first public meeting in Liberty Hall and launched its Charter

1976 Contraceptive Action Programme (CAP) launched by Irishwomen United
(February) Equal Pay directive from European Commission made binding
(March) European Commission rejected Irish Government's application for derogation from Commission's directive on equal pay
(September) Irishwomen United protest against 'gentlemen only' bathing at Forty Foot, Sandycove, County Dublin
Máirín de Burca and Mary Anderson win their case in the Supreme Court. The conditional exclusion of women from the jury lists is deemed to be unconstitutional, and the Juries Act 1976 is passed
The Family Law (Maintenance of Spouses and Children) Act 1976 is passed and provides for the enforcement of maintenance orders
The Family Home Protection Act 1976 is passed. This ensures that a spouse will not sell or otherwise dispose of the family home unknown to his family or without the prior consent of the other spouse

1976 AnCo (later An Foras Áiseanna Saothar/FÁS), responsible for promoting and providing training at all levels of industry and commerce, adopts an equal opportunity policy

1977 Máire Geoghegan-Quinn (Fianna Fáil) appointed Minister of State at the Department of Industry and Commerce
Employment Equality Act passed, and Employment Equality Agency set up with Sylvia Meehan as Chairperson
Unfair Dismissals Act passed, which protects employees, including pregnant women, from unfair dismissal

1978 Irish Feminist Information (IFI) established
(May) First Irish Conference on Lesbianism held at Trinity College Dublin
(October) Women Against Violence Against Women protest takes place with thousands of women marching on the streets of Dublin

Administrative rules and regulations that discriminated against girls and women teachers are deleted from the rule books of the Education Department
The Colleges of Education (catering for primary school teachers) becomes co- educational

1979   (January) The first Rape Crisis Centre opens in Dublin
(May) '*Women Today* Programme' starts on RTÉ (1979–83). Later, '*The Women's Programme*' (1983–86) was a half-hour programme, five days a week, dedicated to women's issues and, largely, produced by women
Aer Lingus's first woman pilot, Grainne Cronin from Malahide, County Dublin, flew from Frankfurt to Shannon
Máirá Uí Dhálaigh, Pro-Chancellor of Trinity College Dublin, becomes the first woman to confer degrees at an Irish University
First Women's Right to Choose group met and established the Irish Pregnancy Counselling Centre (IPCC)
(July) the Health (Family Planning) Act is passed, restricting the sale of contraceptives to 'bona fide' couples only
Córas Iopair Éireann (CIE/Irish Transport Service) employ their first women bus conductors
Mairin Bean Ui Dalaigh appointed Pro-Chancellor of Dublin University, the first woman to be appointed to such a position in an Irish University
Josephine Airey won her case against the Irish Government in the European Court of Human Rights. The case was instrumental in the introduction of a Civil Legal Aid scheme
As a result of the Supreme Court ruling in Murphy v The Attorney General, sections of the Income Tax Act 1967 were found to be unconstitutional insofar as they provided for the aggregation of the earned incomes of married couples
Máire Geoghan Quinn appointed Minister for the Gaeltacht, the first woman to be appointed to the Cabinet since Constance Markievicz in 1919

1980   Opening of the Dublin Women's Centre
Mella Carroll became the first woman to be appointed as a High Court Judge
The Finance Act passed, following on from the Murphy case ruling that punitive taxation of married women must end

1981   Start of the Pro-Life Amendment Campaign
Civil Legal Aid and Advice Scheme set up
Eileen Desmond (Labour) appointed Minister for Health
Mary Flaherty (Fine Gael) appointed Minister of State for Poverty and the Family
Gemma Hussey appointed Fine Gael Leader in Seanad Éireann
The Family Law (Protection of Spouses and Children Act) passed
Maternity (Protection of Employees) Act passed
Courts Act passed. This simplified the question of jurisdiction in family law cases
Family Law Act passed, abolishing Criminal Conversation
The first Irish women soldiers held their passing out parade. Eight women cadets, the first in the history of the State, received their officer commissions

1982   Máire Geoghegan Quinn (Fianna Fáil) appointed Minister of State at the Department of Education
Tras Honan (Fianna Fáil) appointed Cathaoirleach (Chair of the Senate) of Seanad Éireann
(February) The High Court ruled that married women who are separated are entitled to Unemployment Assistance, following a case taken by Róisín Conroy
(February) The Labour Court, on appeal, holds that upper age limits discriminate against married women
(December) Gemma Hussey (Fine Gael) appointed Minister for Education
Nuala Fennell (Fine Gael) appointed Minister of State for Women's Affairs
(December) The High Court rules that a child born to a woman and a man other than her husband can have the name of the actual father recorded

1983 Anti-Reagan demonstrations by Women Against Disarmament
(January) Nuala Fennell appointed Minister of State for Family Law Reform
(February) Ireland denounces Convention 89 of the International Labour Organisation, which prohibited women from engaging in industrial work at night
(March) Working Party on Childcare Facilities for Working Parents report released
(April) Interdepartmental Working party on Women's Affairs and Family Law Reform is set up, chaired by Nuala Fennell
(April) The report, 'Sex Differences in Subject Provision and Student Choice in Irish Post-Primary Schools' (Hannon Report), together with the response from the Employment Equality Agency, is published and presented to the Minister for Education. This was the first comprehensive examination of sexism in the Irish educational system
(July) The Joint Oireachtas Committee on Women's Rights was set up to consider how discrimination against women can be eliminated. The Committee produced four reports on: Education (October 1984); Social Welfare (May 1985); The Portrayal of Women in the Media (April 1986); Sexual Violence (January 1987)
(July) The Joint Oireachtas Committee on Marriage Breakdown set up to 'consider the protection of marriage and family life, and to examine the problems that follow the breakdown of marriage'. The Committee published its report in April 1985
(September) The electorate voted by referendum to add the following subsection to Article 40 of the Constitution 40.3.3 – 'The State acknowledges the right to life of the unborn and, with due regard to the equal right to life of the mother, guarantees in its laws to respect, and as far as practicable, by its laws to defend and vindicate that right'

1984 Attic Press founded
University College Dublin Women's Studies Forum established
The Programme for Action in Education 1984–87 was published containing the first ever positive commitment by a Government to the elimination of sexism in education. Key components in this policy are the elimination of sex stereotyping in schoolbooks, and the application of the Employment Agency's code of practice at interview boards and appointment procedures
Co-operation North grant to Lesbian Lines North and South
Sylvia Meehan, Chairperson of the Employment Equality Agency is elected Chairperson of the EEC Committee on Equal Opportunities for men and women
Publication of the Employment Equality Agency's Code of Practice for the elimination of sex and marital status discrimination and the promotion of equality of opportunity in employment
(February) Schemes for job-sharing and career breaks were announced in the Civil Service
(November) The Government adopts a policy statement on positive action policies, following which semi-state bodies were expressly asked to appoint equal opportunity officers
(December) An EEC recommendation on positive action in favour of women was adopted during the Irish Presidency of the Council of Ministers
(December) The High Court overturns the Labour Court ruling that age limits are discriminatory against married women because it had not been established that married women were more adversely affected than single women by age limits

1985 Dental, aural, and optical benefits extended to the pregnant wives of insured workers
Capital Acquisitions Tax is abolished on inheritances passed from one spouse to another, relieving many widows of severe financial circumstances following bereavement
(January) Ireland's first Sexual Assault Treatment Unit (SATU) opens in the Rotunda Hospital, Dublin under the Direction of Dr Máire Woods
Senator Mary Robinson takes a case to the European Court of Justice in order to obtain retrospection for a number of women in implementation of the EEC directive on equal treatment for men and women in social security

(April) A national seminar, with participants from Northern Ireland and the Republic, was held at Ballymascanlon House, County Louth, to discuss developments in employment, health, and education during the UN Decade for Women 1976–85
(May) The Family Planning (Amendment) Act is passed, providing a legal basis for the provision family planning services available to all adults
(May) The Agenda for Practical Action report of the Interdepartmental Working Party on Women's Affairs and Family Law Reform is published. The Report recommended changes and improvements in a wide range of areas affecting women
(July) The Conference marking the closing of the United Nations Decade for Women is held in Nairobi, Kenya
(July) The Social Welfare (No 2) Act was enacted, providing for the implementation of the EEC Directive on equal treatment for men and women in matters of social security. For the first time, married women are treated equally with men and single women in the social welfare code
(October) The country's first free cancer screening clinic for women is opened in Hume Street Hospital, Dublin
(October) The Labour Court made an order that sexual harassment at work is a contravention of the Employment Equality Act
(October) An Garda Síochána and the Prison Service are brought within the scope of the Employment Equality Act for the first time and their exemptions from the Act are limited to certain categories of posts
(October) The Council for the Status of Women organised the Irish Women's Forum, to assess the conclusions of the Nairobi End-of-Decade Conference
(December) Ireland acceded with a small number of reservations to the United Nations Convention on the Elimination of All Forms of Discrimination Against Women (CEDAW)
(December) Miriam Hederman O'Brien appointed to the Board of Allied Irish Banks

1986 The Institute of Engineers in Ireland launched Women in Engineering Year, designed to encourage more girls and young women to choose engineering as a career
(January) Official opening of purpose-built refuge for battered wives and their children in Rathmines, Dublin
(February) Gemma Hussey (Fine Gael) appointed Minister for Social Welfare
(February) Avril Doyle appointed Minister of State at the Department of Finance and the Department of the Environment

1987 Supreme Court ruling on abortion information

1990 Mary Robinson elected President of Ireland
Women's Education Research and Resource Centre (WERRC) established at University College Dublin

1992 X Case ruling permits abortion to safeguard 'the equal right to life of the mother'
Abortion information and Right to Travel referenda passed
First legal case awards custody of children to a lesbian mother

1993 Report of the Second Commission on the Status of Women published
Criminal Law (Sexual Offences) Act passed, decriminalising homosexuality
Green Paper on Abortion published

1995 Irish citizens voted in a referendum to allow divorce
The Censorship of Publications Board removed a ban on the sale of *Playboy* magazine, which had existed since 1961. The National Women's Council of Ireland protested against the removal of the ban.

1996	The Fifteenth Amendment to the Irish Constitution was signed into law repealing the absolute constitutional prohibition of divorce (September) The last Magdalene asylum closed in Waterford
1997	Mary McAleese inaugurated as the eighth President of Ireland Mary Robinson appointed UN High Commissioner for Human Rights
1999	The *States of Fear* series, made by Mary Raftery for RTÉ, was broadcast. The series exposed a history of institutional child abuse, which led to questions being raised in the Dáil, and the appointment of a Commission to Inquire into Child Abuse Remaining prohibition orders under the Censorship of Publications Acts relating to contraception or termination of pregnancies were lifted Inez McCormack of UNISON became the first woman President of the Irish Congress of Trade Unions
2002	A referendum to amend the Constitution to remove the threat of suicide as a ground for legal abortion is narrowly defeated Geraldine Kennedy appointed first female editor of *The Irish Times*
2004	Mary McAleese elected unopposed for a second term as President of Ireland
2009	(August) The report of the Commission into Child Abuse (Ryan Report), which investigated abuses of children in industrial schools, is published. (December) The Commission of Investigation, carried out by Judge Yvonne Murphy, begins into the sexual abuse scandal in the Catholic Archdiocese of Dublin
2010	The Health Service Executive began its cervical cancer vaccination (Gardasil 9) campaign in schools Captain Gráinne Cronin, the first female pilot with Aer Lingus, retired after 33 years
2011	The Civil Partnership Act came into effect, affording the same rights in civil partnerships between hetero- and homosexual cohabiting couples
2012	Female Genital Mutilation (FGM) became illegal in Ireland under the Criminal Justice (FGM) Act 2012 (October) Savita Halappanavar died of infection (sepsis) in University Hospital Galway, and after her repeated requests for an abortion were denied because of legal restrictions
2013	(April) The inquest into the death of Savita Halappanavar returned a verdict of 'medical misadventure'
2014	The Protection of Life During Pregnancy Act 2013 came into effect, defining when abortions may be performed
2015	(May) The 34th Amendment to the Constitution, permitting same-sex marriage, was enacted by the Marriage Act 2015, and came into force in November. This was the first time anywhere that same-sex marriage was legalised through popular vote
2017	A 'Women's March' took place in Dublin, organised by the Abortion Rights Campaign, Amnesty International Ireland, European Network Against Racism, ROSA, and the Coalition to Repeal the Eighth Amendment (April) The Citizens' Assembly voted to recommend extensive liberalisation of the grounds on which abortion is available in Ireland

(October) The Oireachtas Committee on the Eighth Amendment voted not to retain Article 40.3.3 in full

2018 (January) Gardaí apologise to Joanne Hayes for the stress and pain she experienced as part of the original investigation into the murder of 'Baby John' in Kerry in 1984
(March) The 2nd stage of the bill to allow for a referendum on the Eighth Amendment passed in the Dáil by 110 votes to 32
(May) A referendum on whether to repeal the ban on abortion in Ireland took place with a landslide win of 66.4 per cent to 33.6 per cent. The Regulation of the Termination of Pregnancy Bill was introduced in the Dáil in October
(December) The National Maternity Hospital in Holles Street announced that it will accept referrals for abortion services from 7 January 2019

2019 (March) Aer Lingus confirmed that its female cabin crew will no longer be required to wear make-up or skirts as part of its new uniform rules
(June) A formal apology was given to former Garda Majella Moynihan, who had been found in breach of discipline after becoming pregnant out of wedlock in 1984

2020 (December) The State formally apologised, after 36 years, to Joanne Hayes for wrongly accusing her of the murder of a baby in 1984

2021 (January) The Mother and Baby Homes Commission of Investigation published its final report. The 3000-page document states that approximately 9,000 children died in Mother and Baby Homes between 1925 and 1998

2023 Taoiseach Leo Varadkar marked International Women's Day by announcing the Government's intention to hold a referendum to enshrine gender equality in the Constitution by amending Articles 40 and 41
(November) Minister for Justice, Helen McEntee sought approval for the repeal of antique censorship laws dating back to 1926

2024 (January) The Supreme Court decided unanimously that an unmarried father, whose partner died, is entitled to a widower's pension

Sources:
Connolly, Linda. *The Irish Women's Movement: From Revolution to Devolution* (Lilliput Press, 2002).
Office of the Minister of State for Women's Affairs, *Irishwomen into Focus 1: The Road to Equal Opportunity: A Narrative History,* Chronology (Dublin, 1987). National Library of Ireland.
Wikipedia 'What Happened in Ireland', https://en.wikipedia.org/wiki/[year]_in_Ireland.

Bibliography

Archival/Electronic Sources:

'After the 8th' National Library of Ireland
'Attic Press/Róisín Conroy Archive' iar.ie/archive/attic-press-roisin-conroy-collection
Banshee: Journal of Irish Women United www.leftarchiveie/document/view/2728
University College Cork, Library Archives Service. IE BL/F/AP
Cherish Archive: National Library of Ireland
Cork LGBT Archive: https://corklgbtarchive.com
Irish Left Archive: https://www.leftarchive.ie
Irish Queer Archive: National Library of Ireland

Bambrick, Laura, https://publications.inmo.ie/view November 2019: p. 48–72.
Banshee: Journal of Irishwomen United Nos. 1 (1970) to 8 (1977). 'Attic Press Collection', Archives of Attic Press, University College Cork Library. (BLF/F/AP).
Barry, Ursula, 'Movement, Change and Reaction: The Struggle over Reproductive Rights in Ireland' in Ailbhe Smyth, *The Abortion Papers: Ireland* (Attic Press, 1992).
Barry, Ursula, *Lifting the Lid* (Attic Press, 1986).
Beaumont, Catríona, 'Women and the Politics of Equality: The Irish Women's Movement, 1930-1943' in Mary O'Dowd and Maryann Gialanella, eds., *Women and Irish History* (Wolfhound, 1997), pp. 185–205.
Binchy, Maeve, *Deeply Regretted By* (Turoe Press, 1979).
Boland, Eavan, *In Her Own Image* (Arlen House, 1980).
——. *Night Feed* (Arlen House, 1982).
——. *The Journey and Other Poems* (Arlen House, 1986).
——. *Carcanet* (Arlen House, 1987).
——. *Selected Poems* (Arlen House, 1989).
Bolger, Pat, *And See Her Beauty Shining There: The Story of the Irish Countrywomen* (Irish Academic Press, 1986).
Boston Women's Health Book Collective, *Our Bodies, Ourselves: A Book By and For women* (Boston Women's Health Book Collective, 1970).
Bourke, Angela, Siobhán Kilfeather, Maria Luddy, Margaret MacCurtain, Gerardine Meaney, Máirín Ní Dhonnchadha, Mary O'Dowd and Clair Wills, eds., *The Field Day Anthology of Irish Writing, Vols. 4 and 5: Irish Women's Writings and Traditions* (Cork University Press, 2002).
Bracken, Claire, *Irish Feminist Futures* (Routledge, 2016).
Brennan, Pat, 'Women in Revolt, *Magill* (April 1979).
——, 'Women Organise in Dublin'. *Magill* (Jan. 1979).
Browne, Kath, *After Repeal: Rethinking Abortion Politics* (E-book) (Bloomsbury Publishing, 2020).
Buckley, Fiona and Yvonne Galligan, eds., *Politics and Gender in Ireland* (Routledge, 2015).
Caherty, Therese, Pauline Conroy, and Derek Speirs, *The Road to Repeal* (Lilliput Press, 2022).
Callaghan, Mary Rose, *Mothers* (Arlen House, 1982).
Clancy, Mary, 'Aspects of Women's Contribution to the Oireachtas Debate in the Irish Free State, 1922-37' in Maria Luddy and Clíona Murphy, eds., *Women Surviving: Studies in Irish Women's History in the 19th and 20th Centuries* (Poolbeg, 1990).
Clark, Clara, *Coping Alone* (Arlen House, 1982).
Clear, Catríona, *Woman of the House: Women's Household Work in Ireland 1922-1961* (Irish Academic Press, 2000).

Condron, Mary, *The Serpent and the Goddess* (Attic Press, 1989).
Conlon, Evelyn, *Reading Rites* (The Blackstaff Press, 2023).
———. 'Escaping the Celtic Tiger, World Music and the Millennium', in *Telling* (The Blackstaff Press, 2000), pp. 212–18.
———. 'The Last Confession', in *Taking Scarlet as a Real Colour* (The Blackstaff Press, 1993), pp. 135–45.
———. *Stars in the Daytime* (Attic Press, 1989).
———. *My Head is Opening* (Attic Press, 1987).
———. 'The Park', in *Taking Scarlet as a Real Colour* (The Blackstaff Press, 1993), pp. 58–72.
———. *Where Did I Come From?* (Dublin: Ard Buí and Arlen House, 1980).
Connolly, Linda, *The Irish Women's Movement: From Revolution to Devolution* (Lilliput Press, 2003).
———. 'The Women's Movement in Ireland: A Social Movements Analysis 1970-1995' in Dooley, Dolores and Liz Steiner-Scott, eds., *Irish Journal of Feminist Studies* 1:1 (1996): pp. 43–77.
Conroy, Róisín, *Attic Book of Special Days for Women* (Attic Press, 1990).
Cork LGBT Archive. https://corklgbtarchive.com/exhibits/show/lgbt-workers-rights/ictu-1987-lesbian-and-gay-work.
Coulter, Coulter, 'Feminist Drive Spearheaded Change in Law on Marital Rape'. *The Irish Times* 19 July 2002.
Criminal Conversations (BAC/RTÉ, 1980), directed by Kieran Hickey.
Crone, Joni, 'Lesbian Feminism in Ireland' in Smyth, Ailbhe, ed., 'Feminism in Ireland' *Women's Studies International Forum* 11:4 (1988): pp. 343–7.
Crozier De Rosa, Sharon, *Shame and the Anti-Feminist Backlash* (Routledge 2018).
Cullen, Mary, *Telling it Our Way: Essays in Gender History* (Arlen House, 2013).
———. Mary Cullen, 'Rational creatures and free citizens: Republicanism, feminism and the writing of history', in Cullen, *Telling It Our Way: Essays in Gender History* (Arlen House, 2013), pp. 249–66; p. 261.
Cullen, Linda, *The Kiss* (Attic Press, 1990).
Cullens-Owens, Rosemary, *Smashing Times: A History of the Irish Women's Suffrage Movement 1889-1922* (Attic Press, 1984).
Dworkin, Andrea, *Right-Wing Women* (The Women's Press, 1983.
Dublin Lesbian and Gay Men's Collectives, *Out for Ourselves: The Lives of Irish Lesbians and Gay Men* (Dublin Lesbian and Gay Men's Collectives and Women's Community Press, 1986).
Enloe, Cynthia, *'The Big Push', Exposing and Challenging the Persistence of Patriarchy* (Myriad Editions, 2017).
Enright, Máiréad, Julie McCandless and Aoife O'Donoghue, eds., *Northern/Irish Feminist Judgements: Judges' Troubles and the Gendered Politics of Identity* (Bloomsbury, 2017).
———. and Emilie Cloatre, eds., 'On the Perimeter of the Lawful: Enduring Illegality in the Irish Family Planning Movement, 1972-1985' in *Journal of Law and Society* 44:4 (Dec. 2017), pp. 471–500.
European Commission. European Care Strategy https://ec.europea.eu/commission/presscorner/detail/ip_22_5169.
Evaso, Eileen, *Against the Grain: The Contemporary Women's Movement in Northern Ireland* (Attic Press, 1991).
Evening Press, 'Bikini Lib Girls Fifth Attack'. 28 July 1974.
Ferrier, Carole and Raymond Evans, eds. *Radical Brisbane: An Unruly History* (Vulgar Press, 2004).
Ferriera, Patricia, 'Claiming and Transforming an Entirely Gentlemanly Artifact: Ireland's Attic Press'. *Canadian Journal of Irish Studies* 19:1 (1993): pp. 97–109.
Ferriter, Diarmaid, *Mothers, Maidens and Myth: A History of the Irish Countrywomen's Association* (ICA, 1994).
Fine Davis, Margaret, *Gender Roles in Ireland: Three Decades of Attitude Change* (Routledge, 2015).
Fischer, Clara and Mary McAuliffe, eds. *Irish Feminisms: Past, Present and Future: Essays in Honour of Mary Cullen and Margaret MacCurtain* (Arlen House, 2015).
French, Marilyn, *The War Against Women* (Hamish Hamilton, 1992).
French, Marilyn, *The Women's Room* (Simon & Schuster, 1977).
Friedan, Betty. *The Feminine Mystique* (Norton, 1963).

Furedi, Ann, *The Moral Case for Abortion: A Defence of Reproductive Choice* (Palgrave Macmillan Cham, 2021).
Galligan, Yvonne, Éilis Ward and Rick Wilford, eds., *Contesting Politics: Women In Ireland, North and South* (Westview Press/Political Studies Assn. of Ireland, 1999).
———, *Women and Politics in Contemporary Ireland: From the Margins to the Mainstream* (Pinter, 1998).
Garvin, Tom, 'The Politics of Denial and Cultural Defence: The Referenda of 1983 and 1986 in Context' in *The Irish Review* 3 (1988): pp. 1–7.
Grainseir, Seosamh, 'Irish Legal Heritage: Marital Rape' in *Irish Legal News* 21 Sept. 2018.
Greer, Germaine, *The Female Eunuch* (MacGibbon & Kee, 1970).
Hardiman, Niamh and Christopher T Whelan, eds., *Values and Social Change in Ireland* (Gill and Macmillan, 1994).
Hayes, Alan, ed. *Hilda Tweedy and the Irish Housewives Association* 2012 (13 essays) (Arlen House, 2012).
Heverin, Aileen, *Irish Countrywomen's Association: A History 1910-2000* (The Irish Countrywomen's Association and Wolfhound Press, 2000).
Huffington, Arianna Stassinopoulos, *The Female Woman* (Random House, 1973).
Hugg, Chrystel, *The Politics of Sexual Morality in Ireland* (Palgrave Macmillan, 1999).
If You Can Talk You Can Write (Women's Community Press in conjunction with the Kilbarrack Women's Writing Group, 1983).
I Hate Mustard (Women's Community Press, 1983).
Inglis, Tom, *Moral Monopoly: The Rise and Fall of the Catholic Church in Modern Ireland* (UCD Press, 1998).
Irish Feminist Review (IFR), Ed., Caroline Butler (Women's Community Press, 1984).
Irish Independent, 'Government pledges Aid to Promote 'Natural' Contraception'. 25 Sept. 1980.
———. 'Preparing the Ground for a Women's Collective'. 16 May 1979.
———. 'Rape Crisis Centre to Open Shortly'. 11 Oct. 1977.
Irish Press, '4000 in City Anti Rape March'. 14 Oct. 1978.
Irish Times, '45% Opt for Abortion After IFPA Counselling'. 19 Feb. 1993.
———. Letters to the Editor. 'The Abortion Referendum'. 17 Feb. 1983.
———. 'Labour to Press for Divorce Bill'. 18 Oct. 1980.
———. 'Therapeutic Termination Distinct from Abortion'. 29 Sept. 1980.
———. Letters to the Editor. 'Abortions'. 27 Sept. 1980.
———. Letters to the Editor. 'Family Planning Act'. 23 Sept. 1980.
Irish Woman's Right to Choose Group, *Abortion: A Choice for Women* [unpublished], 1981.
Irish Left Archive, http://www.leftarchive.ie.
Irish Women's Liberation Movement, *Chains or Change? The Civil Wrongs of Irish Women* (Kevin Clear, 1971).
Jackson, Pauline, 'Outside the Jurisdiction: Irish Women Seeking Abortion' in Curtin, Chris, Pauline Jackson and Barbara O'Connor, eds., *Gender and Irish Society* (Galway University Press, 1987): pp. 203–23.
———. 'Women's Movement and Abortion: The Criminalisation of Irish Women' in Dahlerup, Drude, ed., *The New Women's Movement: Feminism and Political Power in Europe and the US* (Sage, 1986): pp. 48–63.
Jones, Mary, *These Obstreperous Lassies: A History of the Irish Women Workers' Union* (Gill and Macmillan, 1988).
Kane, Eileen, *Doing Your Own Research* (Turoe Press with Marion Boyars, 1983).
Kassarjian, Sevanne, cited in Nancy C Lutkehaus, *Margaret Mead: The Making of an American Icon* (Princeton University Press, 2008), p 261.
Kavanagh, Patrick, *Tarry Flynn* (The Pilot Press, 1948).
Kelly, Laura, *Contraception and Modern Ireland* (Cambridge University Press, 2023).
Kelly, Laura, 'Family Planning Clinics and Activism in the 1970s' Ch. 6 in *Contraception and Modern Ireland: A Social History 1922-1992* (Cambridge University Press, 2023), pp. 184–221.
———. 'Irishwomen United, the Contraception Action Programme, and the Feminist Campaign for Free, Safe and Legal Contraception in Ireland, c1975-1981', *Irish Historical Studies* 43:164 (Nov. 2019), pp. 269–97.

Kelly, Laura, 'A basic issue of women's liberation: The feminist campaign to legalise contraception in 1970s Ireland', in *Nursing Clio* (online) www.nursingclio.org

Kennedy, Stanislaus, *But Where Can I Go? Homeless Women in Dublin* (Arlen House, 1985).

Kenny, Mary, *Something of Myself and Others* (Liberties Press, 2013).

Lagerkvist, Amanda, 'To End "Women's Night": A Resistance Discourse of the Irish Housewives Association in the Media 1961-62' in *Irish Journal of Feminist Studies* 2:3 (1997): pp. 18–34.

Lawrence, D H, *Lady Chatterley's Lover* (Penguin, 1928).

Lentin, Ronit, '"Irishness", the 1937 Constitution and Citizenship: A Gender and Ethnicity View' in *Irish Journal of Sociology* 8 (1998): pp. 5–24.

——- and Geraldine Niland, *Who's Minding the Children* (Arlen House, 1981).

Levine, June and Lynn Madden, *Lynn: A Story of Prostitution* (Attic Press, 1987).

Levine, June, *Sisters: The Personal Story of an Irish Feminist* (Ward River Press, 1982).

Lloyd, Mollie, *The Change of Life* (Arlen House, 1979/81).

Luddy, *Women in Ireland 1800-1918: A Documentary History* (Cork University Press, 1995).

——- and Clíona Murphy, eds., *Women Surviving: Studies in Irish Women's History in the 19th and 20th Centuries* (Poolbeg, 1990).

MacCurtain, Margaret, 'Women, the Vote and Revolution' in MacCurtain, Margaret and Donnachadh Ó Corráin, eds., *Women in Irish Society: The Historical Dimension* (Arlen House, 1978: pp. 46-57.

Mahoney, Rosemary, *Whoredom in Kimmage: Irish Women Coming of Age* (Houghton Mifflin, 1993).

Janet Martin's, *The Essential Guide for Women in Ireland* (Arlen House, 1977).

McAvoy, Sandra, 'From Anti-Amendment Campaigns to Demanding Reproductive Justice: The Changing Landscape of Abortion Rights Activism in Ireland, 1983-2008' in Schweppe, J., ed., *The Unborn Child, Article 40.3.3 and Abortion in Ireland: Twenty- Five Years of Protection?* (Liffey Press, 2008).

McCafferty Nell, *Nell* (Penguin Ireland, 2004).

McGahern, John, *The Dark* (Faber and Faber, 1965).

McAliskey, Bernadette Devlin, "The Class of '68" *The Political Studies Association*. https://www.psa.ac.uk/resources/bernadette-mcaliskey-class-68.

McAuliffe, Mary, 'Irish Feminisms: Past, Present and Future: 100 Years and Beyond' in Clara Fischer and Mary McAuliffe, *Irish Feminism Past, Present and Future: Essays in Honour of Mary Cullen and Margaret MacCurtain* (Arlen House, 2015), pp. 329–36.

McKay, Susan, *Without Fear: 25 Years of the Dublin Rape Crisis Centre* (New Island Press, 2005)

Mead, Margaret, *Male and Female: A Study of the Sexes in a Changing World* (William Morrow, 1949).

Meaney, Gerardine, *Gender, Ireland and Cultural Change* (Routledge, 2010).

Moane, Geraldine, *Gender and Colonialism: A Psychological Analysis of Oppression and Liberation* (Palgrave, 1999/2011).

Mullarney, Máire, *Anything School Can Do, You Can Do Better* (Arlen House, 1983).

Murray, Melissa, *Changelings* (Attic Press, 1989).

Ní Duibhne, Éilís, ed., *Look! It's a Woman Writer* (Arlen House, 2022).

——-. *The Bray House* (Attic Press, 1990)

——-. *Blood and Water* (Attic Press, 1988).

Randall, Vicky, *Gender, Politics and the State* (Routledge, 1998).

O'Brien, Edna, *The Country Girls* (Hutchinson, 1960).

O'Brien, Edna, *The Lonely Girl* (Hutchinson, 1960).

O'Brien, Kate, *Mary Lavelle* (O'Brien Press, 1936).

O'Donnell, Mary, *Jakkurpa* (Wake Forest University, forthcoming).

——-. *Walking Ghosts* (Mercier Press, forthcoming).

——-. *Massacre of the Birds* (Salmon Poetry, 2020).

——-. *Empire* (Arlen House, 2018).

O'Dowd, Mary and Maryann Valiulis, *Women and Irish History* (Wolfhound, 1997).

Office of the Minister of State for Women's Affairs, *Irishwomen in Focus 1: The Road to Equal Opportunity: A Narrative History* (1987).

O'Neill, Cathleen, 'Reclaiming and Transforming the (Irish) Women's Movement' in *f/m* 3 (1999): pp. 41–4.

Pelan, Rebecca, *Two Irelands: Literary Feminisms North and South* (Syracuse University Press, 2005).

Prone, Terry, *Just a Few Words* (Turoe Press, 1985)
——. *Write and Get Paid for It* (Turoe Press, 1977).
Purcell, Betty, *Inside RTÉ* (New Island Press, 2014).
——. *Light After Darkness: An Experience of Nicaragua* (Attic Press, 1989).
Randall, Vicky, *Gender, Politics and the State* (Routledge, 1998).
Richards, Maura, *Single Issue* (Poolbeg, 1998).
Richardson, Sue, and Noreen O'Donohue, eds. *Pure Murder: A Book About Drug Use* (Women's Community Press, 1984).
Riddick, Ruth, *The Right to Choose: Questions of Feminist Morality* (Attic Press, 1990).
Robinson, Mary, 'Women and the Law in Ireland' in Smyth, Ailbhe, ed., in 'Feminism in Ireland' *Women's Studies International Forum* 11:4 (1988): pp. 351–5.
Rose, Catherine, *The Female Experience: The Story of the Woman Movement in Ireland* (Arlen House, 1975).
Rose, Kieran, *Diverse Communities: The Evolution of Lesbian and Gay Politics in Ireland* (Cork University Press, 1994).
Singled Out (Attic Press and Cherish, nd). Camera ready copy available in University College, Cork archive. Reference IE/BL/F/AP/3/7/3/885.
Smyth, Ailbhe, *Irish Women's Studies Reader* (Attic Press, 1993).
——. *The Abortion Papers: Ireland* (Attic Press, 1992).
——. 'Women and Power in Ireland: Problems, Progress, Practice'. *Women's Studies International Forum* 8:4 (1985): pp. 255–6.
——. 'Feminism in Ireland'. *Women's Studies International Forum* 11:4 (1988).
SPUC: A Threat to Irish Women, Factsheet. Socialist Workers Movement, 1989.
Stopper, Anne, *Monday at Gaj's: The Story of the Irish Women's Liberation Movement* (Liffey Press, 2006).
Sunday Independent, 'The Politics of Contraception' 21 Jan. 1979.
——. 'Birth Control March' 3 Dec. 1978.
Sunday Press, 'Girls "Invade" Fitzwilliam' 13 July 1975.
——, 'Round Two at the Forty Foot' 28 July 1971.
Sunday Tribune, 'Feminism is the Radical Notion that Women are People: 25 Years on, What Has Changed for Irish Women?' 21 May 1995.
Tawney, R H, 'The Choice Before the Labour Party' in *The Political Quarterly* 3:3 (July–Sept. 1932), pp. 521–534.
The Attic Diary (Attic Press, 1997).
The Best of Nell: A Selection of Writing Over Fourteen Years (Attic Press, 1984).
The Stationery Office, *Report of the Second Commission on the Status of Women* (Government Publications Office, 1993).
——, *Report of the Second Commission on the Status of Women* (Government Publications Office, 1970).
Trade Union Women's Forum, *Make Sure You Get Equal Pay* (Arlen House, 1977).
Tweedy, Hilda, *A Link in the Chain: The Story of the Irish Housewives Association 1942–1992* (Attic Press, 1992),
Walsh, Deirdre, *Surviving Sexual Abuse* (Attic Press, 1989).
Ward, Margaret, *The Missing Sex: Putting Women Into Irish History* (Attic Press, 1991).
——, *Unmanageable Revolutionaries: Women and Irish Nationalism* (Pluto, 1989).
Who Owns Ireland: Who Owns You? Women in Community Publishing (WICP) Course, 1985.
Women's Political Association Newsletter (June 1976).
Write Up Your Street: An Anthology of Community Writing (Women's Community Press, 1985).

Index

Abbey Theatre 6
Abortion 10, 15, 17, 18, 23, 25–28, 30–31, 39–40, 42–43, 47, 52, 63, 66, 69, 74, 85–86, 88, 91, 96, 104, 106–109, 114–115, 120, 124, 126, 128–131, 139–141
AIM (Action, Information, Motivation) 35, 75, 100, 124, 135
ALLY 72, 75, 124, 135
AnCo ix, 33, 63, 78, 127, 136
Anti-Amendment Campaign 17, 26, 46, 66, 75, 145
Aosdána ix, 8, 61, 98
Arlen House vii, 30–33, 63–64, 77–78, 123–125, 136
Armagh 66, 69, 99, 112
Arts Council 32, 33, 67, 79
Attic Press vii, 8, 49, 64, 68, 75, 77, 78, 80, 105, 109, 123–124, 127–130, 138

Banshee: Journal of Irishwomen United 8–10, 23, 53–56, 59, 61, 81–83, 89, 102, 115, 118, 120–121, 123, 136
Barnes, Monica 35, 43
Bewley's Café 13, 47, 134
Boland, Eavan 31–33, 78, 95–96
Boyd, Róisín 104
Braiden, Olive 38
Browne, Noel (Dr, TD) 60, 100, 134
Byrne, Gay ix, 43, 68, 113
Byrne, Noreen 41

Caherty, Therese 115
Charter viii, 4, 9, 10, 15, 23, 59, 82, 100–102, 112, 114, 117–118, 120, 123, 130, 132, 135–136
Cherish (Children Have Equal Rights in Society Here) vii, xiii, 8, 49, 66, 71-76, 124, 128, 129, 135
Commission on the Status of Women (CSW) 12, 16, 52, 134–135, 139
Condren, Mary 79
Connolly, Linda 11, 15, 24, 103, 123, 125, 130
Conroy, Pauline 115, 131
Conroy, Róisín 49, 62–64, 77, 78–80, 137
Contraception Action Programme (CAP) 5, 15, 24, 27, 53, 75, 103, 113–114, 125, 136
Council for the Status of Women (CSW) 6, 35, 75, 100, 135, 139
Cronin, Maureen 53
Crummy, Frank 40, 41
Cullen, Mary 16, 85, 123–124
Cullen Owens, Rosemary 78

de Burca, Máirín 13, 47, 123, 131, 136
Devlin, Bernadette (now Bernadette McAliskey) 92, 97
Dublin Gay Collective 25
Dublin Lesbian and Gay Collective 25
Dublin Lesbian Line 83, 85
Dublin Rape Crisis Centre (DRCC) vii, xiii, 8, 15, 18–19, 26, 34–38, 49–50, 57–58, 74, 83, 85, 91, 96, 103, 106, 125–126, 130, 137
Dublin Resource Centre (DRC) 64
Duignan, Clare 43
Dworkin, Andrea 7, 93–94, 123, 129–130

Eighth/8th Amendment 17, 26–27, 42, 65–66, 85–86, 95, 121, 128–129, 130–131, 140–141
Employment Equality Act 49, 136, 139
Employment Equality Agency (EEA) 104, 136, 138
Enright, Máiréad 25, 125
Equal Pay Act 49
European Convention on Human Rights 108
European Court of Justice 110, 138
European Court of Human Rights 49, 109, 110, 137
European Union/EU 24, 28, 66, 101, 108, 124
European Economic Community/EEC 12, 42, 108, 113, 124, 138

Farrell, Máiréad 99, 130
Federated Union of Employers/FUE 7, 24, 48–49, 55–56, 90, 101, 113
Fennell, Nuala 35, 76, 100, 135, 137–138
Finucane, Marian 43, 104
Fitzgerald, Frances 43
Fitzgerald, Garret (Dr) 109, 115

Fitzwilliam Lawn Tennis Club 15, 48, 53–54, 90, 114
Fownes Street Group 112
Flynn, Declan 65, 85, 128–129
Forty Foot 15, 24, 53–54, 75, 82, 89, 102, 118–119, 136
Friedan, Betty 8, 93, 116, 129, 131

Gaffney, Maureen 35
Gaj, Margaret 13, 47
Galligan, Yvonne 12, 123
Gannon, Ita 7
Geoghegan Quinn, Máire 49
Gordon, Mary 18
Greer, Germaine 7, 92–93, 110, 116, 129, 131

Halappanavar, Savita 86, 106, 109, 115, 129–131, 140
Harper, Liz 62, 63, 68
Haughey, Charles 36, 103, 114
Hayes, Alan 31, 125
Hayes, Joanne 85, 128–129, 141
Holland, Mary 43, 103, 107
Hussey, Gemma 114, 137, 139

International Women's Year 15, 136
Irish Congress of Trade Unions/ICTU 48, 50, 115, 140
Irish Constitution 12, 17, 26, 107–108, 128, 140
Irish Council for Civil Liberties/ICCL 48
Irish Countrywomen's Association/ICA 6, 13, 133
Irish Gay Rights Movement/IGRM 45
Irish Housewives' Association/IHA 6, 12–13, 124
Irish Feminist Information/IFI 49, 63–64, 77, 136
Irish Feminist Review 18, 19, 66
Irish Transport and General Workers' Union/ITGWU 112
Irish Women's Diary 63, 77–78, 146
Irish Women's Liberation Group/IWLG 4, 51, 59
Irish Women's Liberation Movement/IWLM 6, 12–15, 24, 27, 43, 47, 54, 92, 101, 103, 112, 116, 120, 124, 126, 128, 134–135
Irish Women Workers' Union/IWWU 49, 64, 78, 127–128, 133

Johnston, Máirín 13

Kelleher, Patricia 62–63
Kelly, Laura 40, 115, 124–126, 131
Kennedy, Stanislaus 31

Kerry Babies Case 65, 77, 128–129
Kilbarrack Local Education for Adult Renewal/KLEAR 68

Labour Women's Group 101
Late Late Show (The) ix, 12, 43, 46–47, 113
Law Reform Commission 35, 53
Lentin, Ronit 31
Lesbian Line 46, 83, 85, 138
Levine, June 4, 47, 49, 103, 124, 126–127
Liberty Hall 10, 59, 91, 107, 135–136
Lovett, Ann 65, 77, 85, 109, 128–130
Luddy, Maria 14, 124, 142

MacCurtain, Margaret 31
Magdalene Laundries 84
Maher, Mary 13, 43, 47, 49
'Marriage Bar' 11, 47, 104, 111, 113, 126
Martin, Janet 31
Maynooth 4, 6, 18, 85, 93
McAleese, Mary xiv, 8, 35, 43, 126, 140
McAuliffe, Mary 17, 123
McCafferty, Nell 3, 43, 45, 48, 50, 54, 57, 64, 78, 90, 96, 101, 103, 113, 119, 124, 127, 130
McCormack, Inez 140
McKay, Susan 34
McGee Case (1973) 113, 135–136
Meehan, Sylvia 85, 104, 136, 138
Molloy, Maura 115
Mother and Baby Homes 69, 72, 84, 128, 141
Mullarney, Máire 31, 40
Murphy, Christina 10, 31

National Council for One Parent Families/NCOPF 73, 128
National Gay Federation 46
Ní Mhurchú, Padraigín 49, 64, 78
Norris, David xiii
Northern Ireland Women's Movement/NIWM 90

O'Brien, Anne 100, 114–115
O'Brien, Joanne 45
O'Brien, Mags 49
O'Dea, Maura 66
O'Donohue, Noreen 62–63, 66–67, 128
Open Door Counselling 26, 107, 109–110, 115
Open Line Counselling 25, 109
Orpen, Hilary 104

Pembroke Street xiii, 3–4, 8, 10, 23, 45–46, 53, 74, 81, 88, 99, 117
Prone, Terry 31–32
Prostitution 7, 49, 83, 127

Purcell, Bernie 38

Quinn, Nicola 35, 49, 51

Reclaim the Night 25, 36, 75, 84
Redmond, Marie 115
Repeal Referendum (2018) 17, 26–27, 42, 121, 128–131, 140–141
Richardson, Sue 63, 67, 128
Right to Choose Organisation 25–26, 66, 103, 106–107, 130, 137
Robinson, Mary 3–4, 8, 66, 73, 75, 86, 97, 99, 113, 130, 134–135, 138–140
RTÉ (Raidió Telefís Éireann) ix, 24, 31, 36, 43, 48, 68, 90, 103–105, 113, 124, 126, 130, 137, 140
Rose, Catherine 30–33, 64, 78, 125

Same-sex Marriage 42, 140
Short, Constance 31
Smyth, Ailbhe 14, 18, 27, 85–86, 95–96, 123, 129
Spare Rib 78, 88, 90, 120,
Speirs, Derek 56, 65, 115, 131
Status of Children Act (1988) 75–76
Suffragettes 6

The 'Troubles' ix, 32, 66, 111
Trade Union Women's Forum 31
Trades Union Congress/TUC 112
Trinity College Dublin/TCD 34, 40, 45, 57, 59–60, 76, 85, 95, 134, 136–137
Tweedy, Hilda 12, 43, 124

University College Cork/UCC 55, 57, 69, 110, 127
University College Dublin/UCD 4, 27, 31, 44, 48, 60, 81, 85, 88, 95–96, 99–100
University College Galway/UCG 85
Unmarried Mother's Allowance 73, 135

Virago Press 32, 63, 78

Waking the Feminists 6
Women in Community Publishing/WICP 78
Women in Publishing Network/WIPN 77
Women Today 43, 104, 137
Women's Aid 25, 36, 49–50, 75, 96, 124, 136
Women's Coalition Group 26–27, 86
Women's Community Press/WCP 63–69
Women's Disco 7, 83–84, 126
Women's Education Bureau/WEB 32
Women's Education Research and Resource Centre/WERRC 96, 139
Women's Press, The 64, 78, 123, 129
Women's Representative Committee/WRC 15, 135
Workplace Relations Commission/WRC 49
Women's Right to Choose/WRC 25, 66, 106–107, 137
Women's Social and Progressive League 6, 134
Women's Studies Forum 27
Woods, Máire 13, 41, 138

X Case 27, 86, 129, 139